Ebony Jr!

The Rise, Fall, and Return of a Black Children's Magazine

Laretta Henderson

THE SCARECROW PRESS, INC.
Lanham, Maryland • Toronto • Plymouth, UK
2008

SCARECROW PRESS, INC.

Published in the United States of America
by Scarecrow Press, Inc.
A wholly owned subsidiary of
The Rowman & Littlefield Publishing Group, Inc.
4501 Forbes Boulevard, Suite 200, Lanham, Maryland 20706
www.scarecrowpress.com

Estover Road
Plymouth PL6 7PY
United Kingdom

British Library Cataloguing in Publication Information Available

Library of Congress Cataloging-in-Publication Data

Henderson, Laretta.
  Ebony jr! : the rise, fall, and return of a Black children's magazine / Laretta
Henderson.
    p. cm.
  Includes bibliographical references and index.
  ISBN-13: 978-0-8108-6134-3 (hbk. : alk. paper)
  ISBN-10: 0-8108-6134-8 (hbk. : alk. paper)
 1. Ebony jr! I. Title.

PN4900.E36H46 2007
051--dc22
                                    2007052566

∞™ The paper used in this publication meets the minimum requirements of
American National Standard for Information Sciences—Permanence of Paper for
Printed Library Materials, ANSI/NISO Z39.48-1992.
Manufactured in the United States of America

To my great nieces and nephews:
Erin, Bria, Nia, Brian, Trinity, and Isreal.
You are my Ebony Juniors.

Contents

Acknowledgments

As with any project of this magnitude, there are many people who have contributed to the fruition and success of this book. As this journey began as a dissertation, I thank the members of my committee—Carolyn Colvin, Doris Witt, Jim Marshall, and Katrina Sanders—for their guidance and support. As co-chair of my dissertation, Donnarae Mac-Cann's scholarship, patience, and concern for me as a budding scholar made this specific project possible. She generously shared her expertise in children's literature, African American history and culture, and editing with me and asked for nothing but this book in return. Finally, of all the faculty I encountered at the University of Iowa, my adviser, Cynthia Lewis, made the most powerful impact upon me. From the time she began to "mentor me to tenure" as a new graduate student until now, she has served as my model of a scholar. Like the kids say, "I want to be like her when I grow up." I know no better compliment.

Others from the University of Iowa who supported me in bringing this book to fruition include members of my writing group, Bonnie K. Sonnek and Pam Coke. While Bonnie and I actually wrote our dissertations together at the Java House in Iowa City, Pam contributed her expertise in the writing process to both of us. I love you both. For the very idea of studying *Ebony Jr!*, I thank Elizabeth Tsukahara and Shanti Roundtree.

Other friends and colleagues at Central Michigan University aided in this process. Pamela Gates provided monetary support; Susan Griffith was ever present with advice on children's literature, offers to edit, and dinner invitations; Rene Shingles offered friendship; and Diyonne and

Brad Falhman provided the comic relief. Finally, Janice Hartwick-Dressel contributed her voice, a calm and wise whisper, to me during the process.

New friends and colleagues at the University of Wisconsin–Milwaukee have added their contribution to the final stages of the project. Johannes Britz contributed time and money, Hope Olson contributed the insight of a full professor, Carolyn Washburn served as a reader, and Cheryl Ajiro-tutu rounded off my support group as my devoted cheerleader.

For their love and their spiritual and financial support, I thank my immediate family: Erma Jean Henderson, Sharon Kinzer, Derral Anderson, Bernita McKinney, and Stephen Anderson. Yet "it takes a village to raise a child," and members of my village who supported my education are Elder Samuel DuBois, Mother Bridges, and Shelia Carpenter.

Again, it was the backing I received from this village that made this project possible. Thank you all.

Introduction

[W]e only become what we are by the radical and deep-seated refusal of that which others have made of us.—Franz Fanon

I was raised in the suburbs of Chicago during the late 1960s and 1970s, and was ten when *Ebony Jr!* (*EJ*) was inaugurated. While my mother did not subscribe to it, nor do I remember it being available in my school library, I do recall seeing it in the doctor's and dentist's offices and in friends' homes. Although I cannot remember why, I was not particularly interested in reading *EJ*, and I do recall that *Ebony* (Johnson Publishing Company's adult magazine) was viewed within my local community as a little out of touch with the political positions of most Blacks, as we were known then.[1]

We considered their portrayal of the Black community to be conservative, stagnant—lost somewhere in the 1950s and 1960s—and rarely critical. But I do remember *EJ* being considered rare in that it was a children's magazine written for and containing images of Black children like me.[2] While I was not a regular reader, I remember getting *EJ* when the Jackson 5 were either on the cover or featured in an issue. This was during the time when it seemed that the Jackson 5 were always on *Billboard*'s Rhythm & Blues Top 40 list and Michael Jackson was a pre- or early teenager sans plastic surgery. Although *EJ* went out of print in 1985, it has returned on the Internet at Ebonyjr.com.[3] While I discuss the Internet magazine in this text, I am more interested in the print version.

My work puts *EJ* in historical, political, educational, and cultural contexts to examine how *EJ* worked to "strengthen the preparedness of Black

ix

children" for a racialized and educational future.[4] To do this, I investigate how the various political and educational ideologies of the 1970s and 1980s informed and were represented in *EJ*. How did the Black Liberation Movement, in its various class and religious configurations, as well as educational theories about Black children influence the types of articles and activities that were included in or excluded from *EJ*? Further, how did these same ideologies inform *EJ* as a piece of Black children's literature of the late 1970s and early 1980s? Finally, what might be some causes for *EJ*'s demise in the mid-1980s and its rebirth in the early 2000s?

EJ is undoubtedly a cultural artifact of the African American community of the 1970s and 1980s; as such I have chosen to view it through the lens of Black Studies. I am interested in the way both Black Studies and *EJ* are cultural enterprises grounded in the African American experience. In addition, Black Studies as an academic discipline was developed in the late 1960s, just prior to *EJ*'s appearance. It offers an African American perspective with which to analyze *EJ*'s genesis, contents, and context within African American children's literature. Furthermore, "Black Studies has historically endeavored to provide the intellectual and academic space for Black people to 'tell their own story'" and to analyze our own historical record.[5] Black Studies is, by nature, interdisciplinary; it includes historical studies, cultural studies, and social and behavioral studies.

Children's literary critics such as Rudine Sims Bishop, Violet Harris, Dianne Johnson, Donnarae MacCann, and Katherine Capshaw Smith have documented the history of African American children's literature and identified stereotypes and issues of White supremacy in the literature.[6] They have also contributed to the production of Black children's literature that supports "racial pride, strength, and self-definition" (features that historians associate with Black Power activism).[7] Yet an in-depth analysis of *EJ* has been absent from this body of criticism. A study of periodicals is important, since, according to writer and critic Carolyn Gerald, "the direction and developing quality of black literature can be but imperfectly seen if these journals are ignored."[8] Following in the footsteps of Dianne Johnson and her work with *The Brownies' Book*, I have chosen to study *EJ*, a popular periodical targeting African American children from five to eleven years old.[9] With respect to related research, only one brief critical study of *EJ* has been published: Courtney Vaughn-Roberson and Brenda Hill's "*The Brownies' Book* and *Ebony Jr!*: Literature as a Mirror of the Afro-American Experience."[10] The authors conducted a content analysis of both texts and highlighted seven significant ideologies posited in both periodicals. Other than my work, *EJ* has been mentioned only in passing in research on the history of African American children's literature.[11] My work fills this void by offering an extended analysis of *EJ*, its context, and its influences. But a clear perception of this enterprise for children will remain ill defined unless we start with how the project is structured.

ORGANIZATION

In this section, I discuss the organization of this project, the research question, and the theory used to investigate this question. In chapter 1, I profile *EJ*, discussing its layout, audience, content, and overall trends. In chapter 2, I investigate the market for *EJ* in the field of children's periodicals at its inception. In so doing, I note the lack of culturally conscious African American children's literature and present an overview of mainstream children's periodicals as well as African American periodicals similar to *EJ*. I discuss *EJ* in relation to all of these categories in an effort to align it with the intentions of both African American and mainstream children's publishing. To provide a corporate context and its influences on *EJ*, chapter 3 contains a brief biography of John H. Johnson, followed by an overview of Johnson Publishing Company (JPC).

The next section deals with historical trends and their implied connections with *EJ*. Chapter 4 reveals the importance of the political socialization of children. Chapter 4 is therefore about how the Black Liberation and the Black Feminist movements' ideologies were manifested in JPC and *EJ*. The Black Liberation Movement consists of three primary political ideologies: Racial Uplift, the Civil Rights Movement, and Black Nationalist Movements. The proponents of Racial Uplift believed "that an emphasis on self-help, racial solidarity, temperance, thrift, chastity, social purity, patriarchal authority and accumulation of wealth . . . [would help alleviate] . . . 'the Negro problem.'"[12] Those who subscribed to this ideology were accommodationists, and Booker T. Washington is sometimes viewed as an important nineteenth-century forefather.

The proponents of the Civil Rights Movement did not agree with the accommodationist ideology of the older generation. They moved in the direction of explicit and vigorous political activism. They did not believe that Whites would grant them their human and civil rights based upon Whites' benevolence and guilt complex. They saw the need for more direct action in the form of protests and sit-ins. Many of the proponents of the Civil Rights Movement followed the leadership of Dr. Martin Luther King Jr. But many young people of the late 1960s thought King's leadership, as well as the Racial Uplift ideology, were far too accommodating and slow.

The Black Nationalists (as this group was called) were disillusioned by a century of failed integration efforts and thought that cultural separatism, and, to a lesser degree, political separatism, were the solution.

This group would have concurred with John H. Stanfield's observation that assimilation "is rooted more in liberal ideals regarding the inevitable goodness of U.S. democracy as a utopian belief than in empirical realities."[13] The Black Nationalists sought "to strengthen in-group values while holding those promoted by the larger society at arm's length. . . . [T]he hope [was] to win and maintain sociocultural autonomy."[14]

All three political approaches were represented in the administration of JPC. John H. Johnson, the publisher and founder, aligned himself with the Racial Uplift agenda, and this position is evident in all of JPC's ventures. But Johnson stated in his autobiography, *Succeeding against the Odds*, that JPC was involved in the Civil Rights Movement not only through media coverage, but through monetary contributions and participation in movement activities, including marches. The Black Nationalist philosophy was apparent in the JPC magazine *Black World*, which gave explicit support to the Black Arts Movement. Another indicator was the presence of Lerone Bennett Jr., a known Black Nationalist and scholar, on the editorial staff of many JPC publications.

Another component of the politicization of children includes gender roles. While not central to my analysis, I use Black Feminist theory, which was articulated during the years of *EJ*'s publication, to evaluate how gender roles were represented in *EJ*. Black women of the 1970s found that neither the Black Liberation Movement nor the (White) Feminist Movement addressed the intersection of race, class, sexuality, and gender. Many Black women found the various Black Liberation Movements to be sexist and the Feminist Movement to be racist. In 1974 a group of Black women formed the Combahee River Collective, which was "actively committed to struggling against racial, sexual, heterosexual, and class oppression and saw as their particular task the development of integrated analysis and practice based upon the fact that major systems of oppression are interlocking."[15] Eventually Black Women's Studies began to appear in college courses, although not to the degree that either Black Studies or Women's Studies were instituted. By 1981 there was a Black Feminist publisher, Kitchen Table: Women of Color Press, founded by Barbara Smith. By the 1980s those who were interested would have had access to Black Feminist theory, classes, and literature. Again, how this theory was represented in *EJ* and how it evolved as the Black Feminist Movement progressed will be considered here.

Chapter 5 takes up the turbulent educational trends and practices of the 1960s, 1970s, and 1980s, and how they were manifested in *EJ*. The magazine's educational content reflected the call for culturally conscious pedagogy and content made by various factions of the community—Black educators and Black Nationalists. It also mirrored an elementary school curriculum with the addition of a discourse on racial identity. These subjects, among others, in chapter 5 lead to a description of how *EJ* was shaped as an educational tool.

The final section includes one chapter. Chapter 6 deals with how the Black child of the late 1960s and early 1970s was posited in various sectors of the Black community (the middle class, the church, the Black Panther Party, etc.). In the conclusion, I situate *EJ* within the field of African American children's literature. In this connection I use Rudine Sims's *Shadow and Substance: Afro-American Experience in Contemporary Children's Fiction*. Sims conducted a survey of literature with Black characters in which she noted some trends relevant to *EJ*. Basically, Sims, like other proponents of the Black Aesthetic, postulated that literature written for Black children should reflect their culture and be written *for* them. In this chapter, I also investigate possible causes of the demise of *EJ*. To do so, I look to various scholars and activists for possible reasons for the downfall of *EJ*. Finally, I discuss the return of *EJ* in an online format and speculate about its future.

Since I have chosen a magazine produced by a company solely owned by African Americans and guided by a racialized goal statement, an African American perspective is fundamental to my work. Yet alongside this framework, I take note that African Americans are, for all intents and purposes, "bicultural and share in varying degrees some of the same values, attitudes, beliefs, social goals and characteristics as white America."[16] In the end, however, this project can be characterized as Black in orientation, interdisciplinary in scope, and reformist by nature.

NOTES

1. I will use the terms *Black* and *African American* interchangeably.

2. According to Ada Rose, a magazine is "a printed periodical containing a miscellaneous collection—or storehouse of stories, articles, poems, and other features suitable for a given audience" ("Are Children's Magazines Dying on the Vine?" *Catholic Library* 47 [1976]: 370), while Margaret Koste stated that a magazine is a "publication which appears at regular intervals and which may be general or specific in nature or content. It is bound with a paper cover and usually contains many illustrations" ("An Evaluation of Magazines Published for Children in America" [PhD diss., The Ohio State University, 1962], 13). I will use the terms *periodical* and *magazine* interchangeably.

3. For clarity's sake, references to *EJ* imply the print version. I will use "*EJ* online" to refer to the contemporary online version of *EJ*.

4. "Johnson Introduces Magazine Designed for Black Children," *Jet*, May 10, 1973, 52.

5. Ronald W Bailey, "Black Studies," in *The Concise Oxford Companion to African American Literature*, ed. William L. Andrews, Frances Smith Foster, and Trudier Harris (New York: Oxford University Press, 1997), 82.

6. I follow Donnarae MacCann's lead and use the term *White supremacy* instead of *racism* since the latter has suffered from overuse and is laden with multiple meanings. The ideology of White supremacy, as defined by George M. Fredrickson,

> refers to the attitudes, ideologies, and policies associated with the rise of blatant forms of white or European dominance over "nonwhite" populations. . . . At the public level, this myth of superiority entails restriction of meaningful citizenship rights. . . . It suggests systematic and self-conscious efforts to make race or color a qualification for membership in the civil community.

Donnarae MacCann, *White Supremacy in Children's Literature: Characterizations of African Americans, 1830–1900* (New York: Garland, 2001), xi.

7. William L. Van Deburg, *New Day in Babylon: The Black Power Movement and American Culture, 1965–1975* (Chicago: University of Chicago Press, 1993), 2.

8. Carolyn Gerald, cited in Abby Arthur Johnson and Ronald Maberry Johnson, "Scholarly Journals and Literary Magazines," in *The Concise Oxford Companion to African American Literature*, ed. William L. Andrews, Frances Smith Foster, and Trudier Harris (New York: Oxford University Press, 1997).

9. Dianne Johnson-Feelings, "The Pedagogy and the Promise of Du Bois' *The Brownies' Book* Magazine," in *Telling Tales: The Pedagogy and Promise of African American Literature for Youth*, ed. Dianne Johnson-Feelings (New York: Greenwood Press, 1990).

10. Courtney Vaughn-Roberson and Brenda Hill, "*The Brownies' Book* and *Ebony Jr!*: Literature as a Mirror of the Afro-American Experience," *Journal of Negro Education* 8, no. 4 (1989).

11. Violet J. Harris, "African American Children's Literature: The First One Hundred Years," *Journal of Negro Education* 59, no. 4 (1990).

12. Kevin Gaines, *Uplifting the Race: Black Leadership, Politics, and Culture in the Twentieth Century* (Chapel Hill: University of North Carolina Press, 1996), 2.

13. John H. Stanfield and Rutledge M. Dennis, *Race and Ethnicity in Research Methods* (Newbury Park, CA: Sage, 1993), 5.

14. William L. Van Deburg, *New Day in Babylon: The Black Power Movement and American Culture, 1965–1975* (Chicago: University of Chicago Press, 1992), 25.

15. Combahee River Collective, "A Black Feminist Statement," in *All the Women Are White, All the Men Are Black: But Some of Us Are Brave*, ed. Gloria T. Hull, Patricia Bell Scott, and Barbara Smith (New York: Feminist Press, 1982).

16. Talmadge Anderson, *Black Studies: Theory, Method, and Cultural Perspectives* (Pullman: Washington State University Press, 1990), 7.

I

EBONY JR!'S PLACE IN THE WORLD OF CHILDREN'S PERIODICALS

1

✝

Ebony Jr!: A Profile

Because many of society's concerns are reflected in children's literature more rapidly than in other literary studies . . . critics of children's literature are uniquely able to reach out from their studies and embrace other critical and social concerns.—Samuel Pickering

[Y]ou have to change images before you can change acts and institutions.—John H. Johnson

Ebony Jr! was published by Johnson Publishing Company, a Black-owned, privately held company, from 1973 until 1985. JPC is a multinational, multimillion-dollar company that produces a cadre of books and other magazines, including *Ebony* and *Jet*. It also manufactures Fashion Fair Cosmetics (a very important Black cosmetic line), produces the Ebony Fashion Show, and has owned a number of radio stations and two other cosmetics lines: Ebone Cosmetics and Supreme Beauty. Throughout its history JPC has maintained an Afrocentric focus for its ventures and target audience.[1] *EJ*, JPC's only magazine for children, was published monthly eight times a year, with two bimonthly summer issues. It was geared toward Black children from five to eleven years old and contained "stories, articles, word and mathematical games, songs, contests, and a calendar of events in the lives of black Americans."[2] To begin, I will present an overview of *EJ*'s layout, content, audience, various editors and their influences, and its new online version.[3] Underlying this discussion is the pervasive educational component of the magazine.

LAYOUT AND CONTENTS

During its entire run, *EJ* measured 9¾ x 6½ inches, larger than the pocket-sized *Jet* but significantly smaller than *Ebony*. When *EJ* was first published in 1973, it cost fifty cents per issue, with a one-year subscription rate of five dollars for ten issues if payment was enclosed, or six dollars if billed. When it went out of print in 1985 it cost a dollar per issue, with a subscription costing eight dollars. An article in *Jet* described *EJ* as follows:

> From the colorful characters on the front cover to the *Ebony Jr!* Art Gallery on the back cover, the monthly publication is jammed packed with puzzles, letters from *Ebony Jr!* fans, short stories, arts and crafts, poetry, cartoons, articles on their favorite entertainers and Black history.[4]

Although some of the features changed with the editors and the changing educational, political, and economic climates facing the African American community during *EJ*'s run, each issue usually followed a theme related to events relevant to children and current trends. Themes included summer break, the Olympics, and holidays. Whatever the topic, the layout of *EJ* usually began with a multicolored theme-related cover featuring cartoon drawings of children. For example, the August/September 1981 back-to-school issue featured a cover showing a classroom packed with active multiracial children (multiracial scenes are uncommon in *EJ*). The first narrative of this issue was "Welcome to Success" by Lynn Norment, a story about the famed Chicago teacher Marva Collins and her Westside Preparatory School.[5] Even the Phonics Loonicans, a stock cartoon family used to teach phonics, was shown in a scene about the first day of school.[6]

The first page of the magazine featured a calendar for the month, followed by a table of contents. Above the calendar was an illustration of children playing around the name of the month in a month-related scene. Noted dates on the calendar specifically referred to the theme and to Afrocentric concerns, with key events repeated on subsequent calendars (e.g., the anniversary of the date that Joseph Cinqué led the *Amistad* mutiny of 1839 was noted in the June/July 1973 and 1975 calendars).[7] Another regular component of *EJ* was the *Ebony Jr!* Art Gallery, which premiered in August/September 1973 on the back cover of the magazine. Under the guidance of the first editor, whom I discuss below, the art gallery was covered with readers' artwork, and the images were almost exclusively drawings of faces of African American children. When the editor changed, so did the images; the art gallery then included any image the child readers sent in for publication.

In addition to the art provided by readers, colorful cartoons were peppered throughout *EJ*. Photographs of children were used in the arts and crafts and cooking columns, in the featured interviews with children, and in the reader response columns such as "From the Reader."

The layout and regular content of *EJ* attempted to educate and reflect its audience of Black children. The orientation of the magazine was educational and Afrocentric. The assumption was that most children attended schools that did not include Black history and culture in their curricula, that the child reader was interested in such information, and that the most affirming context was exclusively Afrocentric. The use of colorful cartoons was similar to those included in other children's magazines. The photographs and the art gallery used in *EJ* featured almost exclusively Black children. Thus, *EJ* was rare in that it offered images of Black children at a time when they were not fully integrated into mainstream children's literature. This practice was aligned with John H. Johnson's intention to provide "a medium to make Black people believe in themselves, in their skin color, in their noses, in their lips."[8] By teaching Black children about their history and culture as well as showing them accurate and positive images of themselves, Johnson hoped to encourage racialized self-esteem in his young readers.[9]

Complementing its themes and illustrations, each issue typically contained approximately five narratives, or stories, as they were called in the index, whose characteristics evolved as the political and economic conditions in the African American community and *EJ*'s editors changed. The narratives were mostly historical and contemporary fiction, with some interviews and biographies of famous leaders, politicians, entertainers, and "regular kids" who did interesting things. Each issue usually contained at least one article on African history, folklore, or, to a lesser degree, culture. Although most of the authors who published in *EJ* on a regular basis were relatively unknown in the field of African American children's and young adult literature (e.g., Frankie Cox and Phyllis Johnson), some went on to become canonical figures in juvenile literature: Sharon Bell Mathis, Eloise Greenfield, and Walter Myers. In an interview with the *Des Moines Register* in 1973, Constance Van Brunt Johnson, *EJ*'s first editor, explained that a controlled vocabulary was used in each story. Whoever the author might be, he or she wrote according to *EJ*'s guidelines, and the editor's hand was consistently apparent, such as when words that might be unfamiliar to the typical reader were set in bold type and defined at the bottom of the page.

These narratives were accompanied by regular columns such as *"Ebony Jr! News," "From Our Readers," and "Writing Readers,"* which were all essentially reader response columns. "Mama Write-On's Scribblin' Scope" was an educational activity that encouraged the development of penmanship. Another staple of *EJ* was the stock characters Sunny, his sister, Honey, and their nameless doll, who premiered in August/September

1973 and remain staples of *EJ*. Although they began the run of the print version of *EJ* as five-year-olds (the beginning age of the target audience), toward the end of the run they were older—approximately ten or eleven. Sunny, Honey, and their doll lived in a world of their own, with few adults. They served as guides for the child reader, sometimes announcing themes, "authoring" articles such as "*Ebony Jr!* News," and reflecting the child reader in gender, age, and possibly lifestyle.

Lastly, as alluded to above, each issue of *EJ* during Van Brunt Johnson's tenure had a comprehensive educational component:

> The materials are designed for comprehension, vocabulary building and perceptual exercises. We are concentrating on reading development because today's culture and technology demand that children become prepared for a highly literate future.[10]

While *EJ* was geared toward academic areas such as reading, math, science, and social studies, arts and crafts were also included on a regular basis. Along with these features, educational activity sheets sometimes followed the narratives. These components provided opportunities for readers to be engaged in the text in an active manner as opposed to just reading. It may have also supported readers' school-based curriculum by providing them an opportunity to use their skills in a leisurely, ungraded environment. And *EJ*'s commitment to education may have been reinforced through the lack of advertising for goods other than those related to *EJ* (e.g., subscription cards, books, and Sunny and Honey dolls).

In geographical orientation *EJ* was a northern, urban publication. There were few references to rural environments, and those that were included were only made in passing. For example, each December issue showed snow, which spoke more to a northern reality than a southern or southwestern one. In addition, most of the characters lived in the North, and participation in the Great Migration was assumed. One such story was "Tough Enough" by Frankie Cox, in which the protagonist had just moved to the North from the South and was trying to learn to ride a bike.[11] I have not found any stories that reversed the Great Migration pattern, with characters moving from the North to the South. Farm families and rural life were shown almost exclusively in historical narratives. Few references were made to the West other than historical narratives about Black cowboys.

Notably absent, and probably related to *EJ*'s public school market, was much discussion of the church in any form. African American literary critics have discussed the importance of including references to the church in African American literature since at least the Harlem Renaissance. Richard Wright defined African American culture as that which should be highlighted in African American literature, the sources of which are the

African American church and folklore.[12] Houston Baker later extended this definition to include traditional African religions and their syncretic forms that are present in the African American community.[13] And although in many ways *EJ* was aligned with the tenets of African American literature, there were only a few brief references to the church. When it was mentioned, it was shown as the setting for events within the story—it was not the focus of the narrative. One such example was "Sneezing Powder," the story of a mischievous little boy who got into some sneezing powder at church: The church was mentioned only as the setting and not an integral component of the plot.[14] Likewise, other religions common in the Black community, such as Islam, were also rarely mentioned, and when they were, only in passing. For example, in periodic salutes to Malcolm X in which Islam might be mentioned, his work in the Black Liberation Movement was highlighted.

Overall, *EJ* was an educationally oriented magazine targeting African American children, supporting their school-based curriculum while supplementing it with an Afrocentric education. Such an educational approach was important to those who purchased *EJ*.

THE BUSINESS OF *EBONY JR!*: AUDIENCE AND MARKETING

Although *EJ* was geared to children, adults had to buy into the product since they were the ones making the purchase. These adult buyers—teachers, librarians, and parents—were primarily working class, urban, and racially conscious. Teachers and librarians looking for culturally relevant literature for their students were a component of *EJ*'s target audience. Initially *EJ* was to be marketed to teachers, who would purchase multiple copies and whose approval of *EJ* would encourage individual sales to parents. The idea was that if teachers approved of *EJ*, educationally invested parents would purchase it for their children. In an article that celebrated *EJ*'s tenth anniversary, the unnamed author wrote, "Circulation is approximately 200,000 and the magazine is used throughout the nation's elementary school system as a learning tool."[15]

Further evidence that *EJ* was marketed as an educational tool was the *Jet* photo that included Manford Byrd Jr., deputy superintendent of the Chicago Public Schools, as a guest at *EJ*'s inauguration. Other prominent African American leaders in the photo were the Reverend Jesse L. Jackson, who was serving as national president of Operation PUSH, and Mayor Richard Hatcher of Gary, Indiana.[16] Even the article itself—reporting on the educational focus of *EJ* in a JPC publication that targeted adults—was a clear marketing ploy, and including prominent leaders to support *EJ* also gave it credibility as an Afrocentric teaching tool. Johnson stated that his marketing strategy for *EJ* consisted of "identification of parents with children in the target age groups and city-by-city sales campaigns focused on boards of education."[17] JPC published "'[a] guide for use of *Ebony Jr!*' [that] describes ways teachers may use the features in each issue for reading comprehension, vocabulary building," and so on.[18] Johnson provided access to the teacher's guide in the subscription cards, which noted that "[a]n additional \$2.50 per year brings you a monthly guide for getting the most out of the learning benefits of EBONY JR!"

The idea that *EJ* was a useful teaching tool in the classroom, and hopefully in the home, was reinforced in a letter to *EJ* from a reader. Christopher Little from Mississippi wrote to "*Ebony Jr!* News": "My teacher, Miss Zackery, subscribes to *Ebony Jr!* for our class. We can hardly wait to receive it. Your magazine features the best articles for kids I have ever seen."[19] This statement may have been published by the editors to appeal to both child readers and adult buyers. The children learned that *EJ* was popular with their peers, while the educational component was attractive to adult buyers, as was the connection between *EJ* and *Ebony*. *EJ* might be considered a primer for *Ebony* in its effort to train children to read Afrocentric literature. For JPC, the goal was to encourage sales.

Again, "*Ebony Jr!* is about learning and exploring," and teachers were encouraged to use *EJ* in their classrooms at a time when racial and cultural awareness, as well as multiculturalism, were becoming more of an issue in schools.[20] And the magazine was initially a success with teachers. As Van Brunt Johnson stated, "We have had an overwhelming response from educators."[21] Parents were encouraged to purchase *EJ* not only as an educational tool, but as racialized instruction written for Black children. By the time *EJ* was published, most Black families were familiar with JPC and had read at least one of its publications. Therefore, it is safe to say that the parent who purchased *EJ* knew that JPC was an African American–owned and operated company that was firmly invested in the issues reflected in the community. Trusting, to some degree, JPC's racialized orientation, the adults who bought *EJ* probably did so "based on the idea that learning is fun."[22] As Johnson stated, *EJ* was a combination of popular culture materials (e.g., those that grab a reader's attention) and an elementary curriculum. Although Michael Jackson might have been on the cover of a given issue, parents could rest assured that the contents contained narratives about African American history and culture, reading and writing activity sheets, a Black history calendar, elementary math worksheets, and simple science articles and experiments.

As an educational tool, *EJ* may well have served as a text for multigenerational reading. The first issue of *Ebony Jr!*, published in May 1973, was highly literary and geared toward the fifth-grade level as calculated according to Fry's Readability Graph.[23] With the June/July 1973 issue, *EJ* began to gear itself toward a reading level appropriate for children aged five to eleven. The subsequent issues had simpler sentences, as seen in Jacob Lawrence's "Harriet and the Promised Land," with sentences like "Harriet, Harriet born a slave./Work for your master/From your cradle to your grave."[24] During this time, Sunny, Honey, and their doll were instituted to offer primary reading material. As an activity sheet in the June/July 1973 issue, the narrative for their column read, "I dance. You dance. We dance? I don't dance."[25] Text written at this level could easily be read by those children at the younger end of the target audience, while the longer narratives were appropriate for those toward the upper end of the age range. In addition, the longer narratives could be read to younger children by more advanced readers.

Although the reading level ranged from approximately first through sixth grade, sometimes the reading level did not coincide with the skill level required for the educational activity that followed the article. For example, "The Haunted Ship in Charleston Harbor" by Norma Poinsett was written at a fifth-grade reading level.[26] Following the short story was an illustration titled "Help Robert Smalls Escape!" that depicted a steamboat at the beginning of a maze that mimicked water waves, with a dock as the goal.[27] Although the task might interest any reader, the skill level required to complete the maze was significantly lower than the reading level required to decode the text. Therefore, a younger reader could have had the story read to him or her and then attempted the maze. This difference may have encouraged and supported an intergenerational and/or multiage reading of the text.

For older readers outside *EJ*'s target audience, there was a lot to be learned from *EJ*.[28] Ethnically centered education, according to Norman Dixon, is not limited to children; it includes all the generations, sometimes learning together. The information about African American history might have been new to them, and they might have been interested in the many columns about adult political leaders, sports figures, and entertainers. And for the older adolescent or adult reader who was unable to read at a sixth-grade level, *EJ* may have been an accessible text. Although these readers may not have been able to decode material written at a sixth-grade level or above, they may have been able to read *EJ*, even under the guise of reading to a child.

In addition to multigenerational reading, intertextuality between various JPC publications was assumed and encouraged, as demonstrated in the cooking segment "A Cookie Painted Picture" in the December 1973 issue. Readers were told that in order to make the cookies needed for the project, they could "use the recipe for 'Old-Fashioned Sugar Cookies found in the *Ebony Cookbook*.'"[29] The sharing of different JPC publications was encouraged by the editors, as demonstrated in their choice of letters from child readers to publish. In the "From Our Readers" column in one 1974 issue appeared a letter from Adrienne, who stated, "My parents read the big *Ebony*. Boy, I am glad that you made one for kids."[30] In another column also published in 1974, after describing her parents, Susan Clark stated, "They read *Ebony* magazine." [31] Again, the reader's family is constructed as reading multiple JPC publications. Further, reading *EJ* was not only educational—it could serve other purposes, such as keeping loneliness at bay.

But *EJ* did not stay the same from its beginning in 1973 until its demise in 1985. As the managing editors and the issues facing the African American community changed, so did *EJ*. Shifts in direction are noticeable in the approaches taken by three of its four editors.

EDITORS

Constance Van Brunt Johnson

As noted earlier, the first managing editor of *EJ*, serving from its inception until April 1977[32] was Constance Van Brunt Johnson, a Harvard-trained teacher who set the primary tone for the magazine, although John H. Johnson, in his roles as publisher and editor, retained ultimate control. The content and philosophy of *EJ* were Van Brunt Johnson's creations, while John Johnson reportedly conceived and initiated *EJ* in response to letters "from readers asking where they could acquire black literature for elementary schoolers."[33] Van Brunt Johnson (who was no relation to John H. Johnson) "finagled a job as a temporary assistant to the library filing clerk at the publishing company to be close to the action."[34] A native of Los Angeles, Van Brunt Johnson graduated from Sarah Lawrence College and earned her master's and teaching and reading specialist degrees from the Harvard University Graduate School of Education.[35] She worked as a teacher and a reading tutor and conducted literacy research on Black children in Guyana.[36] The first years of *EJ* reflected Van Brunt Johnson's commitment to education and her desire to package learning experiences in ways that would readily engage child readers. More so than any of the other managing editors, Van Brunt Johnson made it her mission to motivate reading mastery and prepare Black children for a life as well-educated citizens.[37]

To accomplish this task, Van Brunt Johnson included in each issue approximately twenty pages of activity sheets, ranging from narrative-related mazes, puzzles, and games to lessons in phonics, math, science, and arts and crafts. Additionally, an annual writing contest was instituted for different age groups, with the winners of each division receiving a prize and having their texts printed in *EJ*. Most of the theme-related stories had associated activity sheets that followed the narrative, with some activity sheets highlighting stock characters. For example, the Phonics Loonicans accompanied the phonics lessons, and "Mama Write-On's Scribblin' Scope," removed toward the end of Van Brunt Johnson's tenure, provided readers with incentive to practice penmanship under the ruse that Mama Write-On would tell them something about themselves via their penmanship. The sheets, based upon their text-related topic and with their diversity and quantity, helped make *Ebony Jr!* fun by engaging readers in activities—always a plus for the child and the parent.

Van Brunt Johnson's first two issues, May and June/July 1973, were unlike the remainder of the issues of her run and reflected her vision without the benefit of much reader response. Both were more political than the rest of the run, using, for example, traditional Afrocentric names for characters, such as Kwame and Lucy Mae. Van Brunt Johnson included an article on Africa in each issue, and tried to reach a distinctly "African American child" by lining up content and pedagogy with the contemporary educational discourses about teaching African American children. But to make this educational material "fun" and something that children would want to engage in, she inserted popular culture items that were "hip" and "cool." In this vein, Van Brunt Johnson incorporated language and language patterns thought to be common in the community in response. There was a significant amount of rhyming and rhythm in Van Brunt Johnson's first few issues, such as in the article, "Bobbie and Bubba and the B-A-A-D Babble Apple Mystery," a skit about a talking apple that ends with the moral: "If an apple named Fred jumps over your head/or calls itself Clyde and starts to slide,/You can be sure that Willy Worm is hiding inside!"

Featuring African American entertainers and sports figures was another attempt to make *EJ* hip—therefore relevant and hopefully engaging. Under Van Brunt Johnson more than any other editor, entertainers and sports figures of interest to children were featured regularly. The Jackson 5 was a staple, while sports figures such as Arthur Ashe were often on the cover or featured in interviews. The use of Black language patterns and trendy entertainers may have been an effort to ground *EJ* in the then-current Black youth culture to make it appealing to young readers. But evidently this approach was not acceptable to teachers and parents concerned about Black children learning standard English, so by the third issue—August/September 1973—there was a significant decrease in the use of vernacular. The second issue was probably predominantly completed by the time JPC received much response to the first issue, which may account for the change occurring in the third and not the second issue. Evidently the adults did not object to Van Brunt Johnson's choices for personalities to feature, since she continued to feature prominent black entertainers and sports figures.

Another aspect of the Black community Van Brunt Johnson incorporated was the Black Nationalist values that emphasized community and
social justice more than individual achievement, which I will discuss in
chapter 4. Black Nationalists criticized the Black middle class for what
they saw as a disinterest in the poor and disadvantaged.[38] Although Van
Brunt Johnson included fashion and popular culture features to appeal to
children, she did not encourage consumerism. At *EJ*'s inception, materialism was strictly incompatible with Afrocentric values, and it was not necessarily aligned with *EJ*'s educational mission. Under Van Brunt Johnson's leadership, there were few stories about children longing for
material objects, and those that did posed a moral lesson about the value
of community.

For example, in "Peter's Tenth Christmas," Peter got the poorest child in
his class, Sarah, for his grab bag partner.[39] Being more affluent, he saved
his money and was proud of the gift he bought her. She, on the other hand,
was poor and could not afford to buy Peter a gift. Ashamed, she gave him
the only present she received: a pink flannel gown. Peter returned the gift
to her and expressed an improved attitude about giving and receiving:
"Well, I didn't get a present from the grab bag that Christmas. I got something a lot better. Even though I left school empty-handed, I had learned
what giving and receiving really means."[40] Peter was not disgruntled because he did not receive a gift. The lesson Peter—and possibly the reader—
learned was that community and giving is more valuable than the acqui-
sition of gifts. Implied was the idea that those who are more fortunate have
a moral obligation to help community members in need. Further, unlike
the bourgeoisie that Black Nationalists disparaged, Peter did not degrade
Sarah for her poverty, nor did he fall prey to class-based superiority; therefore, Peter did not create a division between himself as a representative of
the middle class and Sarah as a member of the lower class.

Because of its community-based values and the educational curriculum, critics generally agreed that Van Brunt Johnson's *EJ* was a hit. In a
brief discussion of children's magazines that were deemed "first purchase" items for every library, influential librarian and reference expert
William A. Katz stated,

> Based on the idea that reading opens the door to opportunity and that learn-
> ing is fun, its [*EJ*'s] purpose is to stimulate pride in and knowledge of black
> history. The themes—black is beautiful and unity among blacks—permeate
> every page from the puzzles to the stories. . . . Educational for the white com-
> munity too. Should be in all public and school libraries.[41]

Katz's *Magazines for Libraries: For the General Reader, and School, Junior College, and Public Libraries* was a staple resource for collection development

in libraries. It is quite possible that teachers and librarians took Katz's suggestion, since circulation for *EJ* was approximately twenty thousand at its tenth anniversary.

Van Brunt Johnson set forth the basic pattern for *EJ*: that is, each issue would have a theme, a group of narratives, multiple reader response columns, and arts and crafts segments. Although *EJ*'s emphasis on academic education would be diminished when Van Brunt Johnson was replaced as managing editor, the academic focus remained a well-rounded one that included reading, math, and science. In addition, the racialized lessons she instituted in the narratives on African and African American history and culture would remain.

Mary C. Lewis

Although Karen Odom Gray[42] served as managing editor from May 1977 through January 1978, no significant changes were made until the editorship changed again, to Mary C. Lewis, who held the position from February 1978 until March 1982.[43] While much of *EJ* remained the same, Lewis expanded the curriculum, reduced the length of the issues, deleted many of the popular culture references, and reflected the economic changes in the Black community of the late 1970s and early 1980s. The educational mission and overall structure of *EJ* remained the same: For instance, narratives emphasizing African and African American history and culture were still included, and fictional materials still played a significant role.

Lewis's changes to the magazine's content included extending the language arts curriculum by encouraging readers to write. Readers were given the beginning of a story—which provided the setting, characters, and conflict—and were then asked to imagine, and hopefully write, possible endings for the story. For example, in Renee King's "Great Galaxies, What a Mess!" readers were asked:

> If you were Sitembile [the protagonist], what would you do? Here's your chance to put yourself in someone else's shoes. After reading this story, think about all the different possible endings this story could have. Then choose the one you think is the best ending and write a story.[44]

This effort was aligned with the writing contest Van Brunt Johnson initiated and may have reflected writing exercises teachers used in school and storytellers used in the community.

Other changes in the educational focus of the magazine included the way historical fiction and nonfiction were presented. History was told more thoroughly, with the assumption of prior knowledge on the reader's part being less apparent than under Van Brunt Johnson's tenure. For example, one of the first narratives Van Brunt Johnson published was Norma Poinsett's "The Haunted Ship in Charleston Harbor," about how Robert Small escaped from slavery.[45] Beginning the metanarrative of African American history with such a story assumes that the reader has basic knowledge of Africans being captured and enslaved in the United States. Under Lewis's direction, the narratives gave more comprehensive information on the historical or cultural events they discussed. Unlike Van Brunt Johnson, Lewis did not assume a certain level of knowledge of history. The backlash from the Civil Rights Movement during the years of the Reagan administration (1980–1988) produced a conservative economic and political climate. There was less discussion of Afrocentric matters in the press in general, which led Lewis not to assume a certain level of knowledge of history on the part of the child reader.

The most noteworthy alteration under Lewis's editorship was the removal of approximately one-half of the educational activity sheets that followed most narratives and that were peppered through each issue. This reduced each issue from an average of sixty pages to fifty pages. Although the narratives and some literacy and science worksheets remained, *EJ* was no longer the educational tool it had been. The removal of many of the activity sheets significantly reduced the types and the level of interaction children could have with *EJ*. Lewis also removed much of the emphasis on popular culture. Gone were the many interviews with Michael Jackson and similar figures, and there was less emphasis on entertainers and sports stars. In short, Lewis removed a significant portion of the entertainment component of this "edutainment" periodical, leaving an education focus that may have made *EJ* less engaging—and may have translated into less "fun" for readers. The removal of the worksheets may have constituted a questionable change to teachers and parents who bought into *EJ* as an educational tool, while the removal of the popular culture references may have made *EJ* less attractive to the child reader. But it is possible that Lewis's reduction in the length of *EJ* and the number of popular culture references may have been influenced by the changing economic conditions of the Black community.

The economic conditions of Blacks changed in the late 1970s: some for the better and others for the worse. The financial status of the Black middle class improved significantly from the mid-1950s through the late 1970s because of the Black Liberation Movement. Some middle-class Blacks gained ground through affirmative action, which facilitated their admission to college and their subsequent employment, which had previously been denied them solely based on their race. Thus, between 1969 and 1974, "earnings of the top 5 percent of all non-white families increased from $17,238 to $24,267, about 74 percent of the level for that of white families of similar background."[46] But the middle class constituted only 7 to 10 percent of the Black community in the mid-1970s. During this same time, the social and economic situation of the majority of Blacks—urban and rural—either stayed the same or became worse. Of course, these issues were noted by JPC's continued coverage of the socioeconomic standing of the African American community in its annual progress reports:

> [Nineteen seventy-four] marked the continued erosion of the economic and social beachheads that Blacks established in the 1960s and 1970s. Whether the public issue was affirmative action in employment or school desegregation, the survival of civil rights organizations, the harnessing of Black political power or the expansion of Black businesses, conditions within Black America deteriorated at an alarming rate.[47]

JPC's awareness of the decline in the economic success of much of the Black community surely informed the construction of *EJ*. Aware that the socioeconomic conditions of the majority of the Black community were stagnant, Johnson and Lewis began to make changes in *EJ*.

The reduction in its length from sixty to fifty pages reduced printing costs and may have made *EJ* more profitable, or at least sustainable. Again, JPC was, and is, a corporate structure primarily concerned with its profits and continued growth. The decrease in popular culture references may have made the way for other changes in *EJ* that both reflected the economic conditions of the community and shifted its values toward preparing readers for their economic future. The most didactic device used to address the worsening economy was the inclusion of a career education component: the "Junior Consumer" column. Career education became a common element of *EJ*'s monthly themes: For example, the theme of the May 1978 issue was "Lights! Camera! ACTION!" which, according to Sunny and Honey, "focus[ed] in on the world of film, photography, and television."[48] The intention was for readers "to learn how to take great photos, and . . . get into movie-making."[49] Readers would also be exposed to "the television scene and . . . learn how to make [their] own cartoons."[50] Features that highlighted photography included "How to Be a Sharpshooter," an article narrated by Carmen Camera. The purpose of the article was to "let [readers] in on some basics of photography so [they'd] be able to take some great pictures."[51] It included a brief history of photography, a description of the mechanics of a camera, and a discussion of which type of camera was most suitable for children before giving instructions on how to take a photograph. The issue also included a biography of the prominent African American photographer James Van-DerZee. Aligned with the elements of children's literature, the article began with VanDerZee as a child longing for a camera before continuing with the story of his career as a photographer in Harlem.[52] The next article, "Super Shutterbug," featured younger photographers in Chicago, where Johnson Publishing Company is located, and offered "Tips on Becoming a Photographer,"[53] encouraging readers to "start NOW" to determine if they were interested in photography; educate themselves by studying photographs, taking pictures, and reading books on the subject; enter contests; and, most importantly, "[r]emember—you *can* be a photographer. Work hard, have confidence and *never give up!*"[54] Cognizant of gender issues, the article also featured a woman photographer. Not to be mired in career education, this issue also featured Mother's Day and *EJ*'s "birthday," as it was labeled in that month's calendar. Other issues featured various themes and careers. Vocational education was a consistent component of *EJ*'s instructional curriculum until its demise in 1985.

Lewis made other changes in *EJ* as well. While they were not as significant as the curricular changes, they slightly altered *EJ*'s reflection of the Black child reader. As stated earlier, one of Johnson and Van Brunt Johnson's initial intentions was to encourage racialized pride in *EJ*'s readers. One of the ways in which Van Brunt Johnson approached this mission was by reflecting Black children exclusively in *EJ*'s illustrations—cartoons, photographs, and, in particular, the *Ebony Jr!* Art Gallery. As noted earlier, Black children were rarely included in mainstream children's literature, be it books or periodicals, during the 1970s. As a teacher, Van Brunt Johnson was concerned with the academic and psychological education of Black children. In order to encourage a positive self-image, she created Afrocentric images of the primary characters and concentrated on faces of Black children in the *Ebony Jr!* Art Gallery. Lewis, on the other hand, deemphasized faces in the art gallery and published various images submitted by readers. For example, the October 1979 issue included pictures of a farm, Spider-Man, a pumpkin, a scarecrow figure, and a cowboy in addition to some faces. Although these new images reflected a variety of children's interests and may have aligned *EJ* with its contemporaries by including various forms of reader art, it failed to celebrate and mirror the image of the Black child reader, as *EJ* had earlier.

Many of the changes instituted under Lewis's tenure (e.g., changes in the narratives and the deletion of worksheets) may have begun the demise of *EJ*. Parents who were accustomed to worksheets as educational tools may have been disappointed with the deletion of half of the activity sheets. And the removal of many popular culture references may have made *EJ* less appealing to children. The addition of career education may have been appealing to parents but possibly less so to children. The general appearance (e.g., quality of illustrations) was less appealing than the format produced under Van Brunt Johnson's leadership. These changes occurred either because of, or concurrent with, the deterioration of the socioeconomic conditions in the Black community for all but the middle class, which may have translated to reduced sales for *EJ*. While the educational focus remained the same, *EJ* evolved into something very literary, with narrative material no longer intermixed with activity sheets. With these changes, *EJ* was no longer "hip" and was far less interesting.

Marcia Roebuck-Hoard

The fourth and final managing editor of *EJ* was Marcia Roebuck-Hoard, who served as editor from April 1982 until October 1985. *Jet* announced her arrival:

> [Under the guidance of Managing Editor Marcia Roebuck-Hoard, staff and freelance writers and artists] produce a top notch children's publication that is designed to challenge youngsters as it develops their reading, spelling, comprehension and creative skills.[55]

An educator like Van Brunt Johnson, Roebuck-Hoard had a degree in educational therapy from National College of Education (now National-Louis University) in Evanston, Illinois.[56] Roebuck-Hoard made multiple changes during her tenure, placing an even greater emphasis on economic and political issues, including images of angry and frustrated people, and reincorporating the use of popular culture into the narratives. Conflict between the classes became apparent, as will be discussed below, and the overt messages defining Blackness were lessened, which will also be discussed below.

Roebuck-Hoard relied heavily on themes and on preparing readers for an economic future in addition to a literary one. For example, Kwanzaa, which had usually been privileged in *EJ* in the 1970s, was emphasized less in the December 1981 issue, and Christmas, with its accompanying consumerism, was the focus. The "Sunny and Honey" cartoon in that issue was particularly noticeable in its shift toward the mainstream and toward consumerism. In that month's feature, both Sunny and Honey were loaded down with packages as they walked through the snow. The text read: "We did our Christmas shopping real early./Because the holiday crowds can be rough./So we really shouldn't be frustrated and gruff./But we can't remember where we hid all that stuff!"[57] Never before had Sunny and Honey been particularly concerned with money, shopping, or material goods.

In addition to demonstrating *EJ*'s changing economic focus, Sunny and Honey also demonstrated the changing political relationships between the middle and lower classes. Poverty was never belittled in *EJ* in the 1970s, but the 1980s comprised a different economic and political moment. In the November 1981 "Sunny and Honey" cartoon, the illustration was of Honey playing the piano, Sunny playing an acoustic guitar, and the doll sitting on the piano. They were all dressed in jeans. All of them were singing, "We love good music, especially if it's bad!"[58] In the next cell, Sunny was in a tuxedo playing a violin and Honey was wiping away tears. The text read, "Music can make you happy, or it can make you sad."[59] In the next cell, Sunny and Honey were back in jeans and the doll was dancing in a ballerina costume. The text read, "It can make you dance slow, or boogie real fast."[60] In the final cell, Sunny and Honey were scowling and covering their ears. Three men with boom boxes were in the background and all appeared to be of a lower socioeconomic status than Sunny and Honey. They all had toothpicks hanging out of their mouths: one had on an apple hat, one wore a big "pimp" hat, and the other wore a baseball cap turned backward. Coming from the men's radios was: "Ah Loves You-u Bay-Bab-y." Coming from Sunny and Honey was the text: "There's also music that can make you sick!"[61]

Never before had the differences between the classes been displayed in such a derogatory manner. The narrative "Peter's Tenth Christmas," as already noted, displayed a difference between the classes, but not a sense of superiority. In 1981, images of high culture that were shown were affiliated more with European culture than African culture, for example, the tuxedo, violin, and references to ballet. Low culture (the culture of "the folk") was defined by the men with boom boxes, fashionable hats, and "jive" mannerisms. There was some distance between the two classes, as in the 1970s, but now the cartoon demonstrated a noticeable disdain for the lower class. Whereas the animosity in this Sunny and Honey article was one sided, history tells us that the lower classes also took issue with the bourgeoisie. In any case, the disdain between the classes in the 1970s was not shown in *EJ*, when racial and ethnic solidarity was the focus. Although there were problems between the classes in the 1970s, the image portrayed in the pages of *EJ* was one of compassion.

Sunny and Honey made another political statement that reflected the economic and educational conditions of many Black children in the May 1981 issue. In this column, Sunny wore a shirt and tie and Honey had on a turtleneck and pants. Neither of them looked as hip as they had in the 1970s. Both held books in their left hands and gestured to a song with their right. The lyrics, to be sung to Sam Cooke's 1960s hit "Wonderful World," are "Don't know much about history-y./Don't know much biology-y./Don't know much about using tools./Sure hope they hurry up and improve our schools."[62] The illustration for the last line is of Sunny and Honey walking past a vacant lot full of trash along a street with low-rise government housing.

This was clearly a statement about the quality of the education curriculum, teachers, and facilities available to most African American children in the late 1970s and 1980s. Sunny and Honey listed the subjects in which they were below standard. They didn't know much about history, biology, or vocational skills. They had neither the liberal arts education that W. E. B. DuBois advocated nor the vocational training that Booker T. Washington favored. The child reader may have lived in such a situation; if not, he or she had most likely heard about the abominable education that many Black children received—and, some would say, still receive. The "projects," as they were known in Chicago then, in the illustration reflect the urbanization, resegregation, and economic decay in the African American community at that time. The text can be read two ways: Because of racial inequality, poor children received an inadequate education, and/or a deficient education led to poverty. Either way, it is clear that a connection was being made between the quality of education one received and the economic implications of such an education.

Needless to say, the lyrics Sunny and Honey sing are different than those written by Sam Cooke, Lou Adler, and Herb Alpert. The third line in verse is not "Don't know much about using tools," but "Don't know much about a science book." I suspect that this reference to tools, or vocational education, connected with Booker T. Washington's enthusiasm for a skills-based education. In his autobiography, John H. Johnson stated that Washington and his accomplishments and philosophies had made a strong impression him.[63] The child reader may have understood that African American children were not being educated with either a liberal arts curriculum or a vocational one in the public schools. I am less sure that the audience in 1981 when this article appeared, who ranged from five to eleven years old, would have known the melody that accompanied the lyrics. The song, although a classic, is still a 1960s song and probably not one considered hip by the five-to-eleven-year-old child reader in 1981. On the other hand, while some children may have heard the song, few would consider it current and a component of Black children's popular culture. By the early 1980s, *EJ* was so far removed from the popular culture interests of the child reader that the beginning of the end was already foreshadowed.

Also noteworthy in this "Sunny and Honey" cartoon were the images of people with scowling faces, which, again, may be in response to the changing economic and political environment. Under Van Brunt Johnson for sure, and Lewis to a lesser extent, the faces of most of the people in *EJ* were pleasant. In the 1980s the adults began to scowl and yell at children, and the children themselves began to have unpleasant, angry, and frustrated looks on their faces. In another column in the May 1981 issue, "Our Ninth Annual Writing Contest," readers were invited to write stories about the adjacent illustration. The man in the illustration was an old, angular, impoverished-looking man who wore a scowl on his face. The boy standing opposite the man had a sarcastic expression. The title of the essay to be submitted was, "Audacious (say: O day shus) Orville

was a fantastic storyteller." Readers were told to assume that the boy had
been challenged to write a story by "Franklinfavorite Tealeington, the
ninety-year-old expert," who, one can assume, was the elderly man in
the illustration.[64] Another example appeared in the July 1981 calendar,
where the illustration was of a group of children who all had scowls on
their faces while they concentrated on a game of marbles. The scowls
were not a fundamental component of the narrative; the children could
have been shown to concentrate without the scowls, but again, the illustrations reflected the times and the adults' perception of children.

In contrast, in the 1970s the adults may have been upset and disappointed, but they did not have scowls on their faces. In the January 1974
story "Nothing to Do," by Eloise Greenfield, two boys were bored and
were throwing rocks.[65] One of the boys threw a rock at a car, and the man
driving stopped and got out of the car. He angrily grabbed the boys and
told them how dangerous their behavior had been to him, his wife, and
their new infant. The boys were appropriately apologetic and appeared to
have learned their lesson. This accentuated Afrocentric values: In the tradition of the axiom "It takes a village to raise a child," this adult taught
the boys how to be, if not productive, at least not destructive members of
the community. Although the man was clearly angry and looked stern, he
did not have the frown on his face that was so prevalent in the 1980s. As
will be discussed in chapter 4, the changing political climate might have
been a factor, given the backlash people were being subjected to over their
earlier involvement in the Civil Rights Movement.

I have already noted how Sunny and Honey's hair and clothes
changed. Other characters changed as well. In "Tina's Present," written
by Karen T. Taha and illustrated by Buck Brown, the family was not encoded, as such families had been in the past, as African American. Fashion was no longer racialized or used to make a statement; clothes were
mainstream and boring.[66] Historically in the 1970s, there was a distinctly
African American fashion sense, although to a lesser degree, Afrocentric
style was also apparent in the 1980s. But it was not exhibited in the pages
of *EJ*. Accordingly, the hair was relaxed and curled on both mothers and
daughters, something I will discuss further in a subsequent chapter.

Roebuck-Hoard tried to make *EJ* hip and thereby appealing to children,
with a return to the use of popular culture references and continued use
of thematic issues and reader response columns. But the image of *EJ*
among the magazine-reading public had changed, in part because of the
decreased number of activity sheets, the increased literary nature of the
text, and the references and topics that were less engaging to children
than they had been under a different editor and different socioeconomic
conditions in the African American community. The times had changed—
and so had *EJ*. But, I contend, the changes did not reflect the child reader,

and, more importantly, teachers and parents did not buy *EJ* as they had in the beginning.

EBONY JR! ONLINE

Ebony Jr! was reincarnated during the summer of 2007 in an online version published by JPC.[67] Currently, the Web site appears to be in its infancy, therefore it lacks the depth and breath of the print version. Yet the site is colorful and has engaging music to which Sunny and Honey dance. The Web site has three sections: "What's Up?" "Old Stuff," and "Downloads." The "What's Up?" section welcomes the reader using dialogue bubbles coming from both Sunny and Honey. "Old time" copies of *EJ* are included in the "Old Stuff" section. Coloring sheets and images of Sunny and Honey are available in "Downloads." Based on the silhouette behind Sunny and Honey, which includes the Sears Tower, they are in Chicago. From the perspective of the buildings, they are east of Johnson Publishing Company's Chicago headquarters on Michigan Avenue—probably across the street in Grant Park. On the "What's Up?" page, Sunny and Honey stand in front of a school named JPC Academy.

In the contemporary version, Sunny and Honey appear to be in middle school. In the print version they began as elementary school–aged children and as time progressed they grew older, so that toward the end of the run they appeared to be middle school–aged as well. Like the Honey of the early 1970s, the contemporary Honey wears her hair in a natural-textured style of two Afro puffs. She is dressed in the current style: beige cargo capris, similar to those made by Baby Phat, and a t-shirt with a flower on the front.[68] Like so many young people, Honey holds a cell phone in her hand, with her picture as the wallpaper on the phone. While Honey is "caramel colored," Sunny's skin tone is more in the "chocolate" range. Under a red cap, he wears his hair in cornrows. He also wears a basketball jersey and bounces a basketball. Instead of a basketball player's number and a team's logo, Sunny's shirt has an "S" on it. And like Sunny of the 1970s and 1980s, he wears glasses. On the "Downloads" page, he holds a video game titled "Space Shooters"; red and yellow bursts of color are reflected in his glasses. The doll has been replaced by a gray dog with black hair atop his head (it looks like a wig); lacking hair on a portion of his tail and chest, the dog looks like he has mange.

In the introduction, there are dialogue bubbles coming from Sunny and Honey welcoming visitors. Aligned with its Afrocentric orientation, the new Sunny and Honey use the language of contemporary children and young adults. For example, after introducing themselves—Honey refers to herself as Sunny's sister and his "gorgeous sister"—Sunny states, "It

would be so cool if you hang with us." Honey says, "Yeah, come check
out our school and stuff." "Oh yeah, we've also got wicked games &
music. Whaddya think?" Sunny says. The last line is, "Oh well, thanks
for hanging with us. We'll catch you later."[69] Like the "old time" Sunny
and Honey, these characters use vernacular familiar to most children,
which orients the text toward the child reader, but the language used is
not something that parents would find problematic. Honey's definition
of herself as "gorgeous" might foreshadow JPC's continued concern
about presenting positive images of African Americans and an attempt
to encourage self-esteem in its readers. Further, the relationship between
Sunny and Honey is loving but playful. After Honey says she is gorgeous, Sunny sighs and continues with the introduction. I can just imagine him rolling his eyes at her. This tension is common in contemporary
siblings. Defining Sunny and Honey as siblings—which was not clearly
stated in the print version—removes any sexual connotations from their
relationship.

It appears that *EJ* online is aligned with the print version: Sunny and
Honey are retained as stock characters and the Afrocentric focus is retained. I do not have enough evidence to speculate why the doll was
deleted in place of a mangy dog. Maybe JPC thinks that contemporary
middle school children, who have cell phones and video games, are less
interested in dolls than the Sunny and Honey of the 1970s and 1980s
would have been. Children's entertainment venues have changed in
thirty years, and so Sunny and Honey have been appropriately updated:
Honey holds a cell phone, Sunny has his video game, and their clothes
mark them as current and fashionable children. Based on the skyscrapers
in the background, the characters live in an urban, northern city—which
can be read as Chicago if the reader knows the shape of the skyline. Does
the inclusion of JPC Academy foreshadow an educational component
with activity sheets? If so, it would make the online magazine engaging
for children and approved by parents. At a moment when children want
to be online and parents are concerned about the subject matter to which
this gives the child access, this Web site would be on the approved list.
Once JPC completes the site, it might be engaging for children.

CONCLUSION

To fully understand *EJ*, one has to put it within the context of its historical moment. Given the sociocultural and educational time frame, what
was the JPC trying to teach African American children? Essentially, *EJ*
points to the way the community sought to teach African American children how to live as racialized beings in the United States.

EJ was a dominant and pivotal force most essential to the artistic development and mass circulation of Afrocentric juvenile literature that would not have otherwise been totally accessible to Black children and adults.[70] To support such a statement, my next endeavor will be to contextualize *EJ* within the field of children's periodicals at its inception and Black magazines in general, but specifically those targeting children.

NOTES

1. Aligned with Molefi Asante I define *Afrocentricity* as a philosophical and theoretical framework that looks to Africa and the Diaspora, as opposed to Europe, particularly Greece, as the center of culture and knowledge. In so doing, African peoples become human subjects with agency instead of objects informed by Eurocentric thought and actions. In an Afrocentric view "location takes precedence over the topic or the data under consideration" since Africans have been dislocated from the focus of social, political, philosophic, and economic discourses while all things Eurocentric have taken center stage.

An Afrocentric perspective privileges the experience, culture, and knowledge of the Diaspora and prevents Blacks from being viewed as the "other." Although Afrocentricity is typically oriented toward Africa, this orientation does not preclude the African American community, as part of the Diaspora, from being considered a locus of culture and knowledge. Finally, "Afrocentricity is not a counterpoint to Eurocentricity," and it does not seek to "occupy all space and time as Eurocentricism has often done." Molefi K. Asante, "Afrocentricity," in *The Dictionary of Race and Ethnic Relations*, ed. Ernest Cashmore (London: Routledge & Kegan Paul, 1984), 24.

2. Walter C. Daniel, *Black Journals in the United States: Historical Guides to the World's Periodicals and Newspapers* (Westport, CT: Greenwood Press, 1982), 164.

3. Johnson Publishing Company denied my request for copyright privileges; therefore, I will not include illustrations of the images I discuss in this text.

4. *"Ebony Jr!* Celebrates Its Tenth Anniversary with Special May Issue," *Jet*, May 9, 1983, 14.

5. Lynn Norment, "Welcome to Success," *Ebony Jr!*, August/September 1981.

6. Anne Rowry Jones, "Phonics with the Loonicans," *Ebony Jr!*, August/September 1981, 12.

7. "Calendar," *Ebony Jr!*, June/July 1975.

8. John H. Johnson and Lerone Bennett, *Succeeding against the Odds* (Chicago: Johnson Publishing, 1989), 156–57.

9. I look to Stephen Small's definition of racialization as the

social structures, social ideologies and attitudes [that] have historically become imbued with "racial" meaning. . . . [S]uch meanings are contingent and contested, and . . . they are shaped by a multitude of other variables, economic, political, and religious.

Stephen Small, *Racialised Barriers: The Black Experience in the United States and England in the 1980s*, Critical Studies in Racism and Migration (London: Routledge, 1994), 36.

One who is "racialized" has had to interact with and be informed by a social matrix that views them through a lens colored by various definitions of race.

10. Sherry Ricchiardi, "At 23, She Lands Top Job on Magazine for Black Youths," *Des Moines Register*, May 2, 1973.

11. Frankie Cox, "Tough Enough," *Ebony Jr!*, June/July 1973.

12. Richard Wright, "Blueprint for Negro Writing," in *Within the Circle: An Anthology of African American Literary Criticism from the Harlem Renaissance to the Present*, ed. Angelyn Mitchell (Durham: Duke University Press, 1937; reprint, 1994).

13. Houston A. Baker, *Blues, Ideology, and Afro-American Literature: A Vernacular Theory* (Chicago: University of Chicago Press, 1984).

14. Carol Searcy, "Sneezing Powder," *Ebony Jr!*, January 1974.

15. "*Ebony Jr!* Celebrates Its Tenth Anniversary with Special May Issue."

16. "Johnson Introduces Magazine Designed for Black Children," *Jet*, May 10, 1973, 53.

17. Johnson and Bennett, *Succeeding against the Odds*.

18. Daniel, *Black Journals in the United States*.

19. Sharon Bell Mathis, "Ebony Jr! News," *Ebony Jr!*, February 1974.

20. "Johnson Introduces Magazine Designed for Black Children," 54.

21. Ricchiardi, "At 23, She Lands Top Job on Magazine for Black Youths," 13.

22. "Johnson Introduces," 54.

23. Edward Fry, "Fry's Readability Graph: Clarifications, Validity, and Extension to Level," *Journal of Reading* 21, no. 3 (1977).

24. Jacob Lawrence, "Harriet and the Promised Land," *Ebony Jr!*, June/July 1973.

25. "Sunny and Honey," *Ebony Jr!*, June/July 1973.

26. Norma Poinsett and illustrations by Orville Hurt, "The Haunted Ship in Charleston Harbor," *Ebony Jr!*, November 1973.

27. "Help Robert Smalls Escape," *Ebony Jr!*, November 1973, 12.

28. Norman R. Dixon, "Defining the Situation: Toward a Definition of Black Education," *Negro Educational Review* 14, no. 3 & 4 (1973).

29. "A Cookie Painted Picture," *Ebony Jr!*, December 1973, 29.

30. "From Our Readers," *Ebony Jr!*, January 1974, 39.

31. "From Our Readers," *Ebony Jr!*, December 1974, 60.

32. In an earlier article, "*Ebony Jr!*: The Rise—and Demise—of an African American Children's magazine," I mistakenly stated that Constance Van Brunt Johnson was editor until April 1976 and that Karen Odom Gray began her tenure in May 1976. This transition happened in 1977.

33. Ricchiardi, "At 23, She Lands Top Job on Magazine for Black Youths," 13.

34. Ibid.

35. Ibid.

36. Ibid.

37. "Johnson Introduces Magazine Designed for Black Children," 52.

38. Manning Marable, *Race, Reform, and Rebellion: The Second Reconstruction in Black America, 1945–1990*, 2nd ed. (Jackson: University Press of Mississippi, 1991).

39. Carol Searcy, "Peter's Tenth Christmas," *Ebony Jr!*, December 1973.

40. Ibid., 41.

41. William A. Katz, *Magazines for Libraries: For the General Reader, and School, Junior College, and Public Libraries*, 2nd supp. ed. (New York: Bowker, 1974).

42. Karen Odom Gray later dropped the surname "Gray."

43. Lewis began her work with *EJ* as the assistant editor in December 1977.

44. Renee King, "Great Galaxies, What a Mess!" *Ebony Jr!*, January 1980, 20–21.

45. Poinsett and Hurt, "The Haunted Ship in Charleston Harbor."

46. Marable, *Race, Reform, and Rebellion: The Second Reconstruction in Black America, 1945–1990*, 151.

47. Doris E. Saunders, ed., *The Ebony Handbook* (Chicago: Johnson Publishing, 1974), 118.

48. "A Letter from Sunny and Honey," *Ebony Jr!*, May 1978, 3.

49. Ibid.

50. Ibid.

51. Jan Lowery, "How to Be a Sharpshooter," *Ebony Jr!*, May 1978.

52. Mary C. Lewis, "James Van Der Zee," *Ebony Jr!*, May 1978.

53. Mary C. Lewis, "Super Shutterbug," *Ebony Jr!*, May 1978.

54. Ibid., 33.

55. "*Ebony Jr!* Celebrates Its Tenth Anniversary with Special May Issue," 14.

56. Ibid.

57. Buck Brown, illustrator, "Sunny and Honey," *Ebony Jr!*, December 1981.

58. "Sunny and Honey," November 1981, 22.

59. Ibid.

60. Ibid., 23.

61. Ibid.

62. Brown, "Sunny and Honey," 22–25.

63. Johnson and Bennett, *Succeeding against the Odds*.

64. "Our Ninth Annual Writing Contest," *Ebony Jr!*, May 1981, 14.

65. Eloise Greenfield, "Nothing to Do," *Ebony Jr!*, January 1974.

66. Karen T. Taha, "Tina's Present," *Ebony Jr!*, June/July 1981.

67. "Ebony Jr!: Sunny & Honey," http://ebonyjr.com/.

68. Baby Phat is a female hip-hop clothing line by Kimora Lee Simmons. The clothing line is popular with hip-hop artists and their fans.

69. "Ebony Jr!: Sunny & Honey."

70. Pearlie-Mae Peters, "Ebony Jr!," in *The Concise Oxford Companion to African American Literature*, ed. William L. Andrews, Frances Smith Foster, and Trudier Harris (New York: Oxford University Press, 1997).

2

✛

Ebony Jr!'s Market

The black child growing into adulthood . . . seeing white protagonists constantly . . . experiences [life] in someone else's image . . . sees, in other words, a zero image of [her/himself].—Carolyn F. Gerald

In the late 1960s and early 1970s, there were various literary issues concerning African American children's literature and mainstream children's periodicals that informed the publication of *Ebony Jr!* Within the African American community, while not specifically about children's literature, the Black Arts Movement focused the attention of African American art toward the community and away from what had been its primary focus—namely, interracial issues and the struggle for civil rights.[1] Scholars of children's literature noted the utter lack of literature written for and about Black children.[2] At the same time, the market for children's periodicals was strong. In this chapter, I am interested in an investigation of the market for children's and African American periodicals at *EJ*'s inception. To what degree did *EJ* correspond with the purpose and style of mainstream (White) children's periodicals? And was *EJ* aligned with the purposes and ideologies of African American magazines?

The first factor I will consider in constructing *EJ*'s market is the Black Arts Movement. The Black Power Movement, of which the Black Arts Movement is a component, was a push toward "racial pride, strength, and self-definition" that basically began with the death of Malcolm X.[3] It lasted from approximately 1965 to 1975.[4] The Black Power Movement proposed a Black Nationalist agenda, one that espoused a separate Black nation, culture, and art form with its own symbolism, mythology, critique, and iconology.[5] The leaders of the Black Power Movement understood that the arts were the best forum through which to disseminate their message and to enact material and political change. The Black Arts Movement focused attention on the Black community as the audience for Black art. It moved toward educating the African American community about its collective—and differing—histories, reflected the community and its culture and concerns, and addressed its social, spiritual, and physical needs.

It is within the Black Arts Movement that the discourse of the Black Aesthetic gathered momentum and began to affect the amount and types of art produced. Hoyt Fuller, an African American literary critic and editor of Johnson Publishing Company's *Black World* from 1970 until 1976 (when it ceased publication) stated that a Black Aesthetic needed to be defined, since the "style and language" of White literary forms are not "the appropriate limits and 'frame of reference' for African American literature."[6] The Black Aesthetic is "a system of isolating and evaluating the artistic works of black people which reflect the special character and imperative of black experience."[7] Even with the many differences within the African American community, Fuller stated that because of a shared racial history, "the road to solidarity and strength leads inevitably through reclamation and indoctrination of black art and culture."[8]

However, the Black Arts Movement generated considerable debate within the African American community. Cornell West and bell hooks criticized Afrocentrism (and by extension the Black Arts Movement), saying that it essentializes Blackness, engages reverse racism, stagnates the art form, and perpetuates sexism.[9] The movement has also been cited for its homophobic tendencies. All that said, the Black Aesthetic, as it defines the Black community as the target audience of Black art, is still an essential tool in grounding art in the Black community and in its sensibilities.

The Black Arts Movement displaced White with African and African American culture and experiences as the center of knowledge. African American authors and critics such as Addison Gayle, Hoyt Fuller, and Larry Neal, who aligned themselves with the Black Arts Movement, stated that it is imperative that Africans and African Americans look to their own communities, pasts, and issues, instead of European and European American ideas that are historically and essentially oppressive of African peoples, for validation and direction.[10] And as the needs of the community change, they asserted, so too must art. As African Americans face new challenges, the art should reflect the new sensibilities and values as well as the old. One of the main tenets of the Black Arts Movement is that the art remain identifiable and nourishing to the African American community. As I discuss in the subsequent chapters, Johnson was aware of the Black Arts Movement and the call for literature addressed to the

Black community. His entire empire was built on goods and services that targeted African Americans. He knew that there was a market for African American literature, in its various formats, and that the community purchased and disseminated these publications among themselves. But what other factors influenced his decision to publish *EJ*?

One such factor was the market for children's literature, specifically African American children's literature. *Ebony Jr!* premiered at a moment when African Americans were notably absent from much of children's literature and when children's periodicals were thriving. In her classic article "The All-White World of Children's Books," Nancy Larrick cited the omission of African American children from the text and trade books of the 1960s.[11] She stated,

> Of the 5,206 children's trade books launched by the sixty-three publishers in the three-year period [1962–64], only 349 include one or more Negroes—an average of 6.7 per cent. . . . The scarcity of children's books portraying American Negroes is much greater than the figure of 6.7 per cent would indicate, for almost 60 per cent of the books with Negroes are placed outside of continental United States or before World War II. . . . [Additionally,] [o]f the books which publishers report as "including one or more Negroes," many show only one or two dark faces in a crowd.[12]

Ten years prior to Larrick's 1965 article, textbooks had been criticized for their "blatant racial bias."[13] The advent of the Coretta Scott King Book Award in 1970 and the *Council on Interracial Books for Children Bulletin* in 1966, and the many additional activities of the council (e.g., awarding prizes to new authors, commissioning important studies, and publishing reviews), meant new support for African American–centered literature.[14] The Elementary and Secondary Education Act of 1965, a federal education law geared toward K–12 education, allocated funds for professional development for educators and resources to support programs and parental involvement; most important to this research, it funded instructional materials. Authorized in 1970, this act, along with these other factors, was pivotal in increasing the amount and quality of African American children's literature on the market.

However, Rudine Sims found in her 1982 survey of children's literature that included Black characters that most narratives were neither written for African American children nor designed to reflect their culture and interests.[15] Of the twenty-five hundred children's books published in 1985, only eighteen were written and illustrated by African Americans.[16] While others were published that featured Black characters, few were written and illustrated by cultural insiders. Clearly, throughout *EJ*'s run (1973–1985) there was a need for children's literature that featured and targeted African American children.

CHILDREN'S PERIODICALS OF THE MID-1970s

Another issue Johnson may have considered in determining whether or not to publish *EJ* was the healthy market for children's periodicals. According to the *Wall Street Journal*, in the mid-1970s children's magazines were thriving. Stephen Grover wrote, "Despite an economic climate that has killed a number of adult publications in recent years, there are more children's magazines around today than ever before."[17] Categories of these magazines included

> general magazines, organization magazines, magazines for teachers and pupils, news magazines, handicraft magazines, magazines of natural science, magazines of invention, magazines of sport, hobby magazines, and religious magazines. The boundaries between groups are often not distinct. [The] [o]rganization [of various] magazines overlap[s] into other interests and categories in several directions.[18]

Part of the appeal of children's magazines was that they arrived periodically—monthly or, in some cases, weekly,[19] the assumption being that most children received their magazines by mail since subscriptions, not advertising, funded most children's magazines.[20] Many magazines arrived by mail addressed to the child, who rarely received mail. This rarity made the anticipation and receipt of the magazine an event. Although children may have looked forward to receiving magazines written for them, with the exception of *Stone and Soup* and *Kids*, the magazines were written and produced by adults who took "great pains to conceal [adult authorship] from their readers, [and whose] aim [was] as much to teach as it [was] to entertain."[21] Among the most popular children's magazines of the 1970s were *Sesame Street*, *The Electric Company*, *Cricket: The Literary Magazine for Children*, and *Highlights for Children*.

Highly popular as companions and outgrowths of their television programs, *Sesame Street* (1971–present) and *The Electric Company* (1974–1988, then as *Kid City*, 1988–2001) were edited and published by the Children's Television Workshop in New York. While *Sesame Street* was written for an audience as young as two or three years old, *The Electric Company* was directed toward an audience of five-to-eight-year-olds.[22] According to William Katz, author of *Magazines for Libraries*, both periodicals had similar formats that included "jokes, word puzzles, games, stories, and comics which highlight the various television personalities."[23] Their primary intention was "to teach—in a painless fashion—simple reading, math, and social studies."[24] In a critique of children's magazines for the Council on Interracial Books for Children (CIBC), Deborah Stead stated that both *Sesame Street* and *The Electric Company* generally worked to avoid sex-role stereotyping:

Sesame Street . . . is basically a picture magazine and children of every race and of both sexes appear in the photos and the drawings. . . . [While the magazine contained mostly stock male characters, it did so] without the traditional machismo. Ernie still needs his rubber ducky in his bath.[25]

Stock male characters received more coverage than female characters in *The Electric Company.*

[However,] [t]he June issue attacks sex-role stereotyping directly: readers are invited to judge as "true" or "not true" the following clichés: Girls make better chocolate pudding than boys. A girl can grow up to be president. Girls are as brave as boys.[26]

Cricket: The Literary Magazine for Children (1973–present), also highly popular, targeted an older audience. Katz noted that unlike many other magazines, "*Cricket* is the only truly literary magazine . . . for children ages 6 to 12."[27] In addition to literature, the magazine included puzzles, tongue twisters, games, things to do and make, reviews, and contributions by its readers. Katz thought so highly of the magazine that he stated, "Almost any title in this section can be considered suitable for children, but all libraries should subscribe to *Cricket.*"[28] Continuing her analysis of children's periodicals, Stead noted that in relation to issues of race and gender, "Mariana Carus, the editor of *Cricket* . . . declares, 'We make a real effort to be international and not racist or sexist. Our goal is to provide quality literature for children' (The magazine's editorial staff is all-white)."[29]

The most popular magazine of the 1970s was *Highlights for Children* (1946–present). It was edited by Dr. and Mrs. Garry C. Myers and Dr. Walter Barbe, "leading child specialists, educators, and scientists . . . [whose purpose was] to assist the preschool and elementary child to 'gain in creativeness, ability to think and reason and to learn worthy ways of living.'"[30] With a target audience of elementary school children, *Highlights* had reading material "in a wide variety of subject areas, including social studies, biographies, science, and literature. Games, tricks and teasers, word fun, party and craft ideas are aimed at stimulating thinking."[31] There was no advertising in *Highlights*, which provided a reading guide for parents and teachers. Stead noted: "An attempt to provide a non-racist format is evident. Third World children are *frequently* shown illustrating points about science, nature or human relations. Heroic figures in Black history are celebrated"[32] (italics in the original). Although Stead's definition of "third world" children is unclear, one can assume that it includes African American children. This prompts the question: What about the status of periodicals targeting African American children historically, and specifically in the 1970s?

In her review of children's periodicals of the 1970s overall, Stead concluded that

> there are still racial stereotypes in kids' magazines (some overt, but most
> covert), lots of omissions and some ridicule. Blatant sex-role stereotypes
> abound, and although challenges are offered they appear in a context that is
> overpoweringly sexist.[33]

In contrast, responding to a call for multicultural children's magazines,
Ada Campbell Rose objected to the whole idea. She wrote,

> Today's periodicals have axes to grind; they are not designed to entertain
> boys and girls with interesting information or to help them escape from the
> terrifying world of too-muchness. Instead of being a friend to its readers, the
> typical so-called magazine of today hammers away at ideological goals; it ra-
> diates towards showing that black is beautiful, or that Indian power is com-
> ing to a boil or that things are tough in Madagascar, etc.[34]

Finally, Rose called for a return to the days of *St. Nicholas: Scribner's Illustrated Magazine for Girls and Boys*. Edited by Mary Mapes Dodge, *St.
Nicholas* ran from November 1873 until May 1943. It was, and sometimes
still is, seen by many White children's literary scholars (such as Rose) as
part of the "Golden Age" of children's literature.[35] Dodge stated that the
purpose of *St. Nicholas* was to "[m]ake the spirit of St. Nicholas (Santa
Claus) bright in each boy and girl in good, pleasant, helpful ways. And to
clear away clouds that sometimes shut it out."[36] The assumption here is
that the boy and girl Dodge references are White, for the references to
Blacks in the magazine were consistently degrading and demeaning.[37]

Again, the children's periodicals market of the early 1970s was doing
well, as shown by the distribution of magazines such as *Highlights*, with a
circulation of 1 million in 1972.[38] The majority of the magazines combined
entertainment and education on varying levels. Yet these same magazines, like the texts and trade books that Larrick reviewed in the 1960s,
were, for the most part, written for White children.[39] This was apparent in
the articles, illustrations, and graphics that featured mostly White children and their culture(s). From the work of scholars such as Kenneth
Clark, we know that the absence of positive images negatively affects the
self-image of African American children.[40] But there have been magazines
written for Black children that used their images and addressed their
racialized concerns—or rather, the concerns adults had for these children.

EBONY JR!

One such magazine was *EJ*. Yet JPC demonstrated an interest in children
and parenting issues prior to the publication of *EJ* in the early 1970s.

Throughout his publishing career, John H. Johnson included youth and youth-related issues in most of his magazines. From its inception, *Negro Digest*, like *Reader's Digest*, had articles related to children and parenting. Even JPC's *Tan*, primarily a romance magazine, included a parenting column and articles that featured, and possibly targeted, teenagers. *Ebony*, JPC's mainstay, has always included articles related to children. Johnson used *Negro Digest* to initiate the discussion of how colorism—prejudice based on the shade of, in this case, an African American—affected prospective adoptive parents' selection of children, and in *Ebony* he continued to focus on adoption issues in the 1970s with coverage of the discussion surrounding non–African American parents adopting African American children. Here again, while they might not have been the primary audience, children and parenting issues were nevertheless included in most JPC publications.

Partially because of the Civil Rights Movement, the African American community was becoming more economically stable in the early 1970s (e.g., unemployment for African Americans in 1970 was 6.7 percent, compared to 8.5 percent in 1965 and 14.7 percent in 1975).[41] Added to the phenomenal sales record of White children's magazines (e.g., *Jack and Jill*, with a circulation of seven hundred thousand) and the calls for more African American children's literature, the climate was propitious when Johnson began publishing *Ebony Jr!* in 1973.

Johnson stated in his autobiography, *Succeeding against the Odds*, "Whenever I found a White magazine with strong African American readership, I brought out a black counterpart, using names which tried to capture the color black."[42] Noting the success of *Jack & Jill*, Johnson set out to make a *Jack & Jill* for the African American community, as he had created *Ebony* to emulate *Life*. Johnson stated that he began *EJ* "for the same reasons he began *Ebony* and *Jet*, so Blacks could have a publication to call their own, one that caters to their needs."[43] And, as discussed above, the need was not only for racially relevant literature, it was for racially relevant educational material and pedagogy as well. In relation to the layout, style of illustrations, combination of an educational and an entertainment focus, and age of the audience, *EJ* was similar to *Jack and Jill*. The two differed in that *EJ* maintained an Afrocentric focus, with Black children as its primary audience. Other differences included the price of an annual subscription in 1973 when *EJ* premiered. *Ebony Jr!* was less expensive than some of its contemporaries; as noted earlier, its subscription price was $5.00 for ten issues if payment was enclosed, or $6.00 if billed. An annual subscription to *Jack and Jill* was $5.95; *Highlights* was $7.95. In relation to other children's magazines, *EJ*'s price was competitive: subscriptions to *The Electric Company* and *Sesame Street* sold for $4.50 each; *Cricket* cost $10 annually.

Like its counterparts, *EJ*'s emphasis was educational, and, like various media projects of the early 1970s, children's periodicals were a popular teaching tool. *Ebony Jr!* with its "biographies of famous people, stories, games, science stories and child-centered Black history," was no exception.[44] In producing *EJ* as an educational tool, Johnson was clear on the primary target audience for *EJ*: adults. Parents and teachers purchase children's texts, and Johnson knew that education was an excellent marketing appeal for this audience. But he also knew that children had to enjoy the magazine or they would not request it; therefore, *EJ* presented education as being fun. This dual strategy is clear, as when Johnson stated,

> *Ebony Jr!* is about learning and exploring. It is based on the idea that learning is fun. It is based on the idea that reading is the door to opportunity. It is based on the idea that exploring new worlds—is half the fun of growing up committed and productive. For these reasons, *Ebony Jr!* will be a magazine of action. It will be filled with things to do.[45]

Like some other children's magazines, such as *Highlights*, there was a companion "'Guide for Use of *Ebony Jr!*' [that] described ways teachers might use the features in each issue for reading comprehension, vocabulary building, word attack, and 'bridging' between black and standard English."[46]

From its inception until the early 1980s, when the economic status of the African American community worsened (something I will discuss later), *EJ*'s focus—both academic and racialized—was presented in a manner to engage the reader. It shared key elements such as the structure and educational focus with its contemporaries and was offered at a competitive price. As it defined the African American community as its audience and offered an Afrocentric perspective, it was aligned with the mission of many African American periodicals.

AFRICAN AMERICAN MAGAZINES

In general, the African American press, which includes magazines and newspapers, has enabled African Americans to (1) define their own identity, (2) create a sense of unity by establishing a communication network among literate African Americans and sympathetic Whites, (3) present events from an African American perspective, (4) highlight Black achievements ignored by the mainstream press, and (5) work for African American equality.[47] Specifically, African American cultural and literary magazines have had a primary role in the shaping of African American literature. They have published scholarly and creative work important in framing the critical discourse, which has long focused on the proper function of Black literature, in particular on whether its principal role is as propaganda advancing group interests or as the artistic expression of the individual writer.[48]

According to Walter Daniel, the author of *Black Journals in the United States: Historical Guides to the World's Periodicals and Newspapers*, the purpose and pattern of the African American periodical was established by John Russwurm and Samuel Cornish, the founders of *Freedom's Journal*.[49] Like many of its successors, *Freedom's Journal* reported news of the African American community, served as a "defense against attacks that the *Daily Press* of New York City was making against [local] free blacks," and published "creative writing."[50] This trend changed slightly with W. E. B. DuBois's *The Crisis*, the official journal of the National Association for the Advancement of Colored People (NAACP). While politics and news were still the main focus of the magazine, DuBois also concentrated on literature, noting that it was important for African Americans to tell their own stories. He believed that "[a]ll art is propaganda and ever must be" and that it should be used in the struggle for civil rights."[51] Overall, African American periodicals have

> met the goal articulated by J. Max Berber, dynamic editor of *Voice of the Negro* (1904–1907). He wanted his publication to be "more than a mere magazine," to record current historical and cultural events so accurately and vividly that "it will become a kind of documentation for the coming generations."[52]

These editors, along with many others, fought for and documented the struggle for full civil liberties, resisted the portrayal of African Americans in the dominant press, and provided a forum for the arts.

Magazines targeting African American children, because they were racialized in a different way, contrasted with mainstream (White) children's periodicals. At the same time, these magazines, like their White counterparts of the 1970s, had an academic component. There have been at least three literary magazines written for African American children: *Joy* (1887–?), *The Brownies' Book* (1920–1921), and *Ebony Jr!* (1973–1985).[53] A fourth magazine, *Negro History Bulletin* (1937–2002, now known as *Black History Bulletin*, 2003–present), is primarily nonfiction. Amelia E. Johnson, a minister's wife, founded *Joy*, an eight-page monthly magazine for Black children published by the American Baptist Association.[54] "Johnson was a late nineteenth- and early twentieth-century novelist, poet, editor, and teacher"[55]; concerned about the "moral well-being of African Americans," she wrote *Joy* to address a need for a "literary journal for young people that would also provide a forum for African American women writers."[56] "Filled with short stories, poetry, and literary items of interest, the *Joy* was well received and praised."[57]

Partially in response to similar issues, W. E. B. DuBois began *The Crisis* in 1910 for adults. Each year, beginning in 1912, he published *A Children's Number* in celebration of African American children. This issue was directed at parents and contained little children's literature. The issue was so popular in the barren field of African American children's texts that it spawned *The Brownies' Book*, a monthly journal for children that ran from January 1920 until December 1921.[58] Advertisements in *The Crisis* stated,

> It will be called, naturally, *The Brownies' Book*. . . . It will be a thing of Joy and Beauty, dealing in Happiness, Laughter and Emulation, and designed for Kiddies from Six to Sixteen. It will seek to teach Universal Love and Brotherhood for all little folk—black and brown and yellow and white.[59]

The Brownies' Book was edited by DuBois; Jessie Redman served as the associate editor.[60] *The Brownies' Book* followed the format and arrangement of *The Crisis*. It was thirty-two pages long and had advertisements for the "promotion of books, schools, courses and self improvement through education."[61] While the images of African American children in White literature consisted mostly of unkempt "pickaninnies," *The Brownies' Book* had photos of clean, well-groomed brown (not overtly mulatto) children throughout. Such a contrast was not unintentional, since the objectives of the magazine were to

- make "colored" normalized
- teach Negro history and biography
- teach a code of honor and action in the black child's relations with white children
- turn hurts and resentments into ambition and love of the child's own home and companions
- point out the best amusements and the worthwhile things of life
- inspire children to prepare for definite occupations and duties with a broad spirit of sacrifice[62]

Each issue contained a variety of fictional and nonfictional materials with settings in the African Diaspora. Children were exposed to images of, and issues relevant to, children of African descent around the world. They were also exposed to "Negro history through a series of biographies of black heroic figures."[63] A discussion of world affairs that were relevant to DuBois's mission for the magazine completed each issue.

When *The Brownies' Book* ceased publication at the end of 1921, DuBois introduced some literary material for children in *The Crisis* as "The Little Page." Written by Effie Lee Newsome, the "Little Page" ran from 1925 until 1929. Although the editors of *The Brownies' Book* responded to the negative images of African Americans in the larger society, they also offered a counter to the degradation of African Americans in the most popular juvenile periodical of its time, the *St. Nicholas* magazine. Further, it contributed to DuBois's

> long-standing concern that there was "no place for black children in the world." With this pioneer accomplishment in children's literature, he sought to erase the image of black children that was found in most popular American magazines.[64]

The next magazine written for African American youth was the *Negro History Bulletin*.[65] Established in 1937 by Carter G. Woodson (who served as managing editor until his death in 1950), the "Bulletin was oriented toward black education and black children's urgent need to learn about their cultural heritage."[66] As an extension of Woodson's Association for the Study of Negro Life and History, its *Journal of Negro History*, and Negro History Week, the *Negro History Bulletin* "sought to offset the practice of excluding educational material about Africans and Afro-Americans from most textbooks."[67] Aligned with the *Bulletin*'s educational mission, Woodson included lesson plans and a "Children's Page" that posed challenging questions to the "pupil"; the early issues featured Negro History Week events from schools around the country.[68] Although the *Bulletin* was designed for use in elementary and secondary education, I find given the required reading level it is not accessible to most elementary readers.[69] Yet the material is still relevant to young children and may have been used by primary teachers.[70]

The educational orientation of *Ebony Jr!* was academic and ethnic, and it may have been influenced by the Black Aesthetic, an aspect of the Black Arts Movement, for which JPC's *Black World* was a vehicle. *Black World* addressed the need for literature written for and by African Americans and that reflected their values, culture, and literary tropes. Since JPC is an African American–owned and operated company, its publications tend to reflect, to varying degrees, the community. And as the Black Arts Movement designated the African American community as the intended audience for art, so too did *EJ*. Johnson alluded to this connection in his editorial for the first issue of *EJ*:

> We of *Ebony Jr!* believe that you deserve a magazine which reflects the sounds and sights and colors of your community. . . . [Further] it will challenge you and remind you of the great tradition of which you are a part. Your forefathers created great monuments and dreamed great dramas in Africa. They came here with the first explorers and were among the founders and builders of this nation.[71]

Johnson defined his audience as Black children, racialized the academic curriculum, and attempted to build the child reader's self-esteem. Johnson incorporated some of DuBois's ideas for *The Brownies' Book* in *EJ*. For example, DuBois had stressed Black history, a "code of honor" in interracial relations, a love of home and friends as a response to racially connected "hurts," and an interest in future careers and duties.[72] As DuBois did with *The Brownies' Book*, Johnson wanted to normalize Blackness.

Other similarities between *The Brownies' Book* and *EJ* were the focus of Courtney Vaughn-Roberson and Brenda Hill's article "*The Brownies' Book* and *Ebony Jr!*: Literature as a Mirror of the Afro-American Experience." They found that both magazines focused on racialized pride; attempted to raise the child readers' awareness of class and race; taught Black history; made connections between the Black child reader and the Diaspora; and posited the benefits of education, moral values, and familial loyalty.[73] They concluded that not only did the two magazines share authors such as Langston Hughes and Arna Bontemps, they both "attempt[ed] to generate a bond and commitment to African roots."[74]

These concerns were still impacting African American children even though they resided in a different historical moment than the 1920s of DuBois's *The Brownies' Book*. *EJ* began publication in 1973, toward the end of the Civil Rights Movement, and it was directed toward children who would have benefited from the movement. To these children, Johnson applied the adage that "of those to whom much has been given, much is required." Johnson told the young reader,

> It is your task to prepare for the next chapter in a great human story which began hundreds of years ago. I hope you will remember that more will be required of our generation than of any other generation in the history of Black people.[75]

Using the words of Lorraine Hansberry, Johnson continued, "I hope you will remember that to be young, gifted and Black today is an honor and an opportunity."[76] Holding child readers to some level of responsibility, Johnson told them that *EJ* would help them be racialized beings by teaching them about "[their] life and [their] opportunity."[77]

Always cognizant of the market, Johnson suspected that the buying public would embrace and sustain an African American children's magazine. Even though it was for children, *EJ* was aligned with the JPC traditions and values that targeted and focused on the African American community in a diverse and positive light, and it would maintain a focus on Black history and culture, as all JPC publications did.

CONCLUSION

African American children of the 1960s and early 1970s who looked to mainstream magazines for images of themselves found those publications wanting. Since African Americans were not considered a viable market by White publishers, there were few texts that contained images of African American children and even fewer that targeted them. The mainstream children's magazines of the time may have considered themselves multicultural, but the reality was that African American children were rarely, or only marginally, included. This lack of literature for African American children was not a new concern, and on a few earlier occasions the African American community had published children's magazines. However, with the exception of the *Negro History Bulletin* (which was neither a literary nor a popular culture periodical), they were short-lived. Addressing the need for an Afrocentric children's magazine, John H. Johnson published *EJ*. It differed from the other magazines written for African American children since it was published by a magazine publisher/businessman who was not only interested in racialized concerns, but who had a corporate structure to support the magazines, as opposed to a political or educational organization. Like the African American children's magazines of the past, *EJ* had a highly educational orientation, and it addressed the needs of the African American community of its time.

Underlying this whole study of *EJ* is my belief that it is a historical and cultural artifact demonstrating how JPC sought to educate African American children, academically and racially. Aligned with the metaphor of "roots and wings," the staff at *EJ* attempted to ground children in Black history, culture, and values. This would make them aware of their "roots," while supplementing their academic education in ways that gave them "wings." Yet the market was not the only force that shaped *EJ*'s construction and content. Johnson, as the publisher and editor, created and controlled *EJ* from its conception to its demise. His concerns as a businessman, his political ideologies, and the corporate structure and ventures of JPC influenced the magazine in ways that deserve investigation.

NOTES

1. Larry Neal, "Some Reflections on the Black Aesthetic," in *The Black Aesthetic*, ed. Addison Gayle (Garden City, NY: Doubleday, 1971).

2. Nancy Larrick, "The All-White World of Children's Books," in *The New Press Guide to Multicultural Resources for Young Readers*, ed. Daphne Muse (New York: New Press, 1965; reprint, 1997).

3. The Black Arts Movement began in the late 1960s when LeRoi Jones (aka Amiri Baraka) moved to Harlem and began the Black Arts Repertory Theatre/School.

4. William L. Van Deburg, *New Day in Babylon: The Black Power Movement and American Culture, 1965–1975* (Chicago: University of Chicago Press, 1992), 2.

5. Neal, "Some Reflections on the Black Aesthetic," 184.

6. Hoyt Fuller, "Towards a Black Aesthetic," in *The Black Aesthetic*, ed. Addison Gayle (Garden City, NY: Doubleday, 1971), 9.

7. Ibid.

8. Ibid.

9. Patricia Hill Collins, "When Fighting Words Are Not Enough: The Gendered Content of Afrocentrism," in *Fighting Words: Black Women and the Search for Justice*, ed. Patricia Hill Collins (Minneapolis: University of Minnesota Press, 1998).

10. Addison Gayle Jr., "Cultural Strangulation: Black Literature and the White Aesthetic," in *Within the Circle: An Anthology of African American Literary Criticism from the Harlem Renaissance to the Present*, ed. Angelyn Mitchell (Durham: Duke University Press, 1971; reprint, 1994); Fuller, "Towards a Black Aesthetic"; Neal, "Some Reflections on the Black Aesthetic."

11. Larrick, "The All-White World of Children's Books," 66.

12. Ibid., 19.

13. Ibid.

14. Although it wasn't an "official" ALA award until 1982, the CSK award was organized in 1969 by Glyndon Greer, Mable McKissack, and John Carroll in an effort to "encourage the artistic expression of the African American experience via literature and the graphic arts, including biographical, social, historical, and social history treatments by African American authors and illustrators," as cited in American Library Association, *The Coretta Scott King Book Awards for Authors and Illustrators*, vol. 2007 (Chicago: American Library Association, 2006). Its purpose is "to promote, recognize and celebrate the continued publication of quality literature by African American children's authors and illustrators" according to the American Library Association. "The *Council on Interracial Books for Children Bulletin*, edited by Bradford Chambers, began publication in order to provide support for authors of color. By introducing them to publishing houses, the *Bulletin* played a key role in shaping multicultural children's literature," as reported in Rosa E. Warder, "Milestone in Children's Literature," in *The New Press Guide to Multicultural Resources for Young Readers*, ed. Daphne Muse (New York: New Press, 1997) 15.

15. Rudine Sims, *Shadow & Substance: Afro-American Experience in Contemporary Children's Fiction* (Urbana, IL: NCTE, 1982).

16. Cooperative Children's Book Center, *Children's Books by and About People of Color Published in the United States*, http://www.education.wisc.edu/ccbc/books/pcstats.htm.

17. Stephen Grover, "Children's Magazines Thrive on Devotion, and Get Oodles of It," *Wall Street Journal*, April 21, 1975.

18. L. Felix Ranlet, "Magazines for Tens and 'Teens,'" *Horn Book* 20 (1944).

19. Ibid.; Ada Campbell Rose, "Are Children's Magazines Dying on the Vine?" *Catholic Library World* 47, no. 4 (1976).

20. Deborah Stead, "A Look at Children's Magazines: Not All Fun and Games," *Interracial Books for Children Bulletin* 6, no. 2 (1975): 7.

21. Grover, "Children's Magazines Thrive on Devotion, and Get Oodles of It," 7.

22. William A. Katz, *Magazines for Libraries: For the General Reader, and School, Junior College, and Public Libraries*, 2nd supp. ed. (New York: Bowker, 1974).

23. Ibid., 66.

24. Ibid.

25. Stead, "A Look at Children's Magazines," 6–7.

26. Ibid., 7.

27. Katz, *Magazines for Libraries: For the General Reader, and School, Junior College, and Public Libraries*, 66.

28. Ibid.

29. Stead, "A Look at Children's Magazines," 7.

30. Katz, *Magazines for Libraries: For the General Reader, and School, Junior College, and Public Libraries*, 158.

31. Ibid., 158–59.

32. Stead, "A Look at Children's Magazines," 7.

33. Ibid., 7.

34. Rose, "Are Children's Magazines Dying on the Vine?" 372.

35. Elinor Desverney Sinnette, *"The Brownies' Book*: A Pioneer Publication for Children," *Freedomways* 5, no. 1 (1965); Donnarae MacCann, *White Supremacy in Children's Literature: Characterizations of African Americans, 1830–1900* (New York: Garland, 2001).

36. Mary Mapes Dodge, ed., *St. Nicholas: Scribner's Illustrated Magazine for Girls and Boys*, November 1873, 1.

37. Dianne Johnson-Feelings, "The Pedagogy and the Promise of Du Bois' *The Brownies' Book* Magazine," in *Telling Tales: The Pedagogy and Promise of African American Literature for Youth*, ed. Dianne Johnson-Feelings (New York: Greenwood Press, 1990); MacCann, *White Supremacy in Children's Literature: Characterizations of African Americans, 1830–1900*; Sinnette, *"The Brownies' Book*: A Pioneer Publication for Children."

38. William A. Katz, *Magazines for Libraries: For the General Reader, and School, Junior College, and Public Libraries*, 2nd ed. (New York: Bowker, 1972), 158.

39. Larrick, "The All-White World of Children's Books."

40. Kenneth B. Clark, *Prejudice and Your Child* (Boston: Beacon Press, 1955).

41. Manning Marable, *Race, Reform, and Rebellion: The Second Reconstruction in Black America, 1945–1990*, 2nd ed. (Jackson: University Press of Mississippi, 1991), 124.

42. John H. Johnson and Lerone Bennett, *Succeeding against the Odds* (Chicago: Johnson Publishing, 1989).

43. "*Ebony Jr!* Celebrates Its Tenth Anniversary with Special May Issue," *Jet*, May 9 1983.

44. "Johnson Introduces Magazine Designed for Black Children," *Jet*, May 10 1973.

45. John H. Johnson, "Why *Ebony Jr!*" *Ebony Jr!* May 1973, 3.

46. Walter C. Daniel, *Black Journals in the United States: Historical Guides to the World's Periodicals and Newspapers* (Westport, CT: Greenwood Press, 1982), 164.

47. Abby Arthur Johnson and Ronald Maberry Johnson, *Propaganda and Aesthetics: The Literary Politics of Afro-American Magazines in the Twentieth Century* (Amherst: University of Massachusetts Press, 1979), 567.

48. Abby Arthur Johnson and Ronald Maberry Johnson, "Scholarly Journals and Literary Magazines," in *The Oxford Companion to African American Literature*, ed. William L. Andrews, Frances Smith Foster, and Trudier Harris (New York: Oxford University Press, 1997).

49. Daniel, *Black Journals in the United States*.

50. Ibid., ix.

51. DuBois, cited in Johnson and Johnson, "Scholarly Journals and Literary Magazines," 567–68.

52. Ibid., 567.

53. Other magazines published for African American children include: *Ivy*, *Young Sisters and Brothers* (1991–1996), *Soul Teen* (1974–1983; aka *Black Beat*, 1983–present), and *Right On!* (1971–present). Amelia E. Johnson's *Ivy* was an African American history magazine for youth published near the end of the nineteenth century. *Young Sisters and Brothers* was published by Black Entertainment Television as an extension of its young adult programming (e.g., "Teen Summit"). Both *Black Beat* and *Right On!* are entertainment magazines that currently feature mostly black hip-hop and rap artists. Because these magazines are either specifically historical or entertainment oriented, they will not be discussed.

Another magazine, entitled *The Young Set*, was advertised in W. E. B. DuBois's *The Horizon*, yet no record of it exists. Violet J Harris, "African American Children's Literature: The First One Hundred Years," *Journal of Negro Education* 59, no. 4 (1990).

54. William L. Andrews, Frances Smith Foster, and Trudier Harris, eds., *The Concise Oxford Companion to African American Literature* (New York: Oxford University Press, 1997).

55. Helen R Houston, "Amelia E. Johnson," in *Notable Black Women*, ed. Jessie C. Smith (New York: Gale Research, 1996), 337.

56. Ibid.

57. Maryland State Archives, "Rev. Dr. Harvey Johnson: Last of the Old Guard," Maryland State Archives, http://archive1.mdarchives.state.md.us/msa/stagser/s1259/121/6050/html/12414101.html.

58. Andrews, Foster, and Harris, *The Concise Oxford Companion to African American Literature*; Sinnette, "*The Brownies' Book*: A Pioneer Publication for Children."

59. W. E. B. DuBois, "The True Brownies," *Crisis*, October 1919, 286.

60. Donnarae MacCann, "Effie Lee Newsome: African American Poet of the 1920s," *Children's Literature Association Quarterly* 13, no. 1 (1988).

61. DuBois, "The True Brownies," 286.

62. Ibid.

63. Daniel, *Black Journals in the United States*, 107.

64. Ibid., 106.

65. Andrews, Foster, and Harris, *The Concise Oxford Companion to African American Literature*.

66. Daniel, *Black Journals in the United States*, 276.

67. Ibid.

68. Ibid., 277.

69. Andrews, Foster, and Harris, *The Concise Oxford Companion to African American Literature*.

70. Ibid.

71. Johnson, "Why *Ebony Jr!*"

72. DuBois, "The True Brownies."

73. Courtney Vaughn-Roberson and Brenda Hill, "*The Brownies' Book* and *Ebony Jr.!*: Literature as a Mirror of the Afro-American Experience," *Journal of Negro Education* 8, no. 4 (1989): 497.

74. Ibid., 498.

75. "Johnson Introduces Magazine Designed for Black Children," 54.

76. Ibid.

77. Ibid.

3

Ebony Jr!'s Publisher:
John H. Johnson

I have no hobbies and play no games, and the food and drink of my life is trying to succeed. . . .

I'm a hands-on, hands-in, hands-wrapped-around manager. Both hands. More to the point, I'm a details man. . . .

Ebony. Tan. Copper. Hue. Jet. These were the colors of my personal rainbow, along with the white contributed by advertisers and the green, gold, and silver of money.—John H. Johnson

In order to understand the production and corporate context of *EJ*, one has to know its creator, John H. Johnson. One must know his political leanings, his transformation into an African American media giant, the development of Johnson Publishing Company and its different ventures, aspects of his later life, and the current status of JPC. These issues, combined with his "hands-on, hands-in, hands-wrapped-around" management style, informed the sociopolitical ideologies contained in *EJ*.

THE EARLY YEARS

Johnny Johnson (his original name) was born on January 19, 1918, to Gertrude Jenkins Johnson and Leroy Johnson in Arkansas City, Arkansas.[1] In his autobiography, *Succeeding against the Odds*, Johnson states, "I was born into a strong family and reared in a strong community where every black adult was charged with the responsibility of monitoring and supervising every black child."[2] Growing up as a Black male in the Jim Crow

South of the 1920–30s would inform Johnson's lifelong political and economic principles. Johnson's mother was also a continuous, powerful force
in his life, even more so, perhaps, because his father was killed in a
sawmill accident when Johnny was eight. As were many others during
the Great Depression, Johnson's family was poor. Thus he "was a working child. I learned how to work before I learned how to play."[3]

Johnson would carry this work ethic into his adulthood. Having only
completed the third grade, Gertrude Johnson wanted better for her son.
Like many Blacks throughout history, she "knew that education for us
was a matter of life and death."[4] She believed that education would position Johnny for a more prosperous future. Therefore, she made sure that
he attended Arkansas City Colored [Elementary] School. Gertrude Johnson began making plans to migrate to Chicago so that Johnny could at-
tend high school after she heard from a friend, Mamie Johnson, that
"armies of blacks were flocking to Chicago and that education, good jobs,
and freedom were ours for the asking."[5] There was no Black high school
in Arkansas City at the time. At the end of Johnny's eighth grade year, because Gertrude did not yet have the resources to move to Chicago, she
made him repeat the eighth grade. She wanted to be sure his time was
well spent—which meant that he was in school.[6]

Like many other African Americans who participated in the Great Migration, the Johnsons migrated to a segregated South Side neighborhood
in Chicago in July 1933. Johnny was enrolled in Wendell Phillips High
School until it was badly damaged in a fire and the student body was
transferred to the newly built Jean Baptiste Pointe duSable High School.
Johnson attended duSable from 1933 until 1936.

In the beginning, high school was difficult:

> Most of my classmates were poor, but I was poorer than most—and I paid for
> it. Since money was at a premium I walked to school, even in bitter-cold win-
> ter months. And I wore homemade suits and pants. As if that wasn't enough,
> I was shy, insecure, and inarticulate, and I spoke in a thick down-home coun-
> try brogue.[7]

Determined to not only fit in, but to excel, Johnson worked hard in his
classes and in academically related extracurricular activities. He read self-
improvement books such as Dale Carnegie's *How to Win Friends and Influence People* and Booker T. Washington's *Up from Slavery: An Autobiography*, as well as essays by W. E. B. DuBois and poetry by Langston Hughes.[8]
He practiced his diction by making speeches before a mirror. As a result
of his hard work, Johnson—like Washington—was the student speaker at
his high school graduation. Subsequently, like many of his African American forefathers, Johnson renamed himself. Following a teacher's sugges-

tion, Johnson changed his name from Johnny Johnson to John Harold Johnson because he wanted to appear mature for such a momentous event as his high school graduation speech.

Because he was the graduation speaker, Johnson attended the annual Urban League luncheon for outstanding high school students, where he met Harry H. Pace. President of the Supreme Liberty Life Insurance Company, the largest Black business in the North, Pace was one of Johnson's heroes.[9] Shored up from his reading and speech practice, Johnson introduced himself to Pace and was able to secure a part-time job at Supreme Liberty. This job evolved into a full-time position as Johnson became editor of the company's monthly newsletter, the *Guardian*.[10] Eventually Pace, who "was so light that you'd never believe he was Black unless he told you," moved "to the White suburb of River Forest [Illinois]."[11] Many of the employees of Supreme Life thought Pace was passing for White. At any rate, "the rumormongers said that [Pace] was scared to take Black newspapers home" for fear that he would be identified as Black.[12] Whatever the reason, Pace had Johnson read the newspapers and magazines and "prepare a digest of what was happening in the Black world" for him.[13] An astute entrepreneur, Johnson realized that he could sell the same information and keep the profits for himself.

Using Supreme Life's mailing list of twelve thousand people, Johnson solicited advance subscriptions to *Negro Digest: A Magazine of Negro Comment*. In a brilliant marketing maneuver, Johnson said that the subscription was $3.00 "but in view of the recommendation" that he received from the potential subscriber's friend, Johnson was offering a subscription for $2.00.[14] Johnson received subscriptions from three thousand people. By this time, Johnson had received permission from publishers to publish condensed versions of stories from various Black and White newspapers and magazines. He was twenty-four years old and beginning to build a publishing empire.

THE PROFESSIONAL YEARS

In the tradition of Horatio Alger's stories, which he read as a child, Johnson had evolved from a poor boy from the South to a magazine editor in the urban North. Over the years, he would parlay this initial six thousand dollars into a multimillion-dollar multinational company. The personal fortune he amassed would garner him the honor of being the first African American on the *Forbes* 400 list of the wealthiest Americans.[15] He accomplished this primarily by publishing a string of magazines targeting the Black community at a time when African Americans were either absent from White publications or only present as social pariahs. The foundation of Johnson's empire was *Negro Digest*.

A Solid Foundation: *Negro Digest*

Negro Digest: A Magazine of Negro Comment was first published in November 1942. Patterning his publication after the successful *Reader's Digest*, Johnson began with a blueprint that would continue throughout his publishing career.[16] Like *Reader's Digest*, *Negro Digest* was a condensation of information from various sources. But unlike its White counterpart, *Negro Digest* was grounded in the African American experience. Johnson's intention was that his "magazine would help to spread the idea—that a people without roots is a people without a future."[17] By publishing news and information about the African American community, Johnson hoped to show the community its roots. Evidently he was successful, because within eight months of its inauguration, *Negro Digest* was selling fifty thousand copies a month nationally.[18] This is especially impressive since the United States was at war and rationing was common. As noted above, these extraordinary sales figures were partially the result of Johnson's clever marketing schemes and partially because *Negro Digest* was one of the few magazines targeting African Americans.

Another reason for the success of *Negro Digest* may have been that Johnson, who functioned as the sole employee for quite some time, "presented news and commentary on music, medicine, labor, the press, entertainment, government and politics, war and peace, and creative arts."[19] Also specific to this study, in December 1942 *Negro Digest* included articles about children and parenting. Addressing multiple issues within the African American community, the first article was titled "Color in Social Work" and has a teaser that stated: "Skin shading important in placing children with foster parents."[20] Condensed from an article by Edward Dalton that appeared in *Survey Semi-Monthly*, the column discussed how the color, or shade, of the couple and the child are factors in foster parents' selection of children. The inclusion of this article speaks to the colorism in the African American community and how it might have affected parenting. From this issue and throughout JPC publishing history—although not the focus of any magazine until *EJ*—children and parenting issues would be included in most magazines.

Another trend that began with *Negro Digest* was Johnson's emphasis on Black history and leadership. For example, in January 1943 Johnson began the "Negro Who's Who" column. In a quiz-like format, Johnson printed a group of photographs and another one of brief biographies of six important Black leaders. A blank line was placed under each photograph; the name was to be filled in by the reader. Answers to the "quiz" were on the inside back cover of the issue.[21] This engaging exercise may have introduced readers to important black Americans, or it may have been a tool to test reader knowledge. Either way, it was the beginning of his commitment to highlight successful African Americans as well as educating readers on Black history and current events. Further proof of Johnson's interest in African American history and education is garnered by an evaluation of the *Index to Negro Digest: November 1942 to October 1943* in which the biography section is by far the largest.

Negro Digest was published monthly from November 1942 until November 1951. It was reintroduced in June 1961 and ran until April 1970, at which time it became the more militant *Black World*.[22] *Negro Digest* is monumental in that it was the vehicle through which Johnson began his publishing career and many of the columns and ideologies that would inform all JPC ventures, such as its current cornerstone *Ebony* magazine.

The Color of Money: *Ebony*

Within seven years of founding *Negro Digest*, Johnson was officially a publisher and a millionaire.[23] Although he never resigned from his job at Supreme Life, as *Negro Digest* grew Johnson took a leave of absence to devote his full attention to the magazine. With *Negro Digest* doing well, Johnson set his sights higher; he said, "Whenever I found a White magazine with a strong Black readership, I brought out a black counterpart, using names which tried to capture the color black."[24] Therefore, noting the success of picture magazines such as *Life*, Johnson began publishing *Ebony* magazine in November 1945. Wrote historian Walter C. Daniel, "[A]nd in doing so, it established an unstated assumption that the U.S. was, indeed, a two-society nation. There was a black life and a white life. The two seldom met in self-image."[25] Johnson wanted a monthly magazine that would show "[w]ords and pictures, *Black* words and pictures, and a holistic presentation of the Black image, showing professionals and entertainers, athletes and doctors and preachers and women and men and children, everybody."[26]

Johnson's wife, Eunice, named *Ebony*. According to Johnson she was always aware of new trends in fashion and design. When he asked her for an idea, she suggested "ebony": "The name means, as Eunice said, a tree, the hard, heavy, fine black wood that the tree yields, *and* the ambience and mystique surrounding the tree and the color."[27] As noted below, this naming trend would also continue. Johnson saw a niche for entertainment periodicals, since African American newspapers were

> doing a good job of reporting discrimination and segregation and that we needed, in addition to all that, a medium to refuel the people, and to recharge their batteries. We needed, in addition to traditional weapons, a medium to make Black people believe in themselves, in their skin color, in their noses, in their lips, so they could hang on and fight for another day. . . . We wanted to

create a windbreak that would let them get away from "the problem" for a few moments and say, "Here are some Blacks who are making it. And if they can make it, I can make it too."[28]

Again, he wanted to focus on a more holistic portrayal of the African American experience by including aspects of Black life that were absent from other publications. Therefore, the departments in the inaugural issue of *Ebony* were Race, Youth, Personalities, Culture, Entertainment, and Humor. News and opinion items under those headings included "Catholics of Color," "The Truth about Brazil," "60 Thousand Jobs or Else," "Children's Crusade," "Bye-Bye to Boogie," "Richard R. Wright's Citizens and Southern Bank in Philadelphia," "African Art for Americans," "Book Boom for Negro Authors," and "Film Parade."[29] This list demonstrates the breadth of Black events and issues that Johnson wanted to depict that were missing from the mainstream media.

Continuing a tradition he began with *Negro Digest*, Johnson and his staff included an ethnic awareness component in *Ebony* from the very beginning. Like *Negro Digest*, in 1963 *Ebony* highlighted the African American elite in features such as "Speaking of People," which featured members of the middle class along with brief descriptions of their jobs, and articles like "Football Roundup," which featured sports figures across the nation. Emphasizing interracial education, the cover story for the inaugural issue of *Ebony* was "Children's Crusade," an article written by "Reverend A. Ritchie Low, a White pastor who was trying to eliminate [racial] bias by taking Harlem Blacks to Vermont farms for their annual vacation."[30] Other issues Johnson addressed were the shortage of Black skilled labor after the war and the miseducation dispensed by historically Black colleges. Invoking Johnson's affinity for Booker T. Washington's educational philosophies, Daniel stated that these colleges

> had leaned over backwards to emphasize academic studies at the expense of the vocations, and in making that choice, they had deprived students of a way of making a living in the fast-developing industrial postwar economy.[31]

To supplement the educational component of *Ebony*, and to further sales of Johnson Publishing Company products, the magazine contained advertisements for JPC's hardcover publications, all of which were racialized examples of fiction and nonfiction and probably were not widely available in mainstream bookstores.[32] Missing from the inaugural issue were advertisements from White-owned companies; within a year five hundred thousand magazines were sold monthly, and there still were no advertisements from White-owned companies.[33] Although Johnson was a successful publisher, it took his savvy as a salesman and several meetings with White CEOs before he was able to garner his first White advertisers in 1946: Chesterfield cigarettes and Kimberly-Clark paper products.[34] Two years later *Ebony*'s advertising space grew to forty-eight pages, with additional mainstream companies such as Zenith, Pepsi-Cola, Seagram, and MGM.[35] Clearly Johnson's skill as a salesman was just as vital as his journalistic skill to JPC's success.

Ebony has been so successful that it is now the cornerstone of JPC with a circulation of 1.6 million;[36] because each *Ebony* sold is read by five people, it actually has a much larger readership.[37] In addition,

> A survey conducted by Daniel Yankelovich Inc. ("An Insight into the Black Community") proved that the composition of *Ebony*'s readership mirrors almost exactly the composition by class, income, education, etc. of the total black American community.[38]

Sadly, although the African American community and its political struggles have changed, *Ebony* has not changed substantially. Its tone remains conventionally aligned with the Racial Uplift ideology, something I will discuss in chapter 4.

The Colors of Romance: *Tan* and *Copper*

Noticing the burgeoning romance magazine market of the 1950s, Johnson published two additional magazines, *Tan Confessions* (1950–1971) and *Copper Romance* (1953–1954).[39] Again, trying to present a more complete representation of Black life and taking advantage of the gaps in publishing, Johnson noted the purpose of *Tan Confessions* in the editorial of the inaugural issue:

> We hope to be able to reflect a side of Negro life that is virtually ignored in most publications today. It is that part of everyday living concerning the happiness and triumphs, the sorrows and suffering of the troubled heart. Love and romance, marriage and the family are vital concerns in everyday life.[40]

Yet *Tan* was about more than love and romance. The staff also included regular features on African American hair care, beauty, child care, health, cooking, interior decoration, entertaining, and fashion. Most relevant to this research project is the child care column written by Dr. Edward W. Beasley, then the senior pediatrician at Chicago's Provident Hospital. Saturated with a middle-class perspective, Beasley's column encouraged parents to use child development theory and psychology to manage children. In the feminist vein, although *Tan* was geared toward women, Beasley also wrote articles such as "Father Is Also a Parent" to encourage men to become active parents.[41] Further, there were ongoing columns and articles written for teenagers. "Teen Talk" was a regular column that addressed dating, social graces, and middle-class etiquette and values. There were also articles such as "High School Is Dangerous" in the same issue. Similar to "Teen Talk," the teaser that introduced "High School Is Dangerous" stated, "The small-town girl in the big city found her high school education a liberal lesson in romance and reefers . . . but she had the courage to fight back and win her diploma."[42] Again, aligned with the values of the Black community, education was offered as the objective and the tool that would facilitate social and economic success.

By now popular culture was a corporate staple for JPC periodicals and was included in *Tan* with columns that highlighted the love and romance of African American entertainers (e.g., "How He Proposed," in which the star tells how she got engaged, and "If You Were Married To," which featured what life would be like if the reader were married to a famous person such as Sidney Poitier). When JPC put even more emphasis on entertainment, *Tan* became *Black Stars* (1971–1981).

The Color of Movement: *Jet*

Ever aware of the trends in periodical publication, Johnson began *Jet*, "a newsmagazine that resembles, in coverage, *Time* and *Newsweek*. It was designed, however, as a black response to *Quick*, a pocket-size magazine"[43] Returning to his wife's naming trend of titles that played on the racial designator "Black," Johnson states,

> The word *jet* was tailor-made for my purposes. A talking word that sounds its message, jet means on one level fast, as in the airplane. From these dictionary definitions, it is but one step and not a long one at that, to the Black American definition of "a fast Black magazine."[44]

Aligned with its name, *Jet* is "a convenient-sized magazine that will summarize the week's biggest Negro news in a well-organized, easy-to-read format."[45] The pocket-sized weekly magazine was first published in November 1951; within six months circulation had reached three hundred thousand copies a week.[46] Currently enjoying a circulation of nearly 1 million magazines weekly, *Jet*'s contents are distributed among "business, education, religion, health, medicine, journalism, politics, labor, poverty, and crime sections."[47] *Jet* contains no editorial comment.

The Color of Stars: *Hue*

Johnson was alert to the shift to pocket-sized magazines like *Quick* and responded with *Hue*. Similar in size, intent, and layout to *Jet*, *Hue* was published from November 1953 until October 1959. In his editorial in the inaugural issue, Johnson stated,

Because of America's increasing awareness of the Negro and the accelerated interest generally in what Negroes are doing, we are introducing our new pocket-size feature magazine, *Hue*. Each month *Hue* will present interesting stories and pictures concerning Negroes everywhere. We have elected to do this in a compact, handy-size magazine because in today's swift-pace atomic age, many readers have indicated a desire for a publication which can be quickly read.[48]

The intended audience for *Hue* is questionable. Johnson stated that "America" was interested in the "Negro." Such a differentiation suggests that *Hue* was intended for Whites interested in the lives of African Americans. While some Whites may have read *Hue*, its primary audience was Blacks. *Hue* was similar to *Jet* in that it had little to no editorial comment, included regular pictures of women in bikinis, and contained anonymous articles. Unlike *Jet*, *Hue* focused on entertainment, with many articles about African American stars and the social events of the African American elite. Like most JPC ventures, the middle class tended to be the focus, with articles such as "Ike's New Black Cabinet" and "'Talented Tenth' Builds on Family Prestige."[49] Yet the "folk" were included—albeit to a lesser degree—with articles such as "World's Richest Negro Woman," a story in *Hue*'s first issue about an "eccentric 82-year-old recluse" farmer who wore "tattered" overalls. The source of her income was not indicated, but her father is mentioned as "white, oil-rich Bud Taylor."[50]

In a surprising disregard for the colorism in the Black community, *Hue* and other JPC publications featured a number of brown-skinned models who were not particularly light nor dark skinned. Similar to other JPC magazines, *Hue* emphasized Black history and awareness. Highlighting African American elites, one feature was titled "People You Think You Know but Don't."[51] Similar to the *Negro Digest* article "Negro Who's Who," this article contained photos of entertainers and readers were asked to guess their names; answers and brief descriptions were given on another page. Finally, children were included with articles like "Kid Speed Boat Racer."[52]

Overall, *Hue* was totally aligned with all its JPC ancestors and contemporaries. It was the African American counterpart of a successful White magazine, highlighted the African American middle class but included the folk, contained articles on Black history, and acknowledged that children were members of the community with articles relevant to children and parenting.

The Color and Reach of Radical Politics and Literary Criticism: *Black World*

In response to the changing artistic, political, and civil rights struggle of the 1960s, such as the Black Arts Movement, in May 1970 Johnson transformed *Negro Digest* into *Black World*. While Johnson remained the executive editor and publisher, Hoyt Fuller, a leader in the Black Arts Movement, served as managing editor.

> [Fuller] moved the *Digest* from a collection of reprinted articles and some special features into essentially a literary journal that reflected the controversies and the thrust of the 1960s and 1970s. . . . *Black World*, then, was the appropriate title for a journal that would meld black politics with black art, even as the "radical" periodicals had done decades earlier. Fuller did not lead the movement. He followed it. And with the new magazine, he came to be one of its chief exponents.[53]

Again, JPC, as one of the most stable and profitable African American businesses in the United States, had a substantial customer base, community trust, and circulation that included a cross section of the Black community. Through the literature, graphics, and literary criticism printed in *Black World*, JPC disseminated ideologies of the Black Aesthetic through to a substantial portion of the community.[54]

Visually, the Afrocentric focus of the magazine was apparent in the cover of the inaugural issue, which featured a bronze mask from Benin, Africa. Aware that the reader might not know much about African art, an explanation was offered on the inside cover. Literarily, Fuller set the tone for the magazine in an editorial. Although the African American community was the primary focus of JPC, in *Black World* the focus was "two principle centers of Black population in the world, the African continent and the United States of America.[55] Reminding African Americans of their shared issues with the Diaspora, Fuller stated,

> Black people of both continents have very grave and very similar problems, and . . . these problems have a common source: the experience of colonialism and enslavement. . . . [T]he empowerment of the Black people of Harlem is not possible until Black men in the Congo are in full control of the vast mineral wealth of that country.[56]

At the same time, in the tradition of *Negro Digest*, Fuller's goal was to continue

> publishing the thoughtful essays, the fiction and the poetry of both known and unknown writers, reporting on the arts, educational movements and innovations, and guarding against the opportunists and charlatans who would exploit Black Art and Literature for their own gain and for the spiritual and artistic colonization of Black people.[57]

The language in the above passage alludes to a compromise between Fuller and Johnson. Johnson surely had an affinity toward *Negro Digest*, his first magazine, and wanted it to continue in some form. In regards to marketing, the title had to be changed, since by the 1970s, the most common term used to reference the community was *Black*. Black Nationalism had gained in popularity in the 1960s and Johnson knew there was a market for the discourse. Further, *Negro* was an outdated term used primarily by older African Americans; JPC had grown to a degree that it could produce its own articles and not "digest" them from other sources. Yet Fuller's Black Arts orientation was clearly stated: *Black World* would focus on presenting Black art, grounded in the Black experience, to Black people around the world. He would also defend and protect Black art as a spiritual, historical, and cultural artifact that represents the community against "opportunists and charlatans."

Johnson stated that he discontinued *Black World* in February 1976 because circulation had dropped from one hundred thousand to fifteen thousand.[58] But Jerry Watts does not believe it was that simple. As a political scientist and scholar, Watts noted that even with the reduction in circulation, *Black World* "might have still been a profitable and viable organ. Johnson [whom Watts refers to as a "capitalist"] should have admitted that *Black World* was not losing money when he chose to shut it down but that its profits were not high enough for him."[59] But Haki Madhubuti, in his essay "Blacks, Jews, and Henry Louis Gates, Jr.," poses another reason for the end of *Black World*. Madhubuti was the leader of a boycott against Johnson's decision to fire Fuller and end *Black World*. Madhubuti stated,

> We were not an hour into our demonstration when John Johnson, himself, came outside and asked that we come upstairs to talk about his decision. . . . He stated that Fuller was fired because he refused to cease publishing the Palestinian side of the Middle-East struggle and African support of that struggle. He ceased publication of *Black World* mainly because Jewish businessmen threatened to pull their advertising out of *Ebony* and *Jet* magazines and would have convinced their white friends to do the same if the Middle East coverage did not stop.[60]

Watts questioned this response noting that *Black World* contained "only a very few articles and opinion pieces on the Middle East conflict."[61] And if Fuller was being problematic, Watts observed, he could have been replaced without terminating *Black World*. "The significance of the controversy over the termination of *Black World* lies in the absence of a class analysis of the Black Arts movement."[62] Watts continued by stating that because Johnson is African American, some Black Nationalists assumed that he would "hav[e] an invested interest in publishing this black nationalist intellectual organ. But they overlooked Johnson's primary desire—to make money."[63]

The Color of the Entertainment and Fashion Industries: *Black Stars*, *Ebony Man*, and *Ebony South Africa*

Another magazine that absorbed a publication is *Black Stars*. As noted above, *Black Stars* began in 1950 as *Tan Confessions*, whose name and focus were changed in 1971. Whereas *Tan Confessions* concentrated on romance and included entertainers as a vehicle to drive romance-related articles, *Black Stars* featured interviews of movie, record, and television entertainers. Under the editorship of Ariel P. Strong, it remained a monthly publication until 1981.[64]

Two magazines that had relatively short runs were *Ebony Man* (1985–1998) and *Ebony South Africa* (1995–2000). *Ebony Man* was a men's fashion and entertainment monthly, while *Ebony South Africa*, also a monthly, featured ethnic interests, culture, and beauty and fashion tips for Black women. Because of the low circulation of both magazines and "the hard realities of national and linguistic barriers" of publishing for a South African audience, Johnson canceled *Ebony Man* in 1998 and *Ebony South Africa* in 2000 to concentrate his resources in *Ebony*, one of the mainstays of JPC.[65]

The Color of Children: *Ebony Jr!*

Ebony Jr! was an important element in the publication history of JPC periodicals and can be read within that context. Like *Negro Digest* and subsequent JPC publications, *Ebony Jr!* was grounded in the Black experience and sought to teach its readers about their ethnic identity. Again, JPC's emphasis on Black history and current affairs had begun with *Negro Digest*. And the interactive model of activities following the narratives, so prevalent in the early years of *EJ*'s run, also has its origin in *Negro Digest*. Like the quiz at the end of the "Negro Who's Who" column in *Negro Digest*, "Things To Do" was such a staple of *EJ* that it was listed on the table of contents as such and was an important element of *EJ*'s early marketing appeal. Like *Negro Digest*, through Johnson's marketing and *EJ*'s position as the only children's magazine targeting African American children, circulation reached approximately two hundred thousand.[66]

As discussed earlier, African American children were marginally presented in (White) mainstream children's magazines. Therefore, as he did with *Ebony*, Johnson used *EJ* to present a "holistic" image of African American children. *Ebony Jr!* even received its name from *Ebony*; using the word *Ebony* in the title of *Ebony Jr!* informed the 9 million readers of *Ebony* that *EJ* was a JPC publication, and as such, could be trusted to have an Afrocentric focus. The *Jr* component of the name denoted that it was either the child of *Ebony* magazine and/or for ebony (Black) children.

Like *Tan* (aka *Black Stars*), *Copper*, and *Hue*, popular culture and celebrities were included, to varying degrees, throughout *EJ*'s publication history. In the tradition of *Jet*, *EJ* was compact, well laid out, and easy to read. From *Black World*, *EJ* received a Black Arts orientation, a continued interest in the Diaspora, and a tradition of publishing known and unknown Black children's authors. *EJ*'s orientation toward Black history, one that concentrated on agency, self-definition, and the exclusion of Whites—something I discuss later—may also have been a legacy of *Black World*. Johnson may have learned through his experiences with *Black World* to avoid issues that might be problematic for White advertisers. In particular, he may have directed *EJ*'s orientation away from Whites as perpetrators of oppression over Blacks around the world and toward a version of history and current affairs that uplifted young African American readers while maintaining palatable relations with White advertisers.

The Johnson Publishing Company: Hardcover

In addition to publishing magazines, Johnson developed a book division that evolved in response to the increased political activity preceding the Civil Rights Movement.

> In 1959 . . . I detected a growing interest in black history and authorized a path-finding Black history series. The response was so enthusiastic that we published a book, Lerone Bennett's *Before the Mayflower*, which became one of the most widely read Black history books ever. This marked the beginning of the Johnson Publishing Company Book Division.[67]

Johnson continued to publish in the area of Black history and sociology with books such as Bennett's controversial *Forced into Glory: Abraham Lincoln's White Dream*. He also tapped into African American culture with cookbooks, such as Freda DeKnight's *Date with a Dish*. According to Johnson, he was a leader in book publishing since his "series on 'Black Power' preceded the first call for 'Black Power.'"[68]

Always aware of children as part of the community, and their parents as part of the market, JPC Book Division included titles targeting children. All were racialized and educational. They include Margaret Peters's *The Ebony Book of Black Achievement* (1970), which is a series of biographies of key figures in African American history. In Helen H. King's picture book *The Soul of Christmas* (1972), we see how an urban African American family makes plans to celebrate Christmas. Aligned with the growing interest in Africa that arose in the late 1960s and early 1970s, JPC Books Division published D. W. Robinson's picture book *The Legend of Africania* (1974), an allegorical tale of Africa's struggle against colonialism. It also remembered young children with Lucille Giles's *Color Me Brown* (1972).

A set of children's videos published in 1991 were aligned with the ethnic education agenda of the children's division. The set is titled *The Ebony/Jet Guide to Black Excellence* and has three episodes: *The Entrepreneurs*, *The Entertainers*, and *The Leaders*. All three focused on accomplished African American figures. JPC also published a photopak of 8-by-10 black-and-white photographs intended for classroom use. Titles included *Famous Negroes of the Past*, *Famous Contemporary Negroes*, *Children at School and Play*, and *Young People*.

The book division was more educationally oriented than the magazines division. This is particularly important because during the late 1960s and early 1970s there were not many culturally accurate texts written for or about African American children. JPC attempted to meet this need. Further, during this time, there was a call for racially relevant education at all grade levels. This educational orientation and some of the materials from these publications—for instance, the recipes and articles about Black history—would appear in the pages of *EJ*.

The Beautiful Side of Johnson Publishing Company

While JPC is primarily a publishing company, its role has not been limited to such. To support his major projects and to venture into new markets, Johnson added additional holdings such as Fashion Fair Cosmetics, Supreme Beauty Products, and Ebony Fashion Fair. Beauty, a multimillion-dollar industry, has historically been a prosperous area for African American businesses. Therefore, when Johnson spotted these opportunities, he took risks that often paid off. Fashion Fair and Ebony Fashion Fair are still strong presences in the African American community. Johnson has presented an image of Black beauty in his magazines and fashion shows and then provided some of the tools to attain this beauty through his cosmetic companies. In print, *Jet* has consistently lauded Black women's beauty by including a centerfold of a woman in a bathing suit. Irrespective of one's feminist reading of such material, this presented Black beauty at a time when it tended not to be presented in the White mainstream. Further, these *Jet* women always came in a variety of shades.[69]

Complicating the issue was the difficulty of finding Black models for his magazines. The modeling industry of the 1950s and 1960s was just as racist, if not more so, than many other U.S. institutions. This was such a prevalent dilemma that Johnson advertised for models in various magazines. Others who wanted to highlight Black beauty also had difficulty finding models, as in the case of Ernestine Dent. In 1973, Dent, the wife of President Albert Dent of Dillard University in New Orleans, asked Johnson to help her locate Black models for a charity fashion show.[70] Always the opportunist, instead of just providing the models, Johnson realized that he could turn this into a perpetually profitable venture. He told Dent that he would organize the entire fashion show. He provided models, clothes, and management for what would become the Ebony Fashion Fair. Johnson realized that it was not in his best interest to charge the charity a fee for the show, so he told Dent that she could charge whatever she wanted for admission, if "each ticket could be priced to include the cost of a subscription to *Ebony*. . . . All I want is the $3.00 *Ebony* subscription, which will go to the person buying the ticket."[71] So began, according to JPC, "the world's largest traveling fashion show" and a brilliant marketing tool that substantially increased the circulation of JPC magazines.

In preparation for these fashion shows, Eunice Johnson, the show's producer and Johnson's wife, noticed that the models mixed their own cosmetics because in the early 1970s major cosmetic companies did not carry shades for most Black skin tones. Identifying another opportunity for sales, the Johnsons decided to develop their own cosmetics line: Fashion Fair Cosmetics. In his 1989 autobiography, Johnson stated, "We're now the largest Black cosmetics line in the world, and we rank in the top ten among all cosmetics lines sold in department stores."[72]

Another beauty component of Johnson Publishing Company is Supreme Beauty Products, manufacturers and distributors of hair care products such as Duke and Raveen. Supreme is a spin-off of Beauty Star Cosmetics (1948), Johnson's first nonpublishing venture. "In the early days Johnson was unable to obtain advertising, so he formed his own mail-order business, called Beauty Star, and advertised its products (dresses, wigs, hair care products, and vitamins) through his magazines."[73] This mail-order business was the moneymaker that gave Johnson the financial backing to support his magazines and JPC's overall stability. A partnership between the catalog retailer Spiegel and JPC produced a catalog named *E Style* (1993–1996) and an accompanying credit card geared toward African American women's fashions.

Johnson's business prowess does not end with his investments in publications, cosmetics, fashion, and cosmetics. He also entered other areas of media communication. He bought and sold three radio stations, one of which was WJPC, Chicago's first black-owned station. JPC produces the Ebony Music Awards and the American Black Achievement Awards television shows.[74] For children, JPC supports the Coretta Scott King Award, an African American children's and young adult literature award. From the beginning, Johnson donated an honorarium to the winning authors, and as a result of his "years of financial support," Johnson was awarded a "recognition plaque" for "service above and beyond what anyone would ask."[75] JPC continues to donate the cash award for the winning author.

THE LATER YEARS

JPC's direction was solely based on Johnson's resolve and leadership. Johnson's management skills are noteworthy for a number of reasons, one being his ability to lure White companies, who did not consider the Black market as viable, to advertise in JPC publications. Before this, no African American magazine had been able to lure a sufficient number of White advertising dollars to make it financially stable enough to sustain longevity. Prior to attaining White advertising dollars, the financial stability of JPC was tentative and required that Johnson seek other venues such as beauty products and popular culture magazines, such as *Tan*, to generate revenue. According to *Black Enterprise* publisher Earl Graves Sr.,

> Johnson was the first publisher to open the eyes of Madison Avenue to the multibillion dollar influence of the African American consumer market. By showing the profitability of using Black models and Black-themed campaigns, he literally changed the way American companies market their products to Black consumers. [He also] ushered into being the first generation of African American professionals in publishing and advertising.[76]

Johnson's savvy as a salesman is so legendary that in 1996 he received a Lifetime Achievement Award from the American Advertising Foundation and was inducted into the Advertising Hall of Fame in 2003.[77] The tribute continued even after his death in 2005. In the tributary issue of *Jet* released after Johnson's funeral, there were twenty full-page advertisements. Companies such as Essence, Toyota, Coca-Cola, and Wal-Mart presented advertisements in tribute to Johnson. While Clorox did not include an advertisement dedicated to Johnson, it did occupy four of the twenty placements; no other company had more than one sales pitch. Based on the fact that prior to JPC, White advertisers did not invest in the African American market, Johnson's imprint can be seen on almost every modern African American periodical if for no other reason than that he taught White advertisers that the Black market is worthy of its investment, thereby making various African American publications financially viable.

With monies generated from other JPC ventures such as beauty products plus White advertising dollars, JPC publications such as *Negro Digest* and *Jet* told the story of the African American community. Through the images produced by photojournalists such as Pulitzer Prize winner Monetta Sleet Jr., *Ebony* gave the community a face, one that lovingly reflected our history, current events, and beauty in a manner ignored by the White press. Through it all, Johnson commented on the Black experience. Children were included as the topic and audience for such reporting and commentary. Most noteworthy in this vein was the 1955 *Jet* article featuring the story and pictures of Emmett Till, something I discuss in the next chapter. Whenever a particular article was mentioned at Johnson's funeral or in the various tributary articles, it was the Till article. Chicago mayor Richard M. Daley said, "John Johnson had the courage of his convictions; his difficult decision to print the shocking photos of Emmett Till in his casket shamed America and helped spark the Civil Rights Movement. That wasn't a business decision—that was a cause."[78] This article and accompanying photographs served as an emblem for the mark that Johnson made in publishing, civil rights, and African American history and culture.

Throughout his life, educating others and himself was at the forefront of Johnson's agenda. While he attended both the University of Chicago and Northwestern University, Johnson never earned a degree, but this belies his dedication to education. During the course of his life, Johnson received thirty-one honorary degrees from universities such as Chicago State University, a predominately Black college located on the South Side of Chicago; Harvard University, noted for its academic rigor; and two branches of the University of Arkansas, Fayetteville and Pine Bluff—near where Johnson was born and raised. In 2003 Howard University, which also granted Johnson an honorary degree, renamed its School of Communications the John H. Johnson School of Communications.[79] While these accolades denote Johnson's investment in education, the dedication of the John H. Johnson Cultural and Educational Museum, located in Arkansas City, Arkansas, where Johnson was born, speaks to Johnson's impact to the world.

Johnson's worldwide influence transcended his publication of *Ebony*, *Ebony South Africa*, and *Jet*'s international distribution. Johnson's relationship with U.S. presidents began with Dwight Eisenhower. Among other duties, Johnson traveled to nine African countries in 1957 on a goodwill tour with Vice President Richard Nixon, served as special U.S. ambassador to the Independence Ceremonies of the Ivory Coast in 1961 for President John F. Kennedy, and in 1996 received a Presidential Medal of Freedom (the highest civilian honor of the United States) from President Bill Clinton.[80]

Like the Horatio Alger stories he read as a child, Johnson's life was such a classic "rags-to riches" saga that he received the Horatio Alger Award in 1966.[81] Of Johnson's accomplishments, longtime collaborator Lerone Bennett Jr. said, "Considering the depth from which he came and the heights he climbed and the obstacles he overcame, he was the greatest of all American publishers, Black or White."[82] Although there were several Black magazines before Johnson's *Negro Digest*, it is JPC that set the tone for the African American periodicals of today—entertainment and business oriented. Earl G. Graves Sr. noted, "I'm not exaggerating when I say there would be no Earl Graves without John Johnson."[83] According to civil rights activist Jesse Jackson, "Because of Johnson we have a table of contents . . . [he] chronicled our struggles."[84] Through JPC, Johnson documented Black politics, entertainment, education, and history. And his impact on broadcasting, modeling, and the Black beauty industry is still evident. Because of his tenacity, salesmanship, and management, what began with a borrowed customer list evolved to include a string of magazines (of which *Ebony* is still preeminent), a fashion show, hair care and cosmetic divisions, and multimedia holdings.

On August 8, 2005, at the age of eighty-seven, John H. Johnson died, leaving an indelible mark on business, journalism, and, most importantly, the African American community. At the helm of JPC he left his daughter, Linda Johnson Rice.

THE JOHNSON PUBLISHING COMPANY TODAY: A MULTIMILLION-DOLLAR MULTINATIONAL COMPANY

JPC has consistently ranked in the top ten of *Black Enterprise*'s Top 100 Highest-Grossing Black Businesses list. In 2006 *Black Enterprise* noted that JPC was the nation's eighth-largest Black-owned enterprise in the industrial/service category, with approximately $496 million in sales.[85] In 2002 JPC ranked as Illinois's top-grossing publisher and fourth on the national list of publishers.[86] Top competitors are composed of publishing, cosmetic, and television media businesses such as Essence Communications and L'Oreal.[87] JPC is still a privately owned and family-based business, and Linda Johnson Rice is now president and CEO. A graduate of Northwestern's Kellogg School of Management, Rice's 2002 promotion from COO made her the first African American female CEO of a top-five *Black Enterprise* 100 company.[88] Today the circulation of the company's signature publications is still healthy: *Ebony* sells 1.6 million magazines monthly and *Jet* sells nearly 1 million weekly.[89]

Taking advantage of untapped markets, as her father did, Rice recently began to license *Ebony* brand merchandise in an effort to "help the company diversify, build its revenue stream, and attract more readers."[90] Although licensing is a $108-billion industry, Debbie Turner, president of TurnerPatterson, a company that markets and licenses products, says,

> [T]here's no concentrated effort to target the licensing of products toward African Americans. . . . Further, Johnson Publishing still hasn't fully leveraged its long history with the African American community.[91]

Therefore, in 2006 Johnson joined with American Greetings to form a line of cards named *Ebony* Inspiration, which feature images from *Ebony* magazine.[92] Plans for luxury bed and bath products for the newly developed Ebony Home brand are forthcoming.[93] "'No matter [what, the merchandise] has to be of premium quality—it has to be best in class,' says Johnson Rice. 'I can't do anything less with a product my parents built over 60 years,' she says."[94]

Like her father, Linda Johnson Rice has no plans for selling the company or taking it public.[95]

CONCLUSION

On some levels, Johnson's success story is related to the "rags-to-riches" tales of the popular culture series authored by Horatio Alger.[96] It is the story of a poor African American boy from "uneducated" parents who worked hard and made good. Johnson took the assignment of reading and summarizing the African American newspapers for Pace at Supreme Life and parlayed that into Johnson Publishing Company, which in 2006 was the nation's second-largest Black-owned enterprise and the number-one publisher of African American–oriented magazines.[97] Now under the direction of Johnson's daughter, Linda Johnson Rice, JPC's holdings consist of various magazines, the most well-known being *Ebony* and *Jet*, as well as one of the nation's largest traveling fashion shows, cosmetic and hair care lines, and multimedia enterprises.

Throughout its history, JPC has continued to direct its products toward the African American community. It has tried to represent the people holistically, giving them news and entertainment, and using normal photographs of a people who have historically been—and some say still are—degraded and demeaned in the White press. Like most forms of African American literature, JPC's publications have usually been political in nature in that they have upheld a Racial Uplift agenda—they have shown the middle class in hopes that positive portrayals would further the struggle for human and civil rights.

In addition to the Racial Uplift agenda, I have noted trends in JPC ventures that connect indirectly with *EJ*. For example, childhood and parenting issues appear consistently, though marginally; African American beauty is stressed in narratives and images; Black history is pervasive; key leaders are covered in narratives and columns; and news, current affairs, and entertainment are always part of the menu. Having profiled *EJ* and the context into which it premiered, I provided a brief biography of Johnson and JPC. All the while I have alluded to how various political positions, which arose from the Black Liberation Movement, have influenced *EJ*. The context for the manner in which *EJ* was politicized and how it attempted to socialize its child readers into politics is the subject of chapter 4.

NOTES

1. John H. Johnson and Lerone Bennett, *Succeeding against the Odds* (Chicago: Johnson Publishing, 1989), 215; Jerry G. Watts, *Amiri Baraka: The Politics and Art of a Black Intellectual* (New York: New York University Press, 2001).

2. Johnson and Bennett, *Succeeding against the Odds*, 37.

3. Ibid., 40.

4. Ibid., 47.

5. Ibid.

6. Ibid.

7. Ibid., 66.

8. Ibid.

9. Ibid.

10. Ibid.

11. Ibid., 111.

12. Ibid., 113.

13. Ibid.

14. Ibid., 119.

15. Juliet E. K. Walker, *The History of Black Business in America: Capitalism, Race, Entrepreneurship*, Twayne's Evolution of Modern Business Series (New York: MacMillan Library Reference USA, 1998).

16. Johnson and Bennett, *Succeeding against the Odds*.

17. Ibid., 33.

18. Ibid.

19. Walter C. Daniel, *Black Journals in the United States: Historical Guides to the World's Periodicals and Newspapers* (Westport, CT: Greenwood Press, 1982).

20. Edwin Dalton, "Color in Social Work," *Negro Digest*, December 1942.

21. "Negro Who's Who," *Negro Digest*, January 1943.

22. Daniel, *Black Journals in the United States*.

23. Walker, *The History of Black Business in America*.

24. Johnson and Bennett, *Succeeding against the Odds*.

25. Daniel, *Black Journals in the United States*.

26. Johnson and Bennett, *Succeeding against the Odds*.

27. Ibid., 159.

28. Ibid., 156–57.

29. Daniel, *Black Journals in the United States*.

30. Johnson and Bennett, *Succeeding against the Odds*.

31. Daniel, *Black Journals in the United States*.

32. "The Ebony Bookshop," *Ebony*, December 1963.

33. Walker, *The History of Black Business in America*.

34. Ibid.

35. Ibid.

36. Hoover Report, "Minding Black Business of America: Johnson Publishing Company, Inc." (2002), http://www.blackstocks.com/Features/Bizlegends/jj/jj2.html.

37. "Backstage." (1975, November). *Ebony*, 31, 25.

38. Ibid.

39. Publication of *Tan Confessions* began in 1950, and a year later the name was shortened to *Tan*.

40. John H. Johnson, "Editorial," *Tan Confessions*, November 1950.

41. Edward W. Beasley, "Father Is Also a Parent," *Tan*, November 1950.

42. Jane Walters, "High School Is Dangerous," *Tan*, November 1950.

43. Daniel, *Black Journals in the United States*.

44. Johnson and Bennett, *Succeeding against the Odds*, 206.

45. Ibid., 210.

46. Ibid.

47. Amy Schein, "Johnson Publishing Company, Inc.," *Hoover's* (2007), http://www.hoovers.com/johnson-publishing/—ID__40251—/free-co-fact-sheet.xhtml; Daniel, *Black Journals in the United States*, 214.

48. John H. Johnson, "Why Hue?" *Hue*, November 1953.

49. "Ike's New Black Cabinet," *Hue*, May 1953; "'Talented Tenth' Builds on Family Prestige," *Hue*, May 1953.

50. "'Talented Tenth' Builds on Family Prestige," 12.

51. "World's Richest Negro Woman," *Hue*, May 1953.

52. "Kid Speed Boat Racer," *Hue*, November 1953.

53. Daniel, *Black Journals in the United States*, 93.

54. A. Robert Lee, "Periodicals: Black Periodicals," in *The Concise Oxford Companion to African American Literature*, ed. William L. Andrews, Frances Smith Foster, and Trudier Harris (New York: Oxford University Press, 1997).

55. Hoyt Fuller, "Towards a Black Aesthetic," in *The Black Aesthetic*, ed. Addison Gayle (Garden City, NY: Doubleday, 1971), 4.

56. Ibid.

57. Ibid.

58. Johnson and Bennett, *Succeeding against the Odds*.

59. Watts, *Amiri Baraka*, 215.

60. Haki Madhubuti, *Blacks, Jews, and Henry Louis Gates, Jr. Claiming Earth: Race, Rage, Rape, Redemption* (Chicago: Third World Press, 1994), 68.

61. Watts, *Amiri Baraka*, 215.

62. Ibid.

63. Ibid.

64. Ulrich's Periodical Directory, "Black Stars," ProQuest-CSA LLC, http://www.ulrichsweb.com/ulrichsweb/Search/fullCitation.asp?navPage=1&tab=1&serial_uid=326471&issn=10252665.

65. Johnson and Bennett, *Succeeding against the Odds*, 289.

66. "*Ebony Jr!* Celebrates Its Tenth Anniversary with Special May Issue," *Jet*, May 9, 1983.

67. Johnson and Bennett, *Succeeding against the Odds*, 289.

68. Ibid., 287. Here Johnson considers the "first call for Black Power" to have been made by Carmichael during the Civil Rights Movement of the 1960s. But there has always been Black Nationalism and a call for Black Power in the African American community, a call presented in the literature as early as David Walker's *Appeal*, published in 1829.

69. I am aware that through a Black Feminist lens this same material may be interpreted differently.

70. Johnson and Bennett, *Succeeding against the Odds.*

71. Ibid., 250.

72. Ibid., 343.

73. Hoover Report, "Minding Black Business of America: Johnson Publishing Company, Inc." (2002), http://www.blackstocks.com/Features/Bizlegends/jj/jj2.html.

74. Johnson and Bennett, *Succeeding against the Odds.*

75. Henrietta Smith, ed., *The Coretta Scott King Book Awards: From Vision to Reality* (Chicago: American Library Association, 1994), xii–xiii.

76. "Remembering John H. Johnson, 1918–2005," *Jet*, August 29, 2005, 34–36.

77. "Great Achievements of a Great Man," *Jet*, August 29, 2005.

78. "Thousands Join in Historic Farewell Celebration for Publisher John H. Johnson in Chicago," *Jet*, August 29, 2005, 34–36.

79. "Great Achievements of a Great Man."

80. "Remembering John H. Johnson"; "Great Achievements of a Great Man."

81. "Remembering John H. Johnson."

82. "Thousands Join in Historic Farewell Celebration for Publisher John H. Johnson in Chicago," 8.

83. "Remembering John H. Johnson," 36.

84. "Thousands Join in Historic Farewell Celebration for Publisher John H. Johnson in Chicago," 61.

85. Schein, "Johnson Publishing Company, Inc."

86. Francine Knowles, "Twenty-Eight Black-Owned Illinois Firms on Magazine's Lists of Biggest," http://www.findarticles.com/p/articles/mi_qn4155/is_20020530/ai_n12466027.

87. Schein, "Johnson Publishing Company, Inc."

88. Caroline V. Clarke, "A New Johnson Is CEO," *Black Enterprise*, June 2002.

89. Schein, "Johnson Publishing Company, Inc."

90. Philana Patterson, "*Ebony's* License to Grow," *Black Enterprise*, http://www.blackenterprise.com/exclusivesekopen.asp?id=1203&p=0.

91. Ibid.

92. Schein, "Johnson Publishing Company, Inc."

93. Ibid.

94. Patterson, "*Ebony's* License to Grow."

95. Clarke, "A New Johnson Is CEO."

96. Horatio Alger Jr.'s *Ragged Dick* (1865/1985) and Frances Hodgson Burnett's *Little Lord Fauntleroy* (1887) are typically viewed as among the early idealized versions of American boyhood. Alger's output is estimated as between 118 and 120 titles.

97. In 2006 TLC Beatrice International Holdings Inc. was the largest Black-owned company.

II

CONTEXTS AND ANALYSIS: POLITICS AND EDUCATION

4

The Political Socialization of Black Childhood: The Case for *Ebony Jr!*

Why do we so often assume that it takes ten or twenty years for children to begin to understand exactly what it is that works for or against them in the world?—Robert Coles

Socialization is "the process by which children, born with an enormous potential for different types of behavior, come to adopt the . . . (cultural norms) of their . . . society."[1] Through cultural transmission, the passage of information from one generation to another, children come to understand themselves, society, and their roles within society. "Political socialization," wrote Fred Greenstein, "[is the term] attached to the process of initiation into politics. . . ."[2] It develops as an ongoing awareness of the presence and meaning of political authority, and as children develop, they are able to express their sensitivity to and understanding of such authority. It takes note that the political self is learned at home, school, church, and through the media. It is not innate. Political socialization is concerned with how individuals acquire and develop their ideologies; it notes that the communities to which individuals belong strongly inform the formation of these political ideologies. Based on their status as racialized beings, how have various facets of the African American community attempted to socialize children into political consciousness? How are these political positions and techniques reflected in *EJ*? To investigate these questions I will make the case that African American children have historically been socialized into politics; then I will look at multiple facets of the African American community's attempt to socialize children into political consciousness. Finally, I will demonstrate how various political positions prevalent in the African American community were reflected in *EJ*.

Children "learn" political tendencies in ways that have been found to have a "developmental history."[3] While political values are continually acquired, reevaluated, and discarded, "conventional wisdom as well as historical and contemporary social theory have emphasized the early childhood years as critical for developing personality, social attitudes, and cultural values."[4] Therefore, political socialization theory is particularly interested in the political values acquired during childhood. This fact became abundantly evident when civil rights workers in the 1960s visited families to discuss some action on desegregation or school budgets and a child within earshot would suddenly speak up on the issue.[5] The eavesdropping child had clearly been an alert and longstanding observer, gaining impressions about power and authority from television reports, overheard conversations, and the many encounters with school, church, family, and friends.

These ideas were not simply a parroting of their parents but, according to child psychiatrist Robert Coles, a synthesis of the various discourses the child may have overheard. In light of the fact that "political socialization theory assumes that citizens in different nations [or positions of privilege within a nation] come to feel and believe differently about their political leaders and structures" it makes perfect sense that African American children of the midcentury had different political ideologies than White, mainstream children.[6] Many of the southern African American children whom Coles interviewed noted a disparity between the patriotic discourse of the media, their White teachers, and politicians, and the realities of life in the Jim Crow South. This political insight was imperative for the children's sense of self and their ability to read their world accurately. For the fortunate children of the 1970s and 1980s who read *EJ*, there was another means for absorbing political experience—for gaining both an intuitive and an explicit connection with what worked "for or against them in the world."

The child was politicized in *EJ*, as had been the case historically in the African American community's child-rearing practices. Like his predecessor W. E. B. DuBois, the editor of *The Brownies' Book*, John H. Johnson knew that "being an [African American] adult was a dangerous vocation that required a total commitment to the community and every child in it."[7] In an article in *Ebony*, an anonymous author asserted that JPC's publications extend to the entire African American community: "We reach the conservative and the radical, . . . the young and the old, the male and the female."[8] JPC tried to include and address as many people and ideological orientations as possible. This included the Racial Uplift, Civil Rights, and Black Nationalist political positions; Black Feminist theory; and multiple religious orientations. African American history and culture were of vital importance to Johnson, and he put this subject on his agenda: "My magazine would help to spread the idea—that a people without roots is a people without a future."[9] This cultural education was meant to help African American children formulate, among other things, their political views.

In no way could children be removed from the political world, but children's elders could be selective about when and what to share. JPC made choices that would, from its perspective, touch African American children's lives in the immediate future.

BLACK LIBERATION MOVEMENTS

In order to understand the politicization of the child in *EJ*, one must first consider the political climate of the African American community prior to and during *EJ*'s publication. Three political movements in the African American community have garnered the majority of attention: Racial Uplift, Civil Rights, and Black Power (especially in relation to self-determination). An overview of all three, the backlash because of them, and the Black Feminist Movement is necessary to provide political context and a close reading of how they were manifested in *EJ*. On a continuum, the Racial Uplift agenda is integrationist in orientation, the Black Power agenda is nationalistic, and the Civil Rights activists' range is in the middle. Harold Cruse noted that

> American Negro history is basically a history of the conflict between integrationist and nationalist forces in politics, economics, and culture, no matter what leaders are involved and what slogans used. The pendulum swings back and forth, but the men who swing with it always fail to synthesize composite trends.[10]

The cause of the fluctuation in leadership agendas, according to Cruse, is African American leaders' historic failure to recognize the caste-like quality of U.S. oppression. In the face of skin-based White privilege, African American leaders, who have been "dominated by integrationists" since the mid-1800s, have learned that the success of individuals, or a class, does not lead to group empowerment, because, "power derives from one's group standing."[11] It would be easy to say that since African American leadership has been historically composed of upper-class, educated African Americans with strong ties to the White community, they simply proposed the class-based Racial Uplift agenda because it advanced their social and financial interests. According to DuBois, "The upper-class Negro has almost never been nationalistic, [while nationalism] has always been a thought up-surging from the masses."[12]

Errol Henderson noted that African Americans as a group have always been nationalistic in that we have been separated from Whites, in

> day-to-day existence as political, economic, and cultural outcasts in White-dominated society. Nationalists mobilize on the basis of these castes—more than class—interests while integrationists proffer assimilationist strategies for Black uplift. Integrationists have often made their way by navigating the landscape of the mainstream system, but for the Black masses, many of them poor, the integrationist dream is not representative of their daily—and very separate—reality.[13]

Yet the African American leadership has changed from integrationist to nationalist and back again since the mid-1800s. While each of these ideologies has always been present in the African American community, I present them, and Black Feminist theory, sequentially, and then describe how they impacted JPC in general and *EJ* in particular.

RACIAL UPLIFT AND JOHNSON PUBLISHING COMPANY

While the meaning of Racial Uplift has evolved over time, during the antebellum period, Racial Uplift generally meant "a personal or collective spiritual—and potentially social—transcendence of worldly oppression and misery."[14] Following Martin Delany and Frederick Douglass, Booker T. Washington is often cited as the patriarch of the Racial Uplift movement that eventually, for the educated African American elite, came to mean "an emphasis on self-help, racial solidarity, temperance, thrift, chastity, social purity, patriarchal authority, and the accumulation of wealth."[15] This ideology was used in opposing post-Reconstruction Jim Crow—the systematic and legal segregation, economic exploitation, disfranchisement, and lynching perpetuated on the Black community after the Reconstruction until, some say, the *Brown v. Board of Education* ruling of 1954.

Inherent in the Racial Uplift ideology is the following set of markers: the absence of an activist component, little to no critique of White supremacist behavior, further social stratification of the African American community, and a search for "authentic" middle-class African American values.

Although the NAACP fought the battle in the courts, there was no activist component of the Racial Uplift plan for racial equality. The struggle was to be a "civilized" one, done with style and grace through the courts and with the assistance of powerful Whites, who had historically oppressed Blacks and benefited from their unearned privilege.[16] As such, the Racial Uplift ideology cannot be considered as an "independent Black perspective," since it requires the cooperation and accommodations of the White elite in the struggle for racial equality,[17] and also because

> Black middle-class ideology cannot be isolated from dominant modes of knowledge and power relations structured by race and racism. While Black elites' oppositional claims of self-help may have symbolized their desire for independence and self-determination, this self-image obscured the extent to which self-help also functioned as an accommodation to Blacks' noncitizenship status.[18]

Not only does Racial Uplift require White accommodation, it also predicates that African Americans view themselves as subjects through the gaze of Whites, as opposed to demanding the right of self-definition. Further, this class-based position reified racial, class, and gender hierarchies within the African American community.

Most noteworthy in Racial Uplift ideology is the lack of criticism of White tyranny and supremacy. Other than in passing, there is minimal effort directed toward addressing or rebelling against this oppression—other than, as the saying goes, by "going along to get along."[19] Therefore, since White supremacy was a given, the Racial Uplift agenda focused its prescriptive attention on the African American community.[20] The elite believed that by attaining middle-class status, they would prove their humanity to Whites, who would then grant them their civil rights. The quandary of the African American middle class was the quest for an authentic or "positive" subjectivity.[21] This meant finding their own values and lifestyles, not emulating the White middle class.

As such, middle-class African American ideology, like White society's ideal of social mobility, remained entangled within that which it had denied—or tried to forget:

> that historically, the conditions for social mobility and class formation among all Americans, Blacks, immigrant groups, and other racially marked groups, including whites, have been circumscribed by race and color, and implicated within the legacy of slavery, segregation, and white supremacy.[22]

Middle-class African Americans did not realize that irrespective of what individuals or a socioeconomic class could achieve, oppression in the United States was not founded on achievement or the lack thereof, but on race and an ideology of White supremacy. By buying into the Racial Uplift ideology of socioeconomic progress for a small class of people, "[e]lite African Americans were replicating, even as they contested, the uniquely American racial fictions upon which liberal conceptions of social reality and 'equality' were founded."[23]

The elite tried to distance themselves from "the folk," concentrating on them as the locus of the problem, while also inundating lower-class African Americans with platitudes about the "virtues" of middle-class values. In this move toward "self-help and interdependence," the African American elite worked to educate the lower class on social values and behavior, as in Elise Johnson McDougald's article "The Task of Negro Womanhood."[24] In this article, McDougald offered a sort of ethnography of the African American women of Harlem, outlined many of the social ills facing these women, and encouraged middle-class values. Again,

> [n]ormative assumptions about elite blacks and racial uplift were shackled, so to speak, to the sociological images of urban pathology and, ultimately, to the racist constructions of blackness that uplift ideology purported to transcend.[25]

To some degree, the elite bought into the ideology of the "Negro problem" (which positioned *all* African Americans at the bottom of the social ladder), and the lower classes knew they were ridiculed by members of the African American and White bourgeoisie. But some recognized these values as essentially White, and, moreover, the African American proponents of such were sometimes accused by scholars such as E. Franklin Frazier of "acting White." Alternatively, Gaines stated that the proponents of Racial Uplift were not necessarily "acting White":

> [He wrote,] on the contrary, uplift, among its other connotations, also represented the struggle for a positive black identity in a deeply racist society, turning the pejorative designation of race into a source of dignity and self-affirmation through an ideology of class differentiation, self-help, and interdependence.[26]

For nearly everyone, "uplift" was essentially an illusion.

Since ideological positions are rarely mutually exclusive, there were members of the elite who subscribed to the Racial Uplift agenda and who were also Black Nationalists. Therefore, some of those struggling with the definition of African American bourgeois values looked to the continent of Africa. But this complicated the process of self-definition as it related to gender roles. For example, the concept of Africa (as opposed to a more direct knowledge of the continent's cultural diversity) was commonly invoked as a symbol of the

> normative patriarchal gender relations associated with race progress. The quest for the race's supposed authentic origins in Africa thus came at the expense of black women intellectuals' claim to equal status, although the pressure of patriarchal U.S. political culture also had much to do with the situation.[27]

Not surprisingly the conclusions that were made by either looking to African or White values were unsatisfactory because "Black bourgeois and nationalist ideologies . . . equated race progress with male dominance and Victorian ideals of sexual difference in both political and domestic life."[28]

Class values and gender roles were not the only areas of contention for the elite. Images of African Americans in literature and popular culture were also a matter of deep concern. "This was a complex modern moment of collision between cultures, literary and vernacular."[29] There was a cohort of writers who, seeing themselves through the White supremacist gaze, tried to redefine African American folklore into "high culture" (e.g., the Fisk University Jubilee Singers). While another cohort

> less beholden to "positive" images and racial vindication played with white stereotypes of "authentic" blackness, manipulating minstrelsy, Negro folklore and dialect, and black vernacular forms in search of new forms of black cultural expression, including Negro humor.[30]

Neither approach proved satisfactory in changing the overall image of African Americans in the media.

In his autobiography John H. Johnson alludes to the fact that he was attracted to the Racial Uplift ideology, noting that Booker T. Washington's *Up from Slavery: An Autobiography* was one of the books that most influenced him.[31] Johnson's affinity for the Racial Uplift ideology is also apparent in his inclusion of an article about Washington in his first issue of his first magazine, *Negro Digest*, in 1942. Using Washington's Atlanta Exposition address of 1895 as a resource, the article offers an overview of Washington's philosophy of accommodation, Racial Uplift, and industrial education in an attempt to inform the reader. In a concise rendition of the Racial Uplift ideology, Washington wrote, "when the Negro succeeded in making himself indispensable to his community, when he got wealth and economic security, respectability and influence and even political power would be added unto him."[32]

The *Negro Digest* article also attempted to clarify common misconceptions about Washington. It stated that he did not advocate "industrial training for the Negroes to the exclusion of liberal education. . . . Rather, it was an argument against any kind of learning that did not meet the immediate needs of the learner."[33] Although the original article was written by W. Edward Farrison, it was chosen, condensed, and edited by Johnson. Therefore, I can only assume that Johnson's interests were reflected in the article's publication. Eventually, this same philosophy came to exemplify Johnson's professional trajectory: In a market with few popular periodicals for African Americans, Johnson provided magazines, various other media productions, and beauty products to a community desperate to see themselves portrayed in a realistic manner. He was a millionaire before he was thirty, and because he had the financial status and power to reach the African American community through his publications and possibly inform their behavior, Johnson eventually gained substantial power and influence, as exemplified by his access to various U.S. presidents.

Johnson's Racial Uplift philosophy is also evident in his publication choices. Throughout his entire publishing career, from 1942 until the present, African Americans are presented in a largely positive manner. There is little to no criticism of African Americans' behavior as a group or as individuals, and middle-class values are usually privileged. All of these positions are apparent in his statement about *Ebony*:

> We wanted to emphasize the positive aspects of Black life. We wanted to highlight achievements and make Blacks proud of themselves. We wanted to create a windbreak that would let them get away from "the problem" for a few moments and say, "Here are some Blacks who are making it. And if they can make it, I can make it too." . . . Beyond all that, we wanted to focus on the total Black experience—something no one else was doing then and, I am tempted to say, now. . . . We wanted to show Negroes—we were Negroes then—and Whites the Negroes nobody knew.[34]

Notice Johnson's statement about lower-class African Americans: that irrespective of the various forms of oppression, if middle-class African Americans "make it, I [as a member of the lower-class] can make it too."[35] In addition to being similar to the Horatio Alger stories, this is the essence of the Racial Uplift ideology. By seeing a number of achievers, lower-class African Americans would become increasingly motivated by it and be moved to work hard to become economically successful. As a byproduct, Whites would believe in the humanity of African Americans and grant them their rights. But it did not happen that way.

Although the initial goal was to demonstrate to Whites that not all African Americans were part of the "Negro Problem," Johnson stated that he revised his thinking over time.[36]

> In the early days we followed the consciousness of the times by defining success narrowly in terms of material things. . . . But as the magazine matured and as [the political climate of African Americans] changed, we broadened the formula for success, defining it as the achievement of a positive goal or the attainment of whatever a person set out to do.[37]

This shift in values, for example, defining success in terms of money, may have been informed by the Black Power Movement and its emphasis on community empowerment and self-definition as opposed to the need to acquire wealth as a symbol of success to prove one's merit to Whites.

While Johnson had a strong political and educational mission for his company, he also knew the importance of entertainment and inspiration. Since White-owned newspapers were reporting the news about discrimination, he saw his role as "refueling the people" and making them believe in themselves.[38] Johnson clearly understood the power of images, since even in his entertainment publications he made a strongly affirmative point about being African American. Such assertions were common within the different political philosophies, but even more so in the Racial Uplift philosophy. This message was for both African Americans and Whites. Johnson hoped to "uplift" the race to greater self-esteem, knowledge, and socioeconomic independence. And with the more positive portrayals of the community, barriers between African Americans and Whites would lessen.

Johnson's personal philosophy was closer to Racial Uplift than to other ideologies, such as Black Nationalism. Knowing the value of working within the system while also commenting on the Communist Party, Johnson stated, "I shunned the party because it wanted to destroy the system. I didn't want to destroy the system—I wanted to join it so I could change it and make it more responsive to poor people and Blacks."[39] He sought to change the system through the images and stories he produced for and about African Americans and by being a positive example through his own middle-class (and eventually upper-class) status.

Business practices at JPC also suggested the influence of the Racial Uplift outlook. Johnson noted the value of hiring African Americans, having seen its importance in his own first job at Supreme Liberty Life Insurance. Referencing Booker T. Washington, he stated that "the double-duty dollar" was important in the African American economy in that the dollar was earned by an African American company and paid to an African American, thereby circulating in the community at least twice.[40]

Eventually Johnson came to see the futility of the Racial Uplift paradigm and how "uplift" depended too much on the benevolence of Whites:

> The closer I get to the top the more I realize that I'm never going to be fully accepted on merit and money alone. And that a different generation of Blacks—and a different generation of whites—will know the final victory.[41]

Here it is apparent that the African American elite eventually realized that White guilt and accommodation would not translate into full human and civil rights. Further, there were factions of the community that did not subscribe to the Racial Uplift agenda, its methods, or its time frame.

RACIAL UPLIFT AND *EBONY JR!*

As discussed earlier, Johnson believed that showing positive images of African Americans would increase the self-esteem of the community in general and show Whites that we were fully human and deserving of equal treatment. This Racial Uplift approach can be most clearly seen in the early 1970s. To illustrate, I will highlight two nonfiction articles from *EJ* and then discuss how the Racial Uplift ideology is embedded within them. The first story was Josephine Aspinall's "The Secret," which is "based on an episode that actually happened to her family during the 1860s."[42] An African American boy named Charlie found someone in his family's barn while doing chores. In reporting the incident to his father, Charlie learned that his family and members of the community, such as the preacher, helped slaves over the border into Canada. Charlie's "farm is the very last station before the slaves get to Canada, where they will be free."[43] Once Charlie's father explained what the Underground Railroad was, he said,

> "Son, now you know the secret. Would you like to be the one to drive the wagon over the border this time?" Charlie was so surprised that he couldn't speak. But deep down inside, where it really counts, he felt proud and very important. He knew that he would play a part in the freedom of his people.[44]

The last illustration for this story was one of Charlie driving a wagon of hay to Canada, with the slaves hidden underneath.

The next story, Norma Poinsett's "The Haunted Ship in Charleston Harbor," is also about runaways.[45] It features Robert Smalls, a slave ship pilot who captured a ship, filled it with family and friends, and, "facing great danger," sailed to "freedom" in 1862. The people on board mentioned the danger of "Confederate lookouts," and while the ship was getting ready to depart, an unknown figure came aboard and was jumped by the slave crew.[46] "[A] white, pasty mess was all over the cabin before anyone could see that they were attacking a member of their own crew! He was always late for everything."[47] The tardy crewman went on to explain his plan:

> "I got this flour ready to cover our skin." . . . The tardy crewman tried again to explain his plan of covering their faces with flour paste. . . . Soon they all looked like a group of ghosts that decided to haunt the ship.[48]

The tardy crewman's plan of covering the men in flour and Captain Ripley's hat (a symbol of White authority) assisted them in facing the dangers of their escape.

Suddenly Robert's heart began to pound. The first Confederate check point was ahead. Their escape plan was about to really be tested! Everyone on the *Planter* [the ship] was still. The crewmen on deck stood like statues. Their pasty flour masks had been a good idea. They all showed up white and ghost-like in the moonlight.[49]

Through their own cunning and skill, Smalls and his family and friends were able to escape slavery.

The first illustration was scenes of slaves in which there was an African American woman with a short Afro (presumably Smalls's wife, Hannah) holding a baby. Appropriate to the historical moment, the woman had on a long dress and an apron. There was a large picture of the face of a man, who we can assume is Robert Smalls, in the center of the illustration. He had a small Afro, a beard, and a goatee. There was another picture in the foreground of what I assume is the same man. In this picture, his entire body was included, and one can assume he was a slave, since he wore no shirt, was muscular, and was bent over, picking up what seemed to be a heavy load. Behind this figure was an illustration of a White man looking over his left shoulder. Dressed in suit coat and a hat, he held a cigar and had a mustache; beside him was the mast of a ship. One can assume that he was the White captain Ripley referred to in the narrative. This assumption is easy to make, since the narrative stated, "'Put Ole Captain Ripley's hat on Robert.' . . . 'That way the Rebel lookouts are sure to think you're him.'"[50] Smalls was shown in another illustration with the same hat as the White man from the first illustration. The second illustration of Smalls and his wife, unlike the previous image, portrayed them as modern people. They had small Afros and looked like any other Black people of the 1970s.

Many Racial Uplift ideologies are implied in both articles: a sense of community, self-help, emphasis on the journey toward freedom rather than slavery, and, by all means, no overt criticism of Whites. A sense of a race-based community is evident in both stories. In "The Haunted Ship in Charleston Harbor," there is also the self-help element basic to the Racial Uplift ideology. In both stories, the enslaved people freed themselves, and, in doing so, helped free others as well. In "The Secret," once Charlie learned that a runaway slave was on his family's property, he immediately identified with him and was willing to help the person escape. The idea that he would be willing to risk imprisonment by helping a slave escape was quickly dismissed: Of course he would. He, and by implication the child reader, understood his ethnic and political connections with the unnamed runaway. He was also aware of his privileged position as a free person and his moral obligation to help. By helping the escaping slave, Charlie gained membership into the secret community of an activist family and friends, and gained a sense of pride and agency by driving the slave to Canada.

In "The Haunted Ship in Charleston Harbor," Robert Smalls freed himself, his family, and enough other people to fill the ship. Although not as overtly stated as in "The Secret," Smalls also enjoyed a sense of agency and pride by using his skills as a sailor for the betterment of his community. This idea is important, since in neither story did freedom come at the hand of people outside the Black community. This posited to children that they could make a difference in their own lives and the lives of others, especially since "The Secret," the second story printed, featured a child protagonist—as did most of the stories in *EJ*, even the ones about historical figures, for example, "Harriet and the Promised Land" about a young Harriet Tubman.[51] Also suggesting liberationist values, the writers of both stories stated that the slaves were seeking "freedom" and were not simply "going up North." Using the word *freedom* was important, since a connection could be made between the past and present struggles for the child reader. That is, in the 1960s and 1970s Civil Rights and Black Nationalist movements, there were many references to the Blacks' desire for freedom (e.g., the Freedom Riders).

Another commonality these stories shared was that background knowledge of slavery was assumed. Again, "The Haunted Ship in Charleston Harbor," "Harriet and the Promised Land," and "The Secret" all appeared in the first three issues of *EJ*. Any story that offered an explanation of slavery and the social and economic conditions of the enslaved was noticeably absent from these first three issues, and, in fact, from the entire run of *EJ*. It was assumed that the child reader, between the ages of five to eleven, had basic information about slavery. Their interest in slavery, based on the fact that they were connected through their ancestry to slavery, was assumed. This assumption may not have been an oversight; instead, I suspect that it was quite intentional: Teaching the history of slavery might foster resentment in the racialized reader.

One of the noteworthy differences between the two stories is that in "The Haunted Ship in Charleston Harbor" (which appeared in the first issue, in May 1973), Whites were included in the narrative and illustrations. Although African Americans were the focus of the story, Whites were present as symbols of oppression in the image of Captain Riley, in the references to Confederates and Rebels, and in the Black men applying the paste to their skin so that they would appear White. There was a sense of danger to the story, as represented by the crew jumping the late crewman (who they thought was someone else) and by Smalls's heart beating loudly when they faced the Confederate checkpoint. Even this subtle reference to Whites and their connection to slavery in particular, and oppression in general, never occurred again.

In "The Secret," published in the second issue of *EJ* (after editor Constance Van Brunt Johnson may have received some response from readers—especially adults) Whites were noticeably absent. Even though history tells us that many Whites were active in the Underground Railroad, their possible participation in this escape was missing. Whites, and an extended lesson on slavery, may have been excluded from *EJ* for a number of reasons. There was concern about the possibility of being charged with teaching hate. This issue may have been especially troublesome for conservative African Americans, for White teachers, and, more importantly, for the potential White advertisers in JPC publications.

Initially Van Brunt Johnson, as opposed to John Johnson, may not have been as cognizant of the intricacies of being an African American magazine publisher in a hostile society. Therefore, in her mission to tell African American history, she did just that: She included Whites in their role as slave traders and White supremacists. But for conservative African American parents, who were wary of the way nationalists such as the Black Panthers and Malcolm X would teach history and self-defense, there was a fine line between "defense" (which included knowing Black history) and a hateful mindset. In publishing *The Brownies' Book*, DuBois had faced similar concerns. He acknowledged his responsibility to publish news about the oppression of African Americans, even in the children's issue. Access to such information evoked a letter from a child about hating the White man *"as he hates me."*[52] DuBois responded with a dual reaction: that to hate is "more disastrous to [children] than to be hated" and yet to raise children "in ignorance of their racial identity and peculiar situation is inadvisable—impossible."[53]

The two issues are quite separate: teaching hatred versus teaching African American readers about their history in an effort to make them aware of themselves as racially defined and racially targeted by the "mainstream." The fear of "teaching hatred of Whites" is irrelevant. One need not teach children to hate Whites in order to tell them of their history and status as racialized beings in the United States. Children will naturally react with disapproval to those who have oppressed them historically and those who still benefit from such oppression. The idea that children would not react that way disallows them their humanity. Teaching children their history of subjugation by the state, in and of itself, does not teach them to hate. A privileged White presence underlies this entire discourse, since people do not always want to take responsibility for their actions or for undeserved benefits. One can understand the debilitation of hate as well as the power of anger to move one to action.[54] Adult activists for our human and civil rights had to be angry, on some level, to move against White supremacy, even in a nonviolent manner. If adults were angry, why is it not acceptable for children to be angry? The answer is to be found in the adults' construction of children as innocent, naive, and in need of protection.[55]

Putting the issue of teaching hate in a historical context, during the late 1960s we find the Black Nationalist Movement gaining momentum, with Malcolm X as one of its leaders, and simultaneously being widely condemned and attacked for teaching hate.[56] In response to a White reporter's question about this accusation, Malcolm X replied, "For the white man to ask the black man if he hates him is just like the rapist asking the raped or the wolf asking the sheep, 'Do you hate me?' The white man is in no moral position to accuse anyone else of hate!"[57] But irrespective of the logic of his statement, Malcolm X became saddled with the label of hatemonger. JPC publications contrasted him with Dr. Martin Luther King Jr. and his Christian and nonviolent position. In fact, for the most part *EJ* was a King publication, with Malcolm X mentioned only occasionally during Van Brunt Johnson's run, and almost not at all thereafter. Further, White teachers, who constituted the majority of the teaching force, and politically conservative African American teachers may have been uncomfortable with the portrayal of Whites as oppressors in the stories. Again, teachers were a major component of Johnson's initial market for *EJ*. Since the May and June/July 1973 issues of *EJ* were quite different from the rest of Van Brunt Johnson's run, it could be argued that adult readers' responses may have spurred a more conservative direction.

But more than any of this, I believe it was the risk of losing the newly gained White advertisers that may have been the primary reason for deleting the actions of Whites as agents of African American subjugation.[58] In this autobiography, Johnson discussed the difficulty he had with obtaining White mainstream advertisers and how he oftentimes had to employ his skills as a trickster and adept salesman to obtain accounts like the Zenith Corporation account.[59] Prior to getting such accounts, he had to take less desirable ads from White companies that sold things like skin-whitening creams. Eventually he had to devise subsidiaries of JPC, such as Supreme Beauty, to support his magazines, as it is advertising dollars, not magazine sales, that facilitate the financial health of a periodical. Depending on advertisements for White businessmen—people who may have been weary of race-related issues toward the end of the Civil Rights Movement—Johnson may have chosen to entirely remove images of Whites in *EJ*. Given the dynamics of a Racial Uplift philosophy and given the necessity of White cooperation for commercial success, Johnson undoubtedly weighed the risks and made judicious (e.g., profit-oriented) choices. So what was the strategy, when Van Brunt Johnson (under Johnson's direction) took up the challenge of teaching African American children about their history? How did she manage to excise the White subject? She did so by concentrating on the Black subject, by telling a history of resistance without telling the story of the oppression, as in "The Secret."

An additional Racial Uplift ideology apparent in *EJ* was an emphasis on Black beauty. Cooperation from Whites depended in part upon the image of themselves that Blacks portrayed to Whites. Especially for middle-class Blacks, jobs often required interaction with Whites, and physical appearance needed to counteract the prevalent stereotype of unkempt, unhygienic, lazy Black people. In short, the issue of grooming and appearance has long been an issue for African Americans in relations with Whites. In *Up from Slavery: An Autobiography*, Booker T. Washington, again one of the intellectual patriarchs of Racial Uplift, discussed the lack of good grooming in his students and added this subject to the Tuskegee Institute curriculum.[60] In his own autobiography, Johnson also discusses the issue of grooming and the importance of positive image projection as it concerns race relations:

> For as long as I can remember, I've been fascinated by the idea of going first class. That idea, which has nothing at all to do with money, is part of my management style. It's part of my operating philosophy. It informs my view of men, women, events, and the world. . . . going with class and style.[61]

Image as a projection of success was important to Johnson, as is apparent in the centerfolds of beautiful women in *Jet* and *Hue*, and the images he presented of Blacks in his publications in general. Further, he sold grooming products through his subsidiaries such as Fashion Fair Cosmetics, Supreme Beauty Products, and Ebony Fashion Fair—and these were moneymakers that sustained the company.

Grooming and neatness were seen as important attributes for African American children, and *EJ* made this point in narratives, illustrations, and activity sheets. This was most apparent in the early 1970s, when grooming was not only accentuated, it was highly gendered. Most of the beauty-conscious narratives centered on girls. An excellent example is the story "The Fox Who Came Out of the Hole," written by Robert L. Stevenson and Rosalind E. Woodruff, with illustrations by Michael G. Davis.[62] The title of the story tells a lot about gender politics and Van Brunt Johnson's use of popular forms of African American vernacular. Here, the word *fox* was slang for an attractive girl. The story is narrated by a male classmate:

> [In our class everybody called Cookie Peterson] "Dirt and Grime." That was cold. But she fit the name, and she didn't seem to care. She was one big mess. Her hair was always all over her head. She got her clothes dirty and let them hang half off of her. On top of everything else, Cookie didn't act nice, either.[63]

In the illustration of Cookie for this section of the story, she had unkempt hair that had been straightened, one of her socks had tumbled
down around her ankle, and her fists were balled up. Her physical features were not portrayed as unattractive, but her lack of adequate
grooming made her not only physically unattractive, but also afflicted
with an unpleasant personality. The narrator refers to her as "mean and
ugly," a lethal combination in the African American community. In the
derogatory illustration, Cookie stared longingly at Devon Jackson, who
leaned against a wall while two attractive, well-groomed girls looked
longingly at him. But on the other side of a fence was another boy, who
one assumes is the narrator, looking at Cookie.[64] This unnamed narrator
was well groomed and quite fashionable in his hat and multicolored
pants and shirt.[65] In line with *EJ*'s early policy to deny class tensions and
"blame the victim" insinuations, the narrator continued, "I couldn't figure out why Cookie looked so bad. She had lots of brothers and sisters.
They were all neat and clean. They had tried to talk to her, but it hadn't
done any good."[66] Therefore, we learn that class and family upbringing
are not the issue here, since Cookie's siblings "were all neat and clean."[67]

The problem of Cookie's grooming was expanded upon when the
school planned a picnic and the girls decided to each bring enough lunch
to share with a boy. Cookie wanted to share with Devon, but so did every
other girl in the school. Before the picnic, all the girls started being nice to
Devon to get a date with him—even Cookie. "'Devon, I brought some extra Oreo cookies to share with you.' I heard Cookie say. Devon said, 'No
thanks,' as he looked at the cookies in her filthy, dirty hand."[68] Again, it
was Cookie's lack of grooming that prevented her from getting the most
popular boy in the school.

But Cookie was not totally unattractive. Someone saw beneath the dirt.
The narrator went on to tell the reader how he felt about Cookie,

> To tell the truth I kind of like Cookie. I never told anyone, because they
> would laugh me out of town. I wanted to tell Cookie, and I wanted to try and
> convince her to show everybody how pretty she was under all that dirt and
> grime. I knew I had to find the right time and place. Cookie could be mean,
> and I didn't want anyone around just in case she beat me up.[69]

Although the narrator was attracted to Cookie, he feared what other people might think of him for liking her. The moral: "Girls, boys might not
like you if you aren't well-groomed." As the story continued, Cookie
overheard some boys laughing at her and calling her names, and, since
teasing was always frowned upon in *EJ*, Cookie's feelings were hurt.
Eventually the narrator overcame his fear of Cookie and saw through the
"dirt and grime":

I told her she shouldn't feel bad because of what the guys said, or that Devon was sharing Monique Nash's lunch. "I'd like to share yours," I said. She look at me like I was nuts. "What makes you think I want to share anything with you?" She pouted. "Nothing, except I'd be proud of you if you were proud of yourself."[70]

Again, encouraging self-esteem and racial pride were among *EJ's* goals in an effort to socialize the reader into the Racial Uplift agenda. Although Cookie did not overtly accept the narrator's invitation, he did not take any food to the picnic in hopes that Cookie would bring his lunch. While nervously waiting,

I heard a weird noise that startled me. I stood up and turned around quick. There stood a FOX! I swear, a real fox. There are two kinds of foxes. The four-legged kind is one. Then there are what we guys call the prettiest little girls on two legs. Standing in front of me was Cookie Peterson—the fox who came out of the hole! I couldn't believe my eyes. She had her hair in beautiful corn-rowed braids. She had clean, glowing chocolate skin. To top it off she was wearing red shorts and a halter top. Cookie was outta sight! What a fox! . . . I was proud and she was proud.[71]

This section of the story said a great deal. First, the word *fox* was defined, and that was unusual for *EJ*. Usually when African American vernacular was used, it was assumed that the child reader understood the dual meanings of the term (e.g., "outta sight" is not translated). Second, Cookie's hairstyle had changed drastically. Not only was her hair in the second illustration neatly groomed, it was in an Afrocentric, natural-textured style.

This leads one to notice the intersection of Racial Uplift ideology concerned with grooming and a Black Nationalist approach concerned with natural-textured hair as a political statement. Of course, Racial Uplift and Black Nationalist ideologies are not mutually exclusive, but Racial Uplift is usually associated with straight hair, as it is closer to White hair texture and White definitions of beauty. Also noteworthy is the fact that Cookie was described as having "clean, glowing chocolate skin"; in JPC tradition, Cookie was "brown," not "light skinned" or "yellow." And Cookie's new grooming skills were associated with her newfound pride, and the pride she and her new boyfriend had in one another. She had gotten the boy, and he was no longer ashamed of desiring her because of the "dirt and grime." She had found the value and satisfaction of self-esteem.

Presenting oneself in a neat manner was also a theme in the "Mama Write-On's Scribblin' Scope" column that highlighted the importance of good penmanship. Being directly connected with the way people present themselves to the public, penmanship was an important issue to those in JPC who aligned themselves, to whatever degree, with the Racial Uplift paradigm. And this lesson was not only directed to children, since *Hue* also contained columns that concentrated on script. Furthermore, at that moment, many employers saw good penmanship as a sign of general intelligence and neatness.[72] While "Mama Write-On" could be considered just a column to provide readers with an activity for developing good penmanship, it was more than that, since it was racialized.

Mama Write-On herself didn't look like the typical mother. In October 1973, the illustration was of an attractive Black woman with her hair in Afro puffs, possibly suggesting her social consciousness. Symbolic of her connection to the spiritual realm, she wore star earrings, bangles on her wrists, and a headband with a stone in the center of her forehead (the "third eye"); stars floated behind her head, and below her was a crystal ball. Yet her image changed a bit in August/September 1975, in "Mini-Mysteries from Mama Write-On!" In the illustration, Mama Write-On wore a midriff top and bangles on the upper arms as well as the wrists. Her style of dress had a Middle Eastern appearance and associated her with magic and fortune-telling. Noticeably, although she was a "Mama," the image of Mama Write-On was not that of a stereotypical "mammy," a fat woman with a scarf around her head (e.g., Aunt Jemima). And unlike mammy, Mama Write-On did not resemble a typical Christian, since she was a fortune-teller. Although most African Americans tend to be Christians, there is still an element of traditional African religions in the African American community. Healers, rootworkers, and fortune-tellers have always been a vital, although marginal, part of Black society. Mama Write-On was clearly Afrocentric, as demonstrated by her natural-textured hairstyle and in her connection to traditional religions.

According to the October 1973 issue of *EJ*, "The Scribblin' Scope will help you see what the shape of your future will be!" while some other issues said that Mama Write-On could analyze one's personality based upon penmanship.[73] A text was presented for the child to copy on the lines provided. The text was then repeated in different styles of handwriting. In the October 1973 issue, the analysis stated, "If your handwriting looks like this: You need time to pull yourself together. Try not to spread yourself too thin."[74] The column was presented to the reader not as a penmanship activity, but as a divination device. This begs the question: Did child readers buy into this?

Dawn Lewis wrote a letter to *EJ* that was published in the October 1973 edition of "*Ebony Jr!* News." Dawn wrote, "I don't want to hurt your feelings, but I don't like Mama Write-On. Well, it's not that I don't like it. It's just that it doesn't work."[75] This tells us that on some level Dawn was looking for the response from Mama Write-On that she was promised. She wanted some insight into her personality or her fortune based upon her penmanship and she did not get it. Dawn expected more than a writing exercise. But the editors of *EJ* knew that the real issue was penmanship and its connections with one's presentation of self. Note the response that was printed to Dawn after her letter: "Dawn, Mama Write-On said to tell you that she just tries to remind our readers to make their handwriting as neat as possible. But from the looks of your letter, you are already a very good writer! *Write-on*!!!"[76] To the editors of *EJ*, and the adherents of a Racial Uplift philosophy, good penmanship was important in the effort to resist the stereotype of African Americans as unkempt, lazy, and unintelligent.

The Racial Uplift ideology posited that through the attainment of middle-class status and the embodiment of its values, African Americans could show Whites their humanity, and at the same time sustain self-esteem and an awareness of a rich heritage. Emphasizing Racial Uplift for African Americans, Johnson sought to teach Black history and self-esteem.[77] In relation to Whites, Johnson was conscious of media images: He wanted to "reach out to Whites with the hope that images and ideas can break down the barriers that separate us."[78] This double-edged intention was manifested in *EJ* in the way readers were encouraged to be mindful of the image that they themselves presented. They were encouraged to present neat and clean bodies, as in "The Fox Who Came Out of the Hole," and neat penmanship, as in the Mama Write-On column.

THE CIVIL RIGHTS MOVEMENT

Some proponents of the Civil Rights Movement no longer believed in the accommodationist ideology of the older generation. Although they were committed to ending racial segregation, exercising the right to vote, and eventually achieving economic empowerment, they moved toward explicit and vigorous political activism. They did not subscribe to the belief that Whites would give them human and civil rights based upon Whites' benevolence and guilt. They saw the need for more direct action in the form of protests and sit-ins.

The effects of Jim Crow informed every aspect of the lives of the Black community. Segregation was common nationwide, and it was highly discriminatory vis-à-vis the basic rights of children. Prior to the 1960s—and some would say still—most African American children attended racially segregated schools with inferior resources. These unfavorable conditions prepared them psychologically and academically for menial positions. In the earliest court cases, individual parents and small groups filed cases and began to set precedents. In later cases, the state and national strategies of the NAACP clearly were at work. Having enough to build upon, the NAACP launched its most important court case of the 1950s, *Brown v. Board of Education of Topeka, Kansas* (1954). The ruling overturned the *Plessy v. Ferguson* case (1896), which had established that "separate but equal services" were permissible. Although the courts called for integrated schools and set the tone for integration in general following the *Brown* decision, many state governments resisted desegregation. Growing tired of the slow pace of the NAACP's activities, students and other young activists changed the structure of the struggle for civil rights from adult-led accommodationism to youth-led activism. Even the leadership was, on the whole, far younger than that of Racial Uplift. For example, the Reverend Dr. Martin Luther King Jr. was twenty-eight when he was elected president of the Southern Christian Leadership Conference (SCLC) in 1957.[79]

Although many students still agreed with the assimilationist agenda and the Racial Uplift program of organizations like the NAACP, they disagreed with the *pace* of change.[80] "By 1960 [six years after the *Brown v. Board of Education* ruling] only six percent of public schools were integrated, and those mostly in Washington, D.C."[81] Subsequently the students made a move: They began their own protest activities. Thus, according to many scholars, they initiated the Civil Rights Movement proper with the "sit-in" movement and nonviolent protests.[82] With this approach, the movement shifted from being fought primarily in the courts to the marketplace, and from being focused on adult leadership exclusively to the inclusion of more student-led activism.[83] For the most part protests were, "conceived, planned and carried out by young people—and all the impatience and idealism which characterized youth were an organic and integral aspect of this campaign for racial justice."[84]

One of the first incidents of nonviolent protest was when four African American students from the North Carolina Agricultural and Technical College integrated a "whites-only" Woolworth's lunch counter in Greensboro on February 1, 1961. News of this sit-in spread throughout the country, and similar activities increased in various regions.[85] As the student protests grew, segregationist-led groups harassed and beat protestors while the White police arrested the protesters for trespassing.

In general, white southerners viewed the sit-ins skeptically. Bernard Schweid, a sympathetic white businessman in Nashville, says, "Most people did not take the sit-ins too seriously at the beginning, because they felt . . . they are agitators, these are students, some from New York . . . they're not 'our' Negroes. 'Our' individual Negroes get an even break."[86]

These so-called agitators propelled social change forward, displaced the NAACP as the dominant leader for civil rights, brought into existence "unprecedented rivalry among racial advancement groups," and made nonviolent action the dominant strategy for the next five years.[87]

The Student Nonviolent Coordinating Committee (SNCC) was formed under the mentorship of Ella Baker, the SCLC's executive director and "one of the organization's most militant members."[88] Baker encouraged the students to initiate their own activities. Diane Nash stated that Baker knew "how important it was that students set the goals and directions and maintain control of the student movement."[89] The differences between the SNCC and the SCLC were primarily in organizational methods; whereas the SCLC targeted professional adults for organized activist efforts, the SNCC targeted high school and college students,[90] and where the power was centralized in the SCLC, the SNCC's power base was decentralized.[91] Jean Wiley, a SNCC staff member, noted, "Everyone was their own leader to some extent. Whoever took it upon themselves to do something, generally did it."[92] This decentralized structure allowed more women to take an active role in the organization. Also telling of the difference between the Racial Uplift and Civil Rights activism, according to Paula Giddings, was the difference in class and education levels in the groups' target populations and membership.[93] Aligned with the Racial Uplift ideology, rural African Americans, who tended to be poor and undereducated, were ignored by organizations such the NAACP but were targeted by the SNCC. One resident of a rural southern community stated, "I found out later they [the NAACP] had been in the state for forty years, but we sure hadn't seen 'em."[94]

Of course, there was a backlash of violence directed at civil rights workers, but J. Edgar Hoover, director of the FBI, would not provide protection to civil rights activists in Mississippi.[95] The resulting police brutality only expanded marches in other cities. President Lyndon Baines Johnson responded with a rousing speech to Congress that was instrumental in the passage of the Voting Rights Act of 1965. Within five years, the number of African American adults registered to vote increased significantly: In Mississippi the incidence of African American registration went from 6.7 percent in 1964 to 66.5 percent in 1969.[96] This did not go unnoticed. Manning Marable stated that the passage of the Voting Rights Act "increased the institutional, political and vigilante violence against Blacks across the South."[97] This backlash against the African American community by white politicians and common citizens continued at least through the 1980s. White segregationists and supremacists continued their assault on the African American community, often with the support of local police (e.g., in Gransville, Louisiana, a NAACP Youth Council leader was viciously beaten by a White supremacist under the supervision of the local sheriff).[98] Evidently the legal guarantees of desegregation and voting rights had not been enough to end White terrorism against African Americans.

THE CIVIL RIGHTS MOVEMENT AND JOHNSON PUBLISHING COMPANY

Because JPC was one of the most important African American publishers of the 1960s, its coverage of the Civil Rights Movement was important in that it offered an African American perspective and assisted in keeping the community abreast of the events. The Civil Rights Movement depended heavily upon media coverage and the reaction of Whites and northern African Americans as a result of such coverage. JPC's coverage was responsible for many of the famous photos of the movement, so much so that in 1969 Moneta J. Sleet Jr., a JPC photographer, became the first African American photographer to win a Pulitzer Prize. The winning photograph featured Coretta Scott King and her youngest child, Bernice, during Martin Luther King Jr.'s funeral.[99] According to Johnson, JPC's involvement with the movement did not stop with media coverage:

> [JPC] also became a part of the struggle. I marched and gave tens of thousands of dollars to different arms of the movement. With and without my approval, my editors marched and volunteered for difficult and dangerous assignments. . . . We told the story. More to the point, we were a part of a story that cannot be recalled or told without referring to the pages of *Ebony* and *Jet* and the 2 million photographs in our archives.[100]

In 1955 Emmett Till, a fourteen-year-old African American boy from Chicago who was visiting relatives in Mississippi, was lynched for supposedly whistling at a White woman. *Jet*'s coverage of the lynching and subsequent funeral was a landmark event in newspapers as well as civil rights history. Till's nude body was found

> at the bottom of a nearby river, with a seventy-five pound cotton gin fan tied around his neck. The side of his skull had been crushed in to the bone, an eye had been pushed in, and he had been shot in the head.[101]

Although the Mississippi sheriff wanted to avoid publicity, Mamie Till,[102] Emmett's mother, demanded that the body be returned to their home in Chicago for an open-casket funeral. Mamie Till asked JPC photographers to publish pictures of her son's body, saying, "I want the world to see what they did to my boy."[103] Johnson stated,

There were people on the staff who were squeamish about the photographs. I had reservations, too, but I decided finally that if it happened it was our responsibility to print it and let the world experience man's inhumanity to man. The issue, which went on sale September 15, 1955, sold out immediately and did as much as any other event to traumatize Black America and prepare the way for the Freedom Movement of the sixties.[104]

Notice that even though Johnson was discussing a traumatic event, aligned with his Racial Uplift leanings, Whites are absent from his statement. One can make an assumption about the races of "man's inhumanity to man," but Johnson could not be charged with racism by White advertisers—a common concern of his—because here, and in other publications, he failed to indict Whites explicitly.

Ebony's coverage of the 1963 March on Washington ("Biggest Protest March," 1963) was illustrative of the Racial Uplift tradition. It highlighted King, printed the "I Have a Dream" speech, and featured pictures of African Americans and Whites together at the march. But another article, "Masses Were March Heroes," by Lerone Bennett Jr., centered on the folk. King is nowhere in these photos. Instead, the lead photo, with the caption "Father of the March," is of Asa Phillips Randolph, an important leader of the movement who never garnered the media attention as King. Further coverage in *Ebony* included school desegregation episodes, marches, and reports on a variety of race-based injustices.

THE CIVIL RIGHTS MOVEMENT IN *EBONY JR!*

As one might expect, for the most part, the editors of *EJ* used Dr. Martin Luther King Jr. as the icon of the Civil Rights Movement. Every January the magazine featured articles and possibly activity sheets focusing on King and the movement. These articles took different forms: Some years they were poems, other years one might see plays or short stories. As they had in general, the editors used the readers' responses to support and facilitate their mission statement. For example, the January 1982 issue of *EJ* featured a biographical poem of King written by Janice Taylor, a ten-year-old reader: "Dr. Martin Luther King Jr. was a mighty man/To get equality for all was his plan./He worked very hard for what he thought was right,/But he never, ever chose to fight."[105] The poem, which is substantial, is well informed for a ten-year-old. In addition to King, Rosa Parks was featured in articles such as "From the Back of the Bus" (1974).

An occasional activity sheet focusing on the movement was also included. "Selma to Montgomery" was a maze of Alabama with only Montgomery and Selma identified. The reader was asked, "Can you help

Martin Luther King lead 650 people on a march from Selma to Montgomery? Find path on the map above. In 1965 Martin Luther King really
did lead 650 people on a 50 mile march from Selma to Montgomery Alabama."[106] Even the songs of the movement were mentioned, as in the
sheet music for "If You Miss Me from the Back of the Bus" which is "[a]
traditional song adapted by members of SNCC from We Shall Overcome!
This is one of the songs people sang during the boycott and during the
Civil Rights Movement."[107]

Missing from these issues, in addition to many people other than King
and Parks who contributed to the Civil Rights Movement, was the children's story. Again, many of the marchers and other activists were
young—elementary through college age. Robert Coles documented this
in *Children in Crisis* when he discussed the responses of southern African
American children who experienced the stress of White supremacy and
their political analysis. One would think that since this was children's literature and the protagonists of the narratives should be children, there
would be stories of children's participation in the movement.[108] But in the
late 1970s, many of the children and young adults who participated in the
movement during the 1960s were too young to have their stories published as children's literature. Although there were children's books that
featured adults, there was little to no children's literature about the Civil
Rights Movement that featured child protagonists.

For example, in 1960, Ruby Bridges was a six-year-old when she attended William Frantz Public School in New Orleans. Prior to Bridges's
arrival, Frantz had been a segregated school. According to her autobiography and Coles's biography, both written for children, and his
scholarly works, such as *Children in Crisis*, it was a stressful year for
Bridges. Coles, a child psychiatrist and researcher, served as Bridges's
therapist, assisting her with the trauma of going to school while White
supremacists standing outside the school threatened to kill her. But,
stated Bridges in her autobiography, *Through My Eyes*, at year's end all
the attention was gone and things had returned to normal—and she received no explanation from adults. In fact, Bridges stated that she forgot about her first-grade year until her mother pointed her out on an
episode of *Eyes on the Prize*. While Coles told Bridges's story in *Children
in Crisis* in 1967 and later in *The Story of Ruby Bridges*, a biography written for children and published in 1995, Bridges did not tell her own
story until 1999. So *EJ* was aligned with children's literature in general
in not including stories of children's involvement in the Civil Rights
Movement.

EJ also included another component of the Black Liberation Movement: The Black Power Movement. Again, the Black community is diverse and many of the young people of the late 1960s thought that

King's leadership, as well as the Racial Uplift ideology, as far too accommodating and slow.

THE BLACK POWER MOVEMENT

Some SNCC members eventually lost their confidence in "the efficacy of working with White liberals, their faith in the federal government, and, in a broader sense, the meaningfulness of pursuing civil rights laws when Blacks were at such a perennially low economic level."[109] In addition, they rejected materialism and integration as the ultimate goal. Further, most social critics did not believe that the nonviolent tactics of the southern movement would work in the urbanized, ghettoized North. The gains made by the Civil Rights Movement, while lauded, exposed its weaknesses. Legal advances were "insufficient as an objective in the North, where de facto discrimination was the dominant mode of white supremacism"[110] and where desegregation efforts in the South were often overshadowed by Whites' violent reactions. Also, the economic devastation of the Jim Crow system—sharecropping, little to no access to credit, and the lack of property and contractual rights for Blacks—was only recently being addressed by the Civil Rights agenda. Meanwhile race riots in urban cities led to approximately 250 deaths, 10,000 serious injuries, and 60,000 arrests between 1964 and 1968.[111] In addition to this internal strife, the United States became seriously entangled in the Vietnam War, and the Civil Rights Movement shifted toward a more militant orientation.

Therefore, some turned to the ideologies of Malcolm X and a more militant and efficacious movement in the North. As a link to Marcus Garvey and as an influence on future generations, Malcolm X is considered the father of Black Power. He eventually became the most outspoken minister of the Nation of Islam, preaching a Black Nationalist agenda that included separatism, self-definition, and economic independence. Quickly attracting the attention of non-Muslims, traditional African American leaders, and the media, he came under attack from these groups for what they perceived as teaching a doctrine of hate.[112] But irrespective of what either Whites or conservative African Americans may have thought of Malcolm X, he "changed the lives of thousands of poor and oppressed blacks" and influenced the next generation of civil rights activists.[113] "More than any single personality," wrote Marable, he "was able to articulate the aspirations, bitterness and frustrations of the Negro people."[114] The moment of his assassination in 1965 is considered by scholars to be the beginning of the contemporary Black Nationalist Movement.[115]

The Black Nationalists believed in cultural, and, to a lesser degree, political, separatism. While nationalism in general is "the belief that the cultural and political unit should be congruent," Black Nationalists

> insist that African Americans as a distinct people should pursue collective political action rooted in their common history and their ostensibly common interests. Politically, black nationalists largely pursue racially exclusive political organizations; economically, they advocate for black economic self-sufficiency; and culturally, they emphasize their black and primarily pan-Africanist identity.[116]

As opposed to Eurocentric definitions of *nationalism* that aspire to statehood, Black Nationalism advocates a "pan-Africanist criterion for nationhood wherein historically polyglot black cultural groups are wedded to a common political purpose that suggests group autonomy, though not necessarily statehood."[117] The Black Nationalists sought "to strengthen ingroup values while holding those promoted by the larger society at arm's length. . . . [T]he hope [was] to win and maintain sociocultural autonomy."[118] It was a move toward self-determination, not for separation for its own sake. In segregating and redefining Blackness, nothing was left unconsidered: Everything was included, such as hairstyle, dress, and social values. In the economic sphere, materialism, as a value aligned with Whites, was frowned upon, and socialism was encouraged.

The rise of the 1960s Black Nationalist Movement was, like the others, associated with three factors: African American underemployment in the face of White bounty; "attacks by the white ruling class on civil rights and the promotion of racist vigilantism; and the failure of black leadership to articulate the demands of the black masses through new policies and programs."[119] In addition, Harold Cruse noted the correlation between U.S. involvement in war and the rise of nationalism.[120] While supremacist-induced violence was rampant, the U.S. government simultaneously recruited African Americans for the Armed Forces. Errol Henderson stated,

> Wars provided the opportunity for a redefinition of the status of Blacks inasmuch as their wartime sacrifice in defense of democracy called into question the basis of the racial caste system while exposing the huge disjuncture between the American creed of liberty, equality, and justice and the persistence of white racism, lynch-law, Jim Crow, and Black privation.[121]

In essence, African Americans were asked to "fight for a country" that oppressed them; they were instructed to kill those who did not subjugate them on behalf of those who did. This inconsistency promoted Muhammad Ali's famous reaction to being drafted into service for the Vietnam War: "No Vietnamese ever called me nigger."[122] The exposure of the dichotomy between the myth of American democracy and the caste-based system of White supremacy "stimulated black mobilization, intensified black resistance, and fueled the militancy with which Blacks expressed their grievances."[123] These factors helped set the stage for the modern Black Nationalist Movement.

Unlike integrationists and even pluralists, Black Nationalists did not believe that African Americans, as a racialized group, could coexist with Whites, using the "same societal institutions" in an equal and peaceful manner.[124] Eventually "some component of the social matrix comes to dominate and oppress others" and in the process dissolves "subgroup mores"; therefore, integration was to be "avoided at all costs."[125] The Black Nationalists of the 1960s moved to reify their day-to-day separation from Whites as a means of political, economic, and cultural self-definition and advancement.

Aligned with the more militant orientation of the Black Nationalist Movement is the Black Panther Party for Self Defense, founded in 1966 by Huey P. Newton and Bobby Seale.[126] Influenced by the politics of Malcolm X, the Panthers advocated the restructuring of American society to make it more politically, economically, and socially equitable. They supported the Black Power Movement, and in their original "Ten Point Program" the Panthers set forth a list of demands that included "land, bread, housing, education, clothing, justice and peace."[127] To facilitate self-sufficiency, the Panthers organized community programs, including free health care and free breakfasts for schoolchildren.[128] As a socialist group (numbering five thousand in 1968), the Panthers criticized the African American middle class for what they saw as a disinterest in the poor and disadvantaged.[129]

Threatened by the Panthers' militant, self-defensive agenda (the Panthers advocated the carrying of weapons), the federal government looked for a way to disrupt the party, although it had not, as a whole, "advocated violence against white-owned property, the subversion of authority, or the seizure of state power."[130] Yet blaming the Panthers (instead of the White supremacist system of oppression) for the increasing violence of 1966–1968, the FBI launched a Counterintelligence Program (COINTEL-PRO) to destroy the efforts of militant groups such as the Panthers and the SNCC.[131] By July 1969 the Panthers had been the target of 233 separate actions by the FBI—for example, in 1969 alone, 27 Panthers were killed and 749 were arrested.[132]

In 1969 the federal surveillance of the Black Panther Party came to a head. Under instructions from Edward V. Hanrahan, Cook County's state attorney, fifteen Chicago policemen massacred Panther leaders Mark Clark and Fred Hampton while they were asleep in bed.[133] Hanrahan told the press that the Panthers and the police had a shootout, but physical evidence from the apartment showed that a Panther shot only two bullets, while the police shot approximately two hundred.[134] Although African American members of Congress held a hearing causing the federal jury to indict Hanrahan and thirteen codefendants, Hanrahan was eventually acquitted.[135]

Besides the government, one of the major issues for the movement was a lack of direction caused by a vague definition of Black Power. According to Malcolm X, Black Power was voluntary segregation so that African Americans could focus their energies on themselves and their communities. Concurring with the viewpoint of Malcolm X, Stokely Carmichael and Charles V. Hamilton defined Black Power as "a political framework and ideology which represents the last reasonable opportunity for this society to work out its racial problems short of prolonged destructive guerrilla warfare."[136] Black power would permit African Americans to

> exercise some control over our lives, politically, economically and psychically. We will also contribute to the development of a viable larger society. . . . [T]here is nothing unilateral about the movement to free Black people.[137]

Others, like Amiri Baraka, interpreted Black Power as emphasizing the cultural heritage of African Americans, especially in relation to African roots. "Still another view of Black Power called for a revolutionary political struggle to reject racism and imperialism in the U.S., as well as throughout the world."[138] Marable stated that from its very beginnings, "Black Power was not a coherent ideology, and never developed a unitary program which was commonly supported by a majority of its proponents."[139]

Additionally, the Black Power Movement was co-opted to some degree by President Nixon's notion of Black capitalism. In his presidential campaign of 1968, Nixon defined Black Power as

> the power that people should have over their own destinies, the power to affect their own communities, the power that comes from participating in the political and economic process of society. . . . What most militants are asking is not separation, but to be included in—not as supplicants, but as owners, as entrepreneurs—to have a share of the wealth and a piece of the action. And this is what the Federal central target of the new approach ought to be . . . oriented toward black ownership, for from this can flow the rest—black pride, black jobs, black opportunity, and yes black power.[140]

Of course, once Nixon appropriated the term, most progressive Black Nationalists stopped using it and turned to the ideology of Pan-Africanism—an ideology that unified peoples of the African Diaspora, focuses on Africa as a homeland, and moves against the oppression of African Americans in the United States and Africa.[141]

BLACK NATIONALISM AND JOHNSON PUBLISHING COMPANY

While the Racial Uplift, Civil Rights, and Black Power movements differed ideologically, all had the goals of enfranchisement and equality of
African Americans at their core and all received coverage by JPC. Black
Nationalism and the demand for self-definition were a component of the
civil rights discourse throughout JPC's history; this was apparent in Johnson's inclusion of Black history and culture and displays of Black beauty
of varying shades, even though such features were not rooted exclusively
in the Black Power ideology. According to Johnson, as a result of Black
Nationalism and self-definition, "[f]or the first time Blacks came into their
own. They respected themselves as Black people whether they were very
dark or very light or in between. Color, in fact, lost its importance. . . . JPC
played a leadership role in this process."[142] In addition to the color issue,
from its inception JPC provided its readers with information on Black history and culture. While the majority of JPC publications were influenced
predominantly by the Racial Uplift mindset, with the rise of the Black
Power Movement JPC, according to Johnson, "didn't follow the parade;
we were out front, beating the drums and pointing the way. Our series on
'Black Power' preceded the first call for 'Black Power.'"[143]

One example of coverage of the Black Power Movement is *The Black
Revolution* (1965/1970), a collection of Black Nationalist articles. Origi-
nally the text was a special issue of *Ebony* magazine in August 1969. The
arts, politics, and social condition of African Americans were addressed
by authors such as Lerone Bennett Jr., Larry Neal, Charles Hamilton, and
Huey P. Newton. And, as stated earlier, the JPC magazine *Black World* was
a venue for editor Hoyt Fuller and his ardent support for a Black Aesthetic. Lerone Bennett Jr., a much respected historian, was also on the staff
and covered Black Nationalist concerns.

Because of the many movements for civil rights, significant gains were
made through the joint efforts of various factions of the community. The
Racial Uplift advocates fought the fight in the courts and the legal system;
the youth fought with nonviolent public protests, school desegregation,
and voter registration. The Black Nationalist/Self-Definitionists, such as
the Black Panthers, had a socialist bent and, unlike the nonviolent philosophy of those in the Civil Rights Movement, were poised to use "whatever means necessary."

BLACK NATIONALISM IN *EBONY JR!*

Again, although Johnson's politics were aligned with Racial Uplift and
its agenda was included in *EJ*, so was Black Nationalism, albeit to a lesser

degree. The two often coexisted. Black Nationalist ideologies were evident in the way *EJ* presented an almost exclusively Black world. It emphasized African and African American history and culture, encouraged racial pride, and attempted to bolster self-esteem. Lifestyles were defined as Black through the use of natural-textured hairstyles and Black language patterns, fashions, and foodways. Further, a racially relevant education was a component of the Black Nationalist agenda, and *EJ*'s educational curriculum was, for the most part, racialized in content and form.

More so in the 1970s than the 1980s, Kwanzaa, for example, which was established in 1966 by Maulana Karenga, was privileged over Christmas. As Karenga, a Black Nationalist, attempted to encourage "cultural reaffirmation," he looked primarily to East African harvest festivals and celebrations as a model for a holiday that focuses on socio-centric values.[144] Celebrated from December 26 through January 1, each night of Kwanzaa concentrates on self-awareness and community building. By 1973 Kwanzaa was still primarily celebrated by Black Nationalists who wanted to reify their Pan-Africanism, but it was known well enough by the African American community for inclusion in *EJ*.[145] In the first December issue in 1973, Sharon Bell Mathis introduced the holiday to child readers with the questions, "What is Kwanza? [*sic*], What is Christmas?"[146] While all the children knew what Christmas was, only one out of four readers could define Kwanzaa. Therefore, *EJ*'s editor included a short narrative explaining the holiday and added a relevant activity sheet.

Aligned with Kwanzaa and some definitions of Black Nationalism, consumerism was deemphasized in the *EJ* of the 1970s, particularly around the winter holidays. As mentioned in chapter 1, in the story "Peter's Tenth Christmas," although Peter gave Sarah a gift, she was poor and gave him the only gift she received, a pink nightgown. He refrained from looking down on her, stating, "Well, I didn't get a present from the grab bag that Christmas. I got something a lot better. . . . I had learned what giving and receiving really means."[147] This message was reinforced by the stock characters, too. Sunny and Honey, in their December 1975 cartoon, stated, "Things are really tough./There'll be no big gifts this year./But that doesn't bother me,/as long as love is here!"[148] In the illustration, both Sunny and Honey hugged the doll who served as the narrator. Of course, the message here was that family—and, by extension, community—was far more important than material goods. The Black Nationalist lesson for the 1970s reader was that community was preferable to individualism or materialism. But the economic conditions of African Americans changed in the 1980s, primarily because of the backlash that followed the Civil Rights Movement. The middle class learned that relative access to education and employment did not translate to equal rights, and the working and lower classes grew poorer and poorer. And, of course, *EJ* changed as its editors changed, from Van Brunt Johnson in the early 1970s, to Odom in the mid-to-late 1970s, to Lewis in the late 1970s, and to Roebuck-Hoard in the 1980s.

Whereas Kwanzaa was privileged in the 1970s, Christmas moved to the forefront in the 1980s—although Kwanzaa was still included. For example, the December 1981 cover featured, "Holiday Happenings, Kwanza [*sic*] Wonders, Great Gifts!" Clearly the 1970s Peter (from "Peter's Tenth Christmas") would not have been pleased in the 1980s to have only the joy of giving. Christmas was highlighted, as seen in the illustration above the monthly calendar stating "Merry Christmas" and showing a picture of Santa and two reindeer. Even Sunny and Honey had become materialistic. Loaded down with packages as they walked through the snow, they stated, "We did our Christmas shopping real early. Because the holiday crowds can be rough./So we really shouldn't be frustrated and gruff./ [The illustration then changed to an image of the pair searching for something.] But we can't remember where we hid all that stuff!"[149]

As in the 1970s, in the 1980s the sociopolitical conditions of the Black community were reflected in the pages of *EJ*. Here they were manifested in the need for the child reader to be prepared not only for a literate and racialized future, but for a future in the workforce. Further, the financial strain and the social issues connected with poverty were reflected in the anger the characters expressed on their faces and in the discord shown between the classes. Also reflected were the changing perceptions of gender equality.

ISSUES OF GENDER AND BLACK FEMINISM

The 1960s were not only a time for fighting for African American civil liberties in general; African American women in particular also fought for their rights during this historical moment. Both the Civil Rights Movement and the Black Nationalist Movement have been criticized as sexist, and the White mainstream, including the White feminist movement, is racially biased and sexist.[150] By the 1970s African American women were addressing the intersection of race, gender, class, and sexuality. The founding of the National Black Feminist Organization in New York in 1973 is marked as the official beginning of the movement. In 1974 a group of Black women formed the Combahee River Collective, which was "actively committed to struggling against racial, sexual, heterosexual, and class oppression and see as our particular task the development of integrated analysis and practice based upon the fact that major systems of oppression are interlocking."[151] Eventually Black Women's Studies began to appear in college courses, although not to the degree that either Black Studies or Women's Studies were instituted. In 1981 a Black Feminist publisher, Kitchen Table: Women of Color Press, was founded by Barbara Smith. One of its more well-known titles was *This Bridge Called My Back: Writings by Radical Women of Color* (1981), a collection of Black Feminist essays edited by Cherrie Moraga and Gloria Anzaldua. By the 1980s those who were interested would have had access to Black Feminist theory, classes, and literature.

Of course, Black Feminist theory has evolved over time, and when *EJ* was initially published in 1973, this discourse was not fully formed. Still, Van Brunt Johnson was relatively conscious of gender issues and was commended. Deborah Stead, who critiqued children's magazines for the Council on Interracial Books for Children, stated that most children's magazines (including the Girl Scouts' *American Girl*) were sexist. "From all this *Ebony Jr!* offers much relief [with the] only 'stock character' that is a female of all the publications."[152] (The "stock character" was Sunny, in the "Sunny and Honey" feature.) She applauded Van Brunt Johnson, who stated, "We needed the doll so we could have one character who spoke in simple sentences, but we realized that it should not always be held by only [the female character], so, sometimes the doll is with Sunny."[153] Further, Stead noted the equality in the number of male and female characters shown in *EJ*.

My reading of the sexism or lack thereof in *EJ* is not so generous. I found *EJ* to be sexist in subtle ways. It is true that Van Brunt Johnson consistently placed a girl and a boy in the cooking and crafts columns. And while Sunny did occasionally hold the doll, he usually did so in a very male manner: As opposed to Honey, who often held the doll close to her chest, Sunny usually held the doll by an arm and let her body dangle. Based upon these illustrations, his relationship to the doll was not a nurturing one, which one would expect to be the point of having Sunny hold the doll. And while there tended to be an equal number of boys and girls represented, overall, boys were privileged. More often than not the protagonists of the short stories were boys, and boys were allowed more areas of interest than girls. For example, the May through August/September 1973 issues typically featured only one narrative per issue with a female protagonist.

As time passed, there was an occasional nod to gender equality with stories like "George!" (1974), in which the character everyone thought was a boy baseball player actually turned out to be a girl. But, for the most part, the gender roles were relatively conservative. And it was not until the 1980s that adults were shown in "nontraditional" roles. In the 1970s all the teachers were single women. The first allusion to a married female teacher was made in "Moon," a story in the January 1980 issue. The first male teacher in *EJ* appeared on a cover of a 1981 issue.

Although there tended to be the same number of girls as boys in the illustrations, more often than not the boys were the protagonists and the active agents of the stories. But this reading implies a connection with the Black Feminist Movement, and is therefore stricter in its standards about sexism than was Stead in 1975. As for adults, in the short stories, when men were featured cooking, it was in a traditionally male style: barbecuing. Further, there were few examples of girls doing nontraditional activities, whereas boys were included as active participants in the cooking segment.

CONCLUSION

The African American leadership prior to the 1960s was predominately aligned with Racial Uplift, but faced with the escalating assault on the African American community in the twentieth century, this accommodationist agenda gave way to a more activist approach. The legal advances made by the NAACP were enacted by the grassroots efforts of Civil Rights organizations. While the desegregation of schools and public facilities was applauded, the failure of the many civil rights initiatives and the escalating degree of White-induced violence were taken as reasons for a more militant approach. The rebirth of the Black Nationalist Movement created organizations such as the Black Panther Party and the increase in the popularity of the Nation of Islam. Unlike nonviolent civil rights activism, Black Nationalist organizations taught self-defense for the mind and body. Although they varied in their ideologies, the three approaches to African American civil rights had a shared goal: the elimination of the economic, political, and cultural domination of African Americans by Whites. The struggle touched the lives of African American children, and *EJ*, as the servant of the young, had to take them all into account. In no way could children be excluded from the political world.

The sociopolitical climate the Black community faced in the 1960s–1980s informed the manner in which Blacks were constructed in *EJ*. One of the ways the Racial Uplift agenda was manifested in *EJ* was through the sheer lack of a White subject. Although racialized self-awareness was paramount in *EJ*, African and African American history were reported without a White presence as the cause of Black suffering. This glaring absence of Whites can be considered a maneuver by Johnson not to create any animosity between JPC and its White advertisers. Like the Racial Uplift agenda, Black Nationalist ideologies laud racial pride and self-help, but they do so through racial separation, not integration. Although Racial Uplift and Black Nationalism have ideological differences, they coexist in the pages of *EJ* in a manner that celebrates a Black reality within the context of an academic curriculum.

Another factor that informed the construction of *EJ* was the call for adequate and racially relevant education so prevalent in the Black Liberation Movement of the 1960s and 1970s. Like its counterparts, *EJ* offered an elementary school–based curriculum. *EJ*'s other curriculum—a racialized one—set it apart from its contemporaries and responded to the needs of the Black community. This will be discussed in chapter 5.

NOTES

1. Richard E. Dawson and Kenneth Prewitt, *Political Socialization: An Analytic Study* (Boston: Little, Brown, 1968), 7.

2. Fred I. Greenstein, *Children and Politics* (New Haven, CT: Yale University Press, 1965), 5.

3. Robert Coles, *The Political Life of Children* (Boston: Houghton Mifflin, 1986), 49.

4. Dawson and Prewitt, *Political Socialization*, 41.

5. An example from Robert Coles's book, *The Political Life of Children*, features a ten-year-old who was able to link his own schoolteacher's behavior with actions by the governor of the state. The child commented: "[T]he teachers . . . say bad things to us. They're always calling us names; they make you feel no good. We saw the man on television, the governor, and he wasn't any good either" (p. 28).

6. Dawson and Prewitt, *Political Socialization*, 4.

7. John H. Johnson and Lerone Bennett, *Succeeding against the Odds* (Chicago: Johnson Publishing, 1989), 38.

8. James P. Comer and Alvin F. Poussaint, *Black Child Care: How to Bring up a Healthy Black Child in America: A Guide to Emotional and Psychological Development* (New York: Pocket Books, 1975), 25.

9. Johnson and Bennett, *Succeeding against the Odds*, 33.

10. Harold Cruse, *The Crisis of the Negro Intellectual* (New York: Morrow, 1967), 563.

11. Errol Henderson, "War, Political Cycles, and the Pendulum Thesis: Explaining the Rise of Black Nationalism, 1840–1996," in *Black and Multiracial Politics in America*, ed. Yvette M. Alex-Assensoh and Lawrence J. Hanks (New York: New York University Press, 2000), 339.

12. W. E. B. Du Bois, *The Souls of Black Folk* (1903; reprint, New York: Dover, 1994), 305.

13. Henderson, "War, Political Cycles, and the Pendulum Thesis," 340.

14. Kevin K. Gaines, *Uplifting the Race: Black Leadership, Politics, and Culture in the Twentieth Century* (Chapel Hill: University of North Carolina Press, 1996), 1.

15. Ibid., 2.

16. Ibid.

17. Ibid.; Stephen Small, *Racialised Barriers: The Black Experience in the United States and England in the 1980s*, Critical Studies in Racism and Migration (London: Routledge, 1994).

18. Gaines, *Uplifting the Race*, xiv.

19. Small, *Racialised Barriers.*
20. Ibid.
21. Gaines, *Uplifting the Race.*
22. Ibid., 2.
23. Ibid., 3.
24. Elise J. McDougald, "The Task of Negro Womanhood," in *The New Negro,* ed. Allen Locke (1919; reprint, New York: Simon & Schuster, 1997).
25. Gaines, *Uplifting the Race,* xix.
26. Frazier, as cited in ibid., 3.
27. Ibid., xviii.
28. Ibid.
29. Ibid., xix.
30. Ibid.
31. Booker T. Washington, *Up from Slavery: An Autobiography* (1901; reprint, Garden City, NY: Doubleday, 1963).
32. W. Edward Farrison, "Looking Back at Booker T.," *Negro Digest,* May 1942, 55.
33. Ibid., 57.
34. Johnson and Bennett, *Succeeding against the Odds,* 156–57.
35. Du Bois, *The Souls of Black Folk,* 156.
36. Gaines, *Uplifting the Race,* xv; Johnson and Bennett, *Succeeding against the Odds.*
37. Johnson and Bennett, *Succeeding against the Odds,* 288.
38. Ibid., 157.
39. Ibid., 77.
40. Ibid.
41. Ibid., 21.
42. Josephine Aspinall, "The Secret," *Ebony Jr!,* August/September 1973, 47.
43. Ibid., 49.
44. Ibid.
45. Norma Poinsett and illustrations by Orville Hurt, "The Haunted Ship in Charleston Harbor," *Ebony Jr!,* November 1973.
46. Ibid., 8.
47. Ibid., 9.
48. Ibid.
49. Ibid., 10.
50. Ibid., 9.
51. Jacob Lawrence, "Harriet and the Promised Land," *Ebony Jr!,* June/July 1973.
52. W. E. B. DuBois, "The True Brownies," *Crisis,* October 1919, 285.
53. Ibid.
54. Audre Lorde, "The Uses of Anger: Women Responding to Racism," in *Sister Outsider: Essays and Speeches,* ed. Audre Lorde (Trumansburg, NY: Crossing Press, 1984).
55. Perry Nodelman, *The Pleasures of Children's Literature* (New York: Longman, 1992).
56. Manning Marable, *Race, Reform, and Rebellion: The Second Reconstruction in Black America, 1945–1990,* 2nd ed. (Jackson: University Press of Mississippi, 1991).

57. Malcolm X, "To Mississippi Youth," in *Malcolm X Speaks: Selected Speeches and Statements*, ed. George Breitman (New York: Grove Press, 1965), 201–202.

58. Jerry G. Watts, *Amiri Baraka: The Politics and Art of a Black Intellectual* (New York: New York University Press, 2001).

59. Johnson and Bennett, *Succeeding against the Odds.*

60. Washington, *Up from Slavery.*

61. Johnson and Bennett, *Succeeding against the Odds*, 197.

62. Robert L. Stevenson and Rosalind E. Woodruff, "The Fox Who Came Out of the Hole," *Ebony Jr!*, June/July 1976.

63. Ibid., 19.

64. Ibid.

65. Ibid., 20.

66. Ibid., 19.

67. Ibid.

68. Ibid., 20.

69. Ibid.

70. Ibid.

71. Ibid., 21.

72. As stated before, a penmanship column was presented to the adult readers in *Hue.*

73. "Mama Write-On's Scribblin' Scope," *Ebony Jr!*, October 1973, 24.

74. Ibid.

75. Ibid.

76. Ibid.

77. Johnson and Bennett, *Succeeding against the Odds.*

78. Ibid., 184.

79. King was born on January 15, 1929, making him thirty-one in 1960, which is considered the beginning of the Civil Rights Movement.

80. Paula Giddings, *When and Where I Enter: The Impact of Black Women on Race and Sex in America* (New York: Morrow, 1984).

81. Ibid., 273.

82. The 1960 sit-in conducted by the North Carolina students was not the first, although it is often considered the beginning of the Civil Rights Movement. CORE may have been the first group to sponsor formal nonviolent sit-ins. Students from Fisk University in Nashville were also planning a sit-in in 1961, and students in Wichita conducted a lunch counter sit-in prior to the Greensboro group. Ibid.; Marable, *Race, Reform, and Rebellion.*

83. Marable, *Race, Reform, and Rebellion.*

84. Ibid., 64.

85. Giddings, *When and Where I Enter.*

86. Juan Williams, *Eyes on the Prize: America's Civil Rights Years, 1954–1965* (New York: Viking, 1987), 132.

87. Marable, *Race, Reform, and Rebellion*, 62.

88. The Southern Christian Leadership Conference was begun as a Christian version of the NAACP. The leaders wanted another organization that wasn't a "red flag" to southern Whites as was the NAACP, and that was Christian in ori-

entation and leadership. Martin Luther King Jr. was the SCLC president. Williams, *Eyes on the Prize*, 127.

89. Ibid., 137.

90. Ibid.

91. Giddings, *When and Where I Enter*.

92. Judith Vecchione, *Eyes on the Prize: American Civil Rights Years, 1954–1965* (Alexandria, VA: PBS Video, 1990).

93. Giddings, *When and Where I Enter*.

94. Vecchione, *Eyes on the Prize*.

95. Noam Chomsky has reported that "as late as summer 1965, FBI observers refused to act within their legal authority to protect civil rights demonstrators who were being savagely beaten by police and thrown into stockades (some, who tried to find sanctuary on federal property, were thrown from the steps of the federal building in Jackson, Mississippi, by federal marshals)" as cited in Cathy Perkus and Nelson Blackstock, eds., *COINTELPRO: The FBI's Secret War on Political Freedom* (New York: Monad Press, 1975), 13.

96. Marable, *Race, Reform, and Rebellion*.

97. Ibid., 82.

98. Ibid.

99. Johnson and Bennett, *Succeeding against the Odds*.

100. Ibid., 241.

101. Jeffrey C. Stewart, *1001 Things Everyone Should Know About African-American History* (New York: Doubleday, 1996), 163.

102. In his autobiography, Johnson refers to Till's mother as Mamie Bradley Mobley. For the sake of clarity, I will refer to her as Mamie Till.

103. Johnson and Bennett, *Succeeding against the Odds*, 240.

104. Ibid.

105. Janice Taylor, "Dr. Martin Luther King Jr.—Leader," *Ebony Jr!*, January 1982, 42.

106. "Selma to Montgomery," *Ebony Jr!*, January 1974, 44.

107. "If You Miss Me from the Back of the Bus," *Ebony Jr!*, 1974, 61.

108. Tom Cohen's *Three Who Dared*, published in 1969, features the role of young adults in the movement.

109. Giddings, *When and Where I Enter*, 295–96.

110. Henderson, "War, Political Cycles, and the Pendulum Thesis," 365.

111. Marable, *Race, Reform, and Rebellion*.

112. Ibid.

113. Ibid., 87.

114. Ibid., 91.

115. Ibid.

116. Henderson, "War, Political Cycles, and the Pendulum Thesis," 338–39.

117. Ibid., 341.

118. William L. Van Deburg, *New Day in Babylon: The Black Power Movement and American Culture, 1965–1975* (Chicago: University of Chicago Press, 1992), 25.

119. Marable, *Race, Reform, and Rebellion*, 57.

120. Cruse, *The Crisis of the Negro Intellectual*.

121. Henderson, "War, Political Cycles, and the Pendulum Thesis," 344–45.

122. Ali, as cited in Henderson, "War, Political Cycles, and the Pendulum Thesis," 345.

123. Daniel Kryder, "War and the Politics of Black Militancy in the Twentieth Century U.S." (paper presented at the Annual Conference of the American Political Science Association, Washington, DC, 1997), 17.

124. Van Deburg, *New Day in Babylon*, 25.

125. Ibid.

126. Marable, *Race, Reform, and Rebellion*.

127. The Black Panthers' original Ten Point Program in its entirety is as follows:

We Want Freedom. We Want power to determine the destiny of our Black community.
    We want full employment for our people.
    We want an end to the robbery by the white man of our Black community.
    We want decent housing, fit shelter for human beings.
    We want education for our people that exposes the true nature of this decadent American society. We want education that teaches us our true history and our role in the present day society.
    We want all Black men to be exempt from military service.
    We want an immediate end to *police brutality* and *murder* of Black people.
    We want freedom for all Black men held in federal, state, county, and city prisons and jails.
    We want all Black people when brought to trial to be tried in court by a jury of their peer group or people from their Black communities, as defined by the Constitution of the United States.
    We want land, bread, housing, education, clothing, justice and peace.

Panthers, as cited in Marable, *Race, Reform, and Rebellion*, 109.

128. Ibid.

129. Ibid.

130. Ibid., 110.

131. Ibid; Williams, *Eyes on the Prize*.

132. Marable, *Race, Reform, and Rebellion*.

133. Sharon Harley, *The Timetables of African-American History: A Chronology of the Most Important People and Events in African-American History* (New York: Simon & Schuster, 1995).

134. Williams, *Eyes on the Prize*.

135. Harley, *The Timetables of African-American History*.

136. Stokely Carmichael and Charles V. Hamilton, *Black Power: The Politics of Liberation in America* (New York: Random House, 1967), vi.

137. Marable, *Race, Reform, and Rebellion*, 154.

138. Ibid., 96.

139. Ibid., 99.

140. Ibid., 98.

141. Ibid.

142. Johnson and Bennett, *Succeeding against the Odds*, 287.

143. Ibid.

144. Jessica B. Harris, *A Kwanzaa Keepsake: Celebrating the Holiday with New Traditions and Feasts* (New York: Simon & Schuster, 1995), 13.

145. Ibid.

146. Ibid., 42–43.

147. Carol Searcy, "Peter's Tenth Christmas," *Ebony Jr!*, December 1973, 41.

148. Ibid., 22–23.

149. Ibid., 24–25.

150. Giddings, *When and Where I Enter*.

151. The Combahee River Collective, "A Black Feminist Statement," in *All the Women Are White, All the Men Are Black: But Some of Us Are Brave*, ed. Gloria T. Hull, Patricia Bell Scott, and Barbara Smith (New York: Feminist Press, 1982).

152. Deborah Stead, "A Look at Children's Magazines: Not All Fun and Games," *Interracial Books for Children Bulletin* 6, no. 2 (1975).

153. Ibid.

5

Gaining Skills, Values, and Historically Accurate Knowledge

Get an education, boy, 'cause that's one thing they [White society] can't take away.—John O. Killens

Black students and parents want educational offerings that treat the black experience on a comparable basis to the curriculum that buttresses white nationalism. And most [school] administrations have not removed those sanctions that have been exercised overtly, covertly or inadvertently to prevent blacks from learning about themselves.— William H. McClendon

Access to adequate education in desegregated learning environments was one of the primary educational issues for Blacks from the 1960s through the 1980s. It was thought that following "the money" that accompanied White children would allow Black children access to better curricula, facilities, and teachers than would segregated schools with inadequate funding and resources. Most Blacks were able to access better educational facilities via the *Brown v. Board of Education* decision, political activism, and busing.

All the while, the Black Nationalists never sought desegregation; instead, they sought racially relevant education with Black teachers, administrators, and curricula. They questioned the ability of Whites to administer and teach African American children, and they wanted control of the schools' administration and curricula. They were interested in curricula reflecting their reality, history, and social issues. According to literary critic Talmadge Anderson,

High on the list of priorities were courses in Black Studies. At many colleges and universities black student groups called for departments that would award degrees in Black Studies and that would be controlled by black faculty members. At the elementary and secondary level, control of the decision-making apparatus became a focal point in many community controversies. . . . Black and other minority groups demanded that control of the public schools be transferred from citywide boards of education to elected neighborhood councils of parents.[1]

In addition to the call for a racially relevant curriculum, pedagogical methods were also evaluated and found to be culturally irrelevant. To address these concerns on the elementary level, some educators, such as Haki and Safisha Madhubuti, opened private Afrocentric schools. Others responded through research and writing about the learning styles, history, and values of the Black community so that interested teachers could alter their pedagogy and curricula. While Norman R. Dixon defined Black education in general, others, such as Na'im Akbar and Asa Hilliard, concentrated their efforts on identifying Black children's learning styles.[2] Although their definitions of best practices in Black pedagogy and curricula are limiting, they are indicative of the discourse among Black educators in the late 1960s and early 1970s. Defining education holistically—with regard to academics, community, and multigenerationality—Dixon stated that Black education should be "established, directed and controlled by Blacks," and that it should intentionally address the "individual and institutional needs of Black people."[3]

This should be done in physical structures and in locations that are designed to reflect the community's culture and to address its needs. According to Dixon, this helps build "strong and positive self-concepts" among children, young adults, and adults, which assists them in their struggle against White supremacy—their struggle "to grow" in general, and to act against social issues plaguing the Black community (e.g., police brutality and economics).[4] In the process, Blacks, grounded in their own identity, are enabled to critically evaluate other cultures and use whatever tools they find helpful in addressing community concerns.[5] And, of course, the curricula are grounded in the "longitudinal Black experiences."[6]

Moving from curriculum to learning styles, Akbar, in an address to the Black Child Development Institute in 1975, outlined some attributes of the learning styles of African American children.[7] Again, although his definition does not consider differences within the community, it was a move toward the consideration of culture in relation to pedagogy. Akbar stated that Black children (1) use language utilizing popular, short-lived phrases, (2) prefer oral-aural modalities for learning communication, (3) are sociocentric and people oriented, (4) adapt rapidly to novel stimuli, and (5) feel highly empathetic. To this Hilliard adds that Black children have a "keen sense of justice and are quick to analyze and perceive injustice."[8] Moreover, they have close family ties. For any educational curriculum to be effective, the pedagogy should consider and incorporate these attributes. These features should be considered by teachers and school administrators since, according to Janice Hale-Bensen, "Black children grow up in a distinct culture.[9] Black children therefore need an educational system that recognizes their strengths, their abilities, and their culture and that incorporates them into the learning process."[10]

In response to the educational issues facing the Black community in the late 1960s and early 1970s, JPC responded with *EJ* and its twofold educational curriculum. In addition to an academic curriculum, *EJ* contained a racialized curriculum. While the academic curriculum taught "reading, writing, and arithmetic" (among other things), the racialized curriculum offered lessons on Black history and culture. The ethnically pertinent curriculum and pedagogy were aligned with Dixon's definition: The curriculum of *EJ* was "established, directed and controlled by Black people."[11] Under Van Brunt Johnson's management, the idea that learning was important was presented in a rather didactic manner and through various approaches. Children were told to be like their distant relatives in an activity sheet entitled "A Page for You to Color." The text stated, "In Africa, children sit and listen well to the tales the storyteller has to tell."[12]

In addition, knowing that literacy is highly gendered, that Black boys are vulnerable to peer pressure, and that there is a notion that academics are unattractive, *EJ* targeted boys. In "That February," the protagonist was assigned a paper on African American history, knowing that "[w]riting a good paper took time and work. Lee was so excited about writing his paper he even missed a few days of basketball after school with the rest of the guys."[13] Not only did this text posit boys as academically interested and successful, it also led the reader to believe that, contrary to some assumptions, school was more important than sports. And if readers did not understand any of those messages, the editors stated it plainly: "School is Hip/Stop and Think. Everyone may say it's really a trip, but if you stop and think, _____ __ ___. Use the message in the design above to fill in the spaces."[14]

COMPONENTS OF *EBONY JR'S!* ACADEMIC CURRICULUM

Overall, the educational curriculum of *Ebony Jr!* during the 1970s had more depth and breadth than its contemporaries (e.g., *Jack and Jill*). Although Johnson may have defined literacy as the ability to encode and decode written language, Van Brunt Johnson's definition of literacy was more complex. For Van Brunt Johnson literacy included language arts (reading, phonics, and writing), basic math, social studies (primarily Black history), and arts and crafts. Career education was added in 1976.

The reading curriculum focused on multi-aged narratives. While Sunny and Honey's column was intended for the primary reader, the short stories were typically aimed at elementary readers.[15] The stories tended to be approximately five pages long, with a limited vocabulary, and certain words were printed in bold type and defined at the bottom of the page. In addition, the reading "lesson" took the form of basal readers with theme-related reading activities interspersed throughout the issue. Writing skills were encouraged on multiple levels—for example, a space for practicing penmanship was provided in the "Mama Write-On's Scribblin' Scope" column, while composition and story telling skills were encouraged by the annual writing contest and the many calls for readers' letters and drawings.

The math curriculum was generally theme or story related—usually mazes and puzzles for primary readers and word problems for older readers. On the primary level, "Put It Together" from the October 1973 issue instructed the reader: "[C]ut out the triangles below. Put them together to make a square."[16] Also, many of the primary math activities were story related, for instance, in "Follow the Path to Stardom," the reader was instructed to "[h]elp Aretha follow the path to stardom." This maze was related to a four-page nonfiction poem about Aretha Franklin. The elementary reader's activity "Can You Think Like Imhotep?" following "A Story from the Nile," centered on Imhotep, an Egyptian mathematician, astrologer, and architect.[17]

Word problems built from the general to the specific and from the child's world and knowledge outward. For example, one word problem began, "Can you think of the name of one 45 RPM record? Write the name here. How many minutes does it take the record you named to play?"[18] This portion of the problem focused on the individual reader, allowing for interaction by asking the reader to provide the name of a record and writing it in a specified space. It also included a reference to popular culture. The problem continued by explaining that RPM means revolutions per minute and that a 45 RPM record revolves, or "goes around," forty-five times each minute. This fact was followed by the questions:

> If a 45 RPM record goes around 45 times in one minute, how many times will the record go around if a three-minute song is playing? Which record will make the most full turns in one minute? (circle the right answer) A 33 1/3 RPM record or a 45 RPM record?[19]

While not all the math problems were connected to racial and ethnic identity, many of them were. Again, this was aligned with *EJ*'s culturally relevant educational curriculum.

The science curriculum usually consisted of narratives, with scientific principles explained in short stories or in experimental activities for child readers to complete. In the November 1973 issue, both forms were presented. "The Mystery of Mobius Strip," by Julian Beckford, was an experiment presented according to a scientific method that many elementary school curriculums included and that one can assume most readers would have been either familiar with or ready to encounter. The introduction to the experiment read,

> What gets longer when you cut it in half? The mysterious mobius strip. That's what! When you first look at a mobius strip, you may think that it is just another round band, like a rubber band, maybe. A mobius strip will fool you every time. To discover the difference between a plain round band and a mobius strip, you'll need to make each one. Then you can do some simple experiments and see the differences yourself.[20]

The exercise continues with numbered instructions for making a Möbius strip and a band. The second science lesson in the November 1973 issue was a play by Marlene Cummings titled "Bobbie and Bubba Meet Mellow Mel"; it had a racialized topic. Written in verse, the play used the character Mellow Mel to explain the concept of melanin. Relating the topic to the skin color of the characters, and by extension the child readers, Mellow Mel "jump[ed] right off of [Bobbie's] skin."[21] Mellow Mel was fashionable: He was a stick figure wearing a brimmed hat, sunglasses, and the highly desirable Converse athletic shoes. Not only did Mellow Mel's fashion define him as "cool," he also used slang (e.g., "What's happening, slick!").[22] Bobbie and Bubba were also racialized through language and images. Like Mellow Mel, they both used idioms associated with Black speech, and while Bobbie wore her hair in Afro puffs, Bubba wore an Afro. The play continued with Mellow Mel explaining how melanin "colors" skin. While there was no activity associated with the play, readers were told to look for Mellow Mel in future issues of *EJ*.

As discussed in chapter 1, many such activities were removed from *EJ* in the 1980s, but they were not totally excluded. And while the arts were hardest hit, they still appeared occasionally, as in the December 1981 holiday issue. One activity in this issue, "Tuttle Fluttle," by Helen R. Sattler, was typical of many of the art activities in which readers were told how to construct something to interact with later. After a list of necessary materials and numbered instructions on construction, Sattler gave instructions on how to play the flute. Finally, readers were instructed to "[i]nvite [their] friends to join [them] in a Kwanza [*sic*] concert." This one line, probably added by the editors, related the activity to the winter holiday and to African American culture.

Career-oriented articles such as "Wouldn't You Like to Be an Engineer?" began to appear consistently beginning with the January 1976 issue. But in 1977 the career education pieces become more pervasive. For example, the cover of the June/July 1977 issue read: "Blast off into Space," noting that the issue was devoted to astronomy and astrology. By the 1980s career education was a staple of the curriculum and consisted of related columns and themed issues that highlighted multiple aspects of various careers. To offer children multiple options, professional (e.g., animation), blue collar (e.g., construction work), and artistic (e.g., musician) careers were featured. And pertinent to the evolution in gender politics by the 1980s, a female blue-collar worker was featured on the cover, along with a feature article titled "Bright Ideas from the Everyday World of Work."

Social class issues were addressed in the poem "There's a Job for Everyone," which included various career options in a manner that did not degrade the careers or the employees for their lack of academic education: "Let's search for a job/that requires no college/Just good intelligence/And general knowledge."[23] The illustrations for this poem included construction workers and a photo of JPC headquarters (a point of pride in the African American community) being constructed. The African American history component of this issue was the article "'Mr. Black Labor' Himself, A. Philip Randolph," to which Sunny and Honey directed the reader in their editorial.[24] And since labor was the theme of the issue, the fictional short stories were labor related, as in "The Good Buy Pig (The Three Little Pigs Retold)," in which the construction of the houses was emphasized.[25] The third little pig, being the smart one, went to trade school and "still had his book, *How to Build a House in Eight Easy Steps.*"[26] Telling of class tensions, the "big bad wolf" was illustrated as wearing a white jumpsuit and a large brimmed hat. Whether or not he was intentionally portrayed as a street hustler, he invoked the image of a pimp from the Blaxploitation films of the 1970s.

Other career-themed issues featured fields such as arts and entertainment (e.g., the November 1981 issue featured careers in music) and followed a format similar to the "Bright Ideas from the Everyday World of Work" issue: At least two of the short stories highlighted different jobs in the field, many of the activities were theme related, and articles about prominent African Americans in the industry were included. Unlike the labor issue, a class-based dichotomy between music and high and low culture was noticeable. The biography was of Calvin Simmons, an African American conductor. In the illustration for the activity sheet "Phonics with the Loonicans," Cecilia Loonican played the piano and Cedric played the violin. And in their cartoon, Sunny played the violin while Honey played the piano; as discussed previously, they both criticized men with boom boxes and toothpicks in their mouths. While European classical music (symphonies and opera) and African American classical (jazz) were included, folk and popular music were noticeably absent. The exceptions were two short articles—one that featured Bob Marley and reggae, and one on Patrice Rushen, a musician and producer—but there was nothing about the popular R&B Top 40 list that would have interested most children.

Although changes to *EJ* were made in response to the historical moment and by different editors, the academic content of *EJ* stayed consistent in that it offered a well-rounded curriculum. In addition to reading and writing, math, science, arts and crafts, and career education were also included. Social studies—here defined as the study of history, social values, and culture—was also a component of *EJ*'s academic focus.

COMPONENTS OF *EBONY JR!'S*
RACIALLY RELEVANT CURRICULUM

The foundation of *EJ*'s social studies lessons was Black history. Like Black writers of adult literature during the late 1960s and 1970s, *EJ* "posited four major requisites to a correct understanding of the past: making the pan-African connection, venerating black heroes, celebrating the beauty of black lifestyles, and acknowledging the importance of black culture."[27] They accomplished this task by encoding Blackness in narratives, images of hair, fashion, foodways, and language as signifiers. These same markers of Blackness were being evaluated by adults for their cultural significance, and the discussion was extended to the child reader of *EJ*. Regarding some topics, such as hair, multiple political positions were apparent in *EJ*. While the racially pertinent curriculum changed over time as challenges facing the community changed, a racially relevant curriculum remained. Before an analysis of the signifiers can begin, the conversation must focus on racial identity and its correlation to politics of the late 1960s and 1970s.

RACIAL IDENTITY THEORY AND POLITICS

Although E. Franklin Frazier and Gunner Myrdal set the foundation for African American identity research, Kenneth Clark, along with Mamie Clark, is the "primary architect of Negro identity" research.[28] Basing his

work on Eugene and Ruth Horowitz's research on identity racial preference and self-identification, which defined self-concept as a combination
of personal identity and group identity, the Clarks' work is divergent
from that of their predecessors in that their work was used to advocate for
social change. Even though only 14 percent of the Black children they
studied denoted a preference for White dolls and denigrated the Black
dolls, the Clarks' research was aligned with Frazier, Myrdal, and the
Horowitzes—the leading theorists from 1939 to 1960—in that it posited a
theory of Negro self-hatred based on living in a racist society.[29] Kenneth
Clark's work "The Effects of Prejudice and Discrimination on Personality
Development in Children" was included in the NAACP Legal Defense
Fund's brief to the U.S. Supreme Court in *Brown v. Board of Education*. So
momentous was this report in assisting in ending segregation that the
Court referenced the report. The Clarks' work, and its role in the *Brown*
case, was highlighted in the popular press. Self-hatred was thought to be
the product of segregation and living in a racist society. This theory is also
aligned with the Civil Rights Movement, which is commonly agreed to
have begun with the *Brown* case.

But the proponents of the self-hatred theory failed to see the facets of
African American culture that resisted oppression and that created rich
and nurturing cultural models of racial solidarity. With the propagation
of the Black Power Movement came the Black identity model of racial
identity of 1968–1980, which traced the nature and extent of the movement from Negro-to-Black identity. This model "operationalized the
notion of self-concept through either personal identity or reference
group orientation."[30] It also took a more positive position on Black
Identity and noted the strengths in the Black community, and, like the
Black Power philosophy, called for the development of positive racialized identity.

In the social justice movements, the momentum toward Black self-
definition increased, with Marcus Garvey and his Universal Negro Improvement Association serving as the historical antecedent. Black scholars
and activists moved to define "Blackness" using the African and African
American communities as reference points. Not only was art redefined in
the Black Arts Movement, so too was religion with the Nation of Islam,
with Malcolm X as its frontman, encouraging Christians to abandon their
"slave religion" and education. Likewise, the research on Black identity
during this movement which often replicated research done during the
Civil Rights era, showed a strong preference for the in-group—Blacks—
instead of Whites. This philosophical evolution was evident in *Ebony*, as
the number of advertisements for skin bleachers and hair straighteners,
those products thought to be aligned with the Racial Uplift ideology and
with Black self-hatred in that they changed physical characteristics—skin

color and hair texture—associated with being Black, decreased significantly from 1949 to 1972.[31]

As early research on identity demonstrates, children were not excluded from this discourse on racial and ethnic identity. The average four-year-old has developed and learned to enjoy a sense of autonomy.[32] The next step includes self-definition as children begin "identifying, describing, classifying, evaluating and comparing themselves. . . . Their interest in characteristics or behavior having to do with what adults call race, nationality, or religion is a part of these general interests and inclinations."[33] Therefore, the editors of *EJ* were aligned with child development theorists in assuming that their child readership, including five-year-olds, was interested in defining themselves as racialized beings. Just as the Black Power philosophy called for the development of positive racialized identity, as evident in the slogan "Black Is Beautiful," so too did *EJ*'s curriculum, which presented a positive, Afrocentric definition of Blackness to child readers. For the reader of *EJ*, "Blackness" was encoded in signifiers that were prevalent in the community and that most children would have had some familiarity with.

ETHNIC IDENTITY AND *EBONY JR!*

The racialized curriculum of *EJ* was largely covert, encoded in the presentation of social values, hairstyles, and foodways. Although the emphasis on racial identity changed during *EJ*'s tenure, the Afrocentric focus of the magazine maintained a discourse on the issues and values in the Black community and as such continued to highlight the racialized identity of the child reader. To continue the analysis, I will look to some of the narratives before moving to illustrations and columns.

One of the most didactic lessons on Blackness was contained in a story titled "Saturday."[34] In the text, the protagonist's cousins came for a visit, during which they "taught" him how to be "Black." The story began with Edward (the protagonist) being introduced to his cousins by his mother, during which the cousins were quiet and polite. But as soon as the adults left the room, they began the reeducation of Edward:

> "Don't call us by those old names," Clarence said. "We got new ones. I'm Dink." . . . "What's your cool name?" Weebie asked me. "Sometimes Uncle James calls me Eddie," I said. I knew it wasn't cool, I couldn't think of anything else to say. "You got to get another name, man," Preach said. "All Black dudes have cool names."[35]

This text exemplified the assumption that children are interested in their ethnic identity and whether or not they are, as the saying goes, "Black enough." It also served as an example of how *EJ* offered an encoded and essentialized definition of Blackness, for example, "All black dudes have cool names." Further, this passage referenced the "generation gap" on two levels. As is typical, these children sought to define themselves outside the gaze of adults.

But for Black children of the 1970s, this passage also alluded to the political generation gap between many parents and children. While the NAACP and the Racial Uplift agendas of the 1950s had been organized and led by older, middle-class adults, the Black Nationalist movements, particularly the Black Panthers, largely consisted of young adults who, whatever their class, disassociated themselves from the middle class. Along with their militant and idealistic nature, this was appealing to other young adults. Therefore, when the cousins waited until the adults left the room before negotiating their identity, it is important to note that what they were negotiating was a politicized ethnic identity of which the adults might not approve. Lastly, this passage demonstrated how child readers were assumed to be aware of Black speech rhythms and patterns. The pedagogy of *EJ*, as I will discuss below, attempted to incorporate what editors assumed to be the reader's culture to make the lesson more accessible.

The story continued with Edward describing the cousins further:

> [They] showed me how to jump pretty like a basketball player and how to walk cool. I got some old magazines and we cut out pictures of babies and mamas and daddies and one big picture of Malcolm X, and we taped them all over the walls. My room looked good. They got dashikis out of the suitcases and put them on. I put on one of Dink's. We looked in the mirror and we looked good![36]

Here Blackness was defined in relation to one's body as athletic, as knowing how to walk "properly," and as being dressed in Afrocentric clothing, all of which mirrored some adults' conversations and actions around ethnic identity at the time. Based upon the assumption that African Americans are sociocentric, the importance of family was noted in the pictures of babies, mamas, and daddies on the wall, while community and a rather militant racial pride were symbolized by the picture of Malcolm X.[37]

But Edward was not the only one who had something to learn or teach about Blackness. While Dink, Preach, and Weebie were adept at the outward demonstrations of ethnicity, Edward was the one who really understood one of the most important points in Black ideology: community values and unity. At first Dink, Preach, and Weebie positioned themselves as teachers:

> "We got to teach him how to be Black," Dink said. "You don't have to teach me anything," I said. "I know how to be Black." I was getting kinda mad, so

I sat down on the bed. I was already Black. Anyway, it was bad enough having one teacher at school I sure didn't need three. But Dink said, "I mean really Black. You got to learn about handshakes and unity and all that hard stuff." "Unity?" I said. "What's that?" "That's Black people getting together," Preach said, "and not having arguments." "Yeah," Weebie said. "No fights. And no arguments, right?"[38]

Eventually the boys went outside to cut the grass and Dink, Preach, and Weebie started "fussing and fighting over whose going to go first in taking turns cutting the grass."[39] Reminding them of their own lesson, Edward said, "I thought you said we had to have unity," to which Preach replied, "I know, but he started it."[40] Edward continued to cut the grass while Dink, Preach, and Weebie continued to argue. Finally they saw the futility of their arguing and asked Edward if they could take turns mowing.

The discussion continued later that night:

"Tomorrow, we got to get you a new name, Eddie," Preach said. "We sure taught you a lot, didn't we?" Dink asked me. I said, "Yeah," but I was thinking that I had taught them the most. Anyway I had to think about that new name thing. I wasn't sure I wanted one. I would think about it tomorrow.[41]

While Edward (possibly as an only child or one not living in an urban area) did not know the external indicators used by some factions to indicate ethnic identity, he did understand the most important value: unity.

Ethnic identity also entailed a racialized history, one rarely taught in schools but one that could instill pride and resilience. The use of this history as a "balm in Gilead" is evident in Frankie Cox's "The Big Day." During the winter of 1930, Eva Mae Merrell anticipated the arrival of an important day, Christmas, which also happened to be her birthday. On her way home from school, Eva Mae visited Uncle Firestone, "her best grown-up friend who understood everything about facing hard times."[42] The primary reason she was so enchanted by Uncle Firestone was because he told her stories of the "great things that had happened in the past and that would surely happen again! He told Eva Mae stories about times when Africa had been the greatest civilization in the whole world."[43] At the time, "the Great Depression was sweeping the country. Times were hard. . . . It was especially hard for Black folks. They had very little to live on. When things got really tough, Eva Mae thrilled at traveling back through Uncle Featherstone's stories. 'It won't be this way always child . . . We have had a grand, glorious history and we'll pull through this for the better!'"[44]

She coveted the rare and precious book that "had come all the way from Pittsburgh and was the only one of its kind in the whole town. [The book contained] stories . . . about Africa and they had been written by Mr.

Carter G. Woodson, a famous Black historian."[45] Uncle Featherstone was getting old and considering retiring from his job in the general store that served the African American community. "Eva Mae was alarmed. With no Uncle Featherstone and no book, how would she ever learn the stories that made her feel so good inside?"[46] Hoping beyond hope, Eva Mae longed for the history book as a Christmas/birthday gift. But she knew that times were hard and her family had very little money. On Christmas morning, after the family had eaten breakfast, Eva Mae's father passed out the gifts. He saved Eva Mae's for last. Believing that her first gift was her book, Eva Mae tried not to look disappointed when she saw the pencil box and writing tablet she received. Although the pencil box "was very nice, it wasn't her wonderful book."[47] But Daddy had another gift for Eva Mae, one from Uncle Featherstone: the book! He attached a note that read, "To Eva Mae Merrell, for the Christmas of the Great Depression, nineteen hundred and thirty: May this book on our glorious African past help you live and build for the glorious times to come."[48]

Was it a coincidence that Eva Mae and Jesus had the same birthday? What might this say about Eva Mae's character? It certainly makes the gifts received on this day all the more important, since Christmas and his or her own birthday are any child's two most favorite days of the year, for on both days children receive gifts. Eva Mae's longing for a history book on her birthday/Christmas told of the importance of Black history as a tool to help one get through hard times: "When things got really tough, Eva Mae thrilled at traveling back through Uncle Featherstone's stories."[49] It also connected her, and the child readers, to her prosperous past. Since Black history was not a staple of most schools' curricula, Woodson's history book was a link to a rich past, one that extended further back than U.S. history and one that attested to her value as a member of an ethnic group that had made contributions to world history other than being slaves and being seen as pariahs.

The book was likely *African Myths Together with Proverbs: A Supplementary Reader Composed of Folk Tales from Various Parts of Africa* (1928), which was adapted for use by children in some public schools. Clearly *EJ* was sending a message to readers about the importance of literacy—although she longed for the book, Eva Mae was pleased with the pencil box and tablet. All three gifts are tools of literacy. Again, many African Americans have long considered education to be the gateway to an improved life, financially and socially. As a connection to her past and a bridge to the future, the stories, whether through Uncle Featherstone's oral stories or Woodson's written ones, would help Eva Mae endure the Great Depression and prepare her for the future—because, according to Uncle Featherstone, "It won't be this way always child . . . We have had a grand, glorious history and we'll pull through this for the better!" The stories of

Eva Mae's African past, and by extension the child readers' own past, would provide roots, give strength to endure, encourage self esteem, and inform their future endeavors, which, hopefully, would be more financially sustainable. While not quite as didactic as "Saturday," "The Big Day" nevertheless defined the child reader as Black, with a connection to Africa. And as was its mission, "The Big Day" encouraged literacy and Afrocentric education.

The number of stories about racial identity decreased in the late 1970s and 1980s, but they were still present. There were usually one or two references to Blackness per issue. The glaring exception was the April 1982 issue, whose theme was "Black Publications: Then and Now." As the header suggested, the issues' stories all focused on the history and current status of African American periodicals. Articles included "The Birth of the American Black Newspaper," by Mary Lewis, and "Black Magazines: Then and Now," by Debra Hall. This article was particularly interesting since it featured DuBois's *The Crisis*, which, for me, alluded to Johnson's or some editor's knowledge of *The Brownies' Book*, its mission, format, and sales. Again, the editors may have referenced *The Brownies' Book* as well as *Jack and Jill* in the creation of *EJ*. Another example of Blackness in the 1980s comes from a reader, whose work, "A Black Poem" is printed in the "Writing Readers" column.

> Black, black as the blackboard in school. Black as the blackest dye.
> Black the unfamous and the famous.
> The psychologist, the scientist.
> The rich and the poor.
> From George Washington Carver to Martin Luther King Jr.
> Black is beautiful.
> Black as the even sky
> Will the Black civilization ever die?

Clearly the poet relished the history and diversity within the African American community. He also resuscitated the 1970s adage "Black Is Beautiful" in an effort to instill pride in one's ethnic identity.

In the portions of "Saturday" that I have presented here, Blackness was presented as something that is learned, that children are interested in, and that has been encoded in their lifestyle as well as in their consciousness. In "The Big Day," Blackness was encoded in a connection to Africa and a history and culture that can be called upon to give one strength in trying times. Even the child writer defined Blackness and offered it to the reader as something about which to be proud. But for the most part, the lessons about ethnic identity were not so covert. They were encoded in various aspects of life, as, for example, in *EJ*'s depiction of hair texture and hairstyles.

POLITICAL RELEVANCE OF AFRICAN AMERICAN HAIRSTYLES

In many African societies, hairstyles denote age, occupation, clan, and so-cial status as well as aesthetic.[50] Africans were brought to the Americas without the styling tools necessary to groom their hair. Once in the United States, grooming was relegated to a lesser priority than survival and the maintenance of one's humanity. During slavery, hairstyles moved from being the indicators of tribal affiliation or marriage status as they had been in Africa to their symbolic utilization vis-à-vis free status, parentage, or standards of beauty. Willie Morrow, author of *400 Years without a Comb*, argued that slave owners came to tolerate enslaved Africans' skin color, but not their hair. As a marker of racial difference, interpreted as inferior-ity by white supremacists, African hair texture was used to justify the sub-jugation of Africans. Irrespective to its meaning in West Africa, curly or kinky hair was imbued with inferiority in the United States and therefore was a stamp of racial inferiority. Since many of the free African Americans of the nineteenth century were "the mulatto offspring of the first African arrivals and their European companions, lighter skin and loosely curled hair would often signify free status."[51] Even enslaved mulattos, when their hair was "loosely curled," were identified as having White parent-age and often given preferential treatment. Eventually long, loosely curled hair was considered "good hair," while hair with "kink, tight curls, and frizz [was defined as] . . . [b]ad hair . . . namely African hair in its purest form."[52]

These arbitrary definitions would follow African Americans and Whites into the twentieth century and beyond. Working to resist stereo-types of themselves as uncivilized, ignorant, infantile, and unkempt, and seeking to gain access to White-controlled venues for employment, many African Americans imitated "as many Eurocentric attributes as possi-ble."[53] Particularly for the middle-class proponents of the Racial Uplift ideology, "'When it came to hair for African-Americans,' says image con-sultant Harriette Cole, the goal was 'to have hairstyles that were straight and then curled—organized, with every strand in place.'"[54] Most of the African American periodicals, including JPC publications, sustained themselves through advertisements for hair straighteners as well as skin-lightening products. But they nevertheless participated in the discourse about whether or not women should straighten their hair.

Pushing gender politics aside and considering the issue of class and po-litical affiliation, many of these magazines, such as *"Half Century Magazine*, a leading African American magazine of the first quarter of the twentieth century, never had a cover model with unstraightened hair," although most women, especially older or rural women in the South, wore their hair in the easier-to-manage naturally textured hair styles.[55] Not only was natural-textured hair ignored by some, it was demeaned by others: "Writer Azalia Hackley noted in the early 1900s that while 'kinky hair is an honorable legacy from Africa,' it was nonetheless a trait that she hoped 'constant care' would help make to go away."[56] This statement was consistent with the Racial Uplift conviction that African Americans' humanity and intelligence were judged by Whites—by the people with power over the employment market. To the White employer, hairstyles would ideally be as far removed from African connections as possible, and many African Americans bought into this idea that natural hair was less than desirable, a notion resulting in social stratification and self-hatred.

But for those who did not subscribe to the Racial Uplift ideology, straightened hair was a negative imposition on a racialized identity. Many who aligned themselves with the Black Nationalist ideology believed many hair-grooming practices to be essentially assimilationist in nature: They encouraged African Americans to look to themselves and to Africa for a sense of self and beauty.

> Nannie Helen Burroughs, founder of the National Training School for Girls and Women, wrote in a 1904 article titled "Not Color but Character" that "What every woman who . . . straightens out needs, is not her appearance changed but her mind changed. . . . If Negro women would use half of the time they spend on trying to get White, to get better, the race would move forward."[57]

Of course, Black Nationalist leader Marcus Garvey spoke against hair straightening, stating, "Don't remove the kinks from your hair! . . . Remove them from your brain!"[58]

During the 1960s hair became even more political. The nomenclature used to symbolize the community evolved from "Negro" to "Black," and we adopted a Black Aesthetic in the arts and in hairstyling practices. Eschewing straight hair as a form of self-hatred, Black Nationalist Malcolm X stopped straightening his own hair, stating that getting his first conk was "the first really big step toward self-degradation."[59] For the Black Panthers, natural-textured hair "was about identity and being proud of being Black."[60] In fact, because it was aligned with a political position, natural-textured hair, or an Afro, became the "appropriate" hairstyle of a Black Nationalist.[61]

Many African American women of the 1960s and 1970s straightened their hair using oil and a hot comb or through a chemical relaxer.[62] Black psychiatrists William H. Grier and Price M. Cobbs argued in *Black Rage* that the grooming process, which begins when the African American girl is a "babe in arms," is physically and psychologically painful.[63] Having endured the physical pain of having "kinky" hair styled into "whatever stylish manner the mother may adopt," the African American girl is left with the psychological pain of having been rendered "of an acceptable appearance"—not beautiful.[64] According to Grier and Cobbs, White women also endure painful grooming rituals, but at the end they emerge beautiful—the process "is to enhance her natural appearance which in itself is considered acceptable by her peers," not to make her "presentable," as in the case of African American women.[65]

Grier and Cobbs then recount how for African American women with pressed hair—hair straightened with a hot comb—in various situations, such as swimming, are faced with their hair "going back"—reverting to its natural state—if they partake in the activity.

> It is against this endless circle of shame, humiliation, and the implied unacceptability of one's own person that a small but significant number of black women have turned to the "natural hairdo"; . . . a soft, black, gentle cloche of cropped velvet. The effect is so engaging and feminine, and, in light of the above, so psychologically redemptive.[66]

Clearly for Grier and Cobbs, like other Black Nationalists, natural-textured hair was aligned with the Black Aesthetic, defining African American women, in their natural state, as beautiful. It allowed Black women to define themselves as beautiful, thereby freeing them from the oppressive history that links curly or kinky hair with racialized inferiority. Wearing natural-textured hair during the 1960s and 1970s was, and some say still is, a political act that affirms one's Blackness.

The connections between hair, beauty, and politics were a component of the daily drama of the 1960s and 1970s—*and* of *EJ*'s inception. While Angela Davis, a renowned Black Nationalist, wore the Afro by which she would become known in the 1960s, Coretta Scott King, as a Civil Rights Movement leader, continued to wear her hair straightened. Not only were hairstyles of the early 1970s often indicative of one's political affiliation, they also generated generational conflict. Parents and clergy tended to align themselves with either the Racial Uplift or Civil Rights Movement. At a pragmatic level, they were concerned about the access to employment that straightened hair represented to them. According to journalists Ayana Byrd and Lori Tharps,

> Seventeen-year-old Rochelle Nichols unknowingly declared a battle of wills with her mother when she stopped straightening her hair in 1967. What began as an innocent expression of her changing politics turned into a summer of Nichols's mother leaving notes on the front door that read "No Afros allowed in this house," notes that prompted her daughter to take up temporary residence at the local YWCA. "My mother and my fights were about hair, but it was more than that," explains Nichols. "It was about my growing up and my politics and deciding things on my own. Above my bed, after one of our fights, I hung this poem that I wrote.

It went 'When I die I will be happy. Because Jesus will love me with my hair nappy.'"[67]

On the other hand, some parents who aligned themselves with Black Nationalism had children who wanted to straighten their hair. When Noliwe Rooks was a young adolescent in the late 1970s, she wanted to change her hairstyle to align with her friends and the current styles.[68] Rooks wanted to move from natural-textured to straightened hair. She tried, unsuccessfully, to convince her mother that, as demonstrated in the images of magazines such as *Ebony*, straightened hair held an equal place in the pantheon of African American beauty and culture as natural textured hair. Her mother, who had maintained natural-textured hair for both of them, was quite perturbed. For her, hair, racial identity, self-esteem, and identity were still intertwined in a manner that precluded her from allowing her daughter to straighten her hair. One difference between Nichols and Rooks may be the historical moment: Nichols's story takes place in 1967 at the height of the Civil Rights Movement, during which hair was most strongly aligned with politics, while for Rooks, in the late 1970s, hairstyles represented fashion more than a political statement. Common in both stories is the generational conflict played out over politics and hair, stories that would be replicated in *EJ*.

For the most part, by the late 1970s the Black Power Movement was waning, and for many the natural hair discourse evolved from a political debate to simply a hairstyle. Many young adults wore Afros to emulate Michael Jackson of the Jackson 5, and they were not making a political statement. But for some members of the older generation, such as Rooks's mother, the remnants of the political discourse on hair remained. But for others, by the 1980s access to employment and material gain took precedence over both political and fashion statements, and many African Americans returned to straightened hairstyles. By 2007 the call for natural-textured hair was somewhat less political and more pragmatic: ease of styling and self-acceptance. This evolution of the significance of hair in the African American community was reflected in *EJ*.

HAIRSTYLES AND *EBONY JR!*

Since skin and hair vary not only among different races but within a race, they are the two most significant signs designating race—so it makes perfect sense that hairstyles were included in *EJ*'s agenda on ethnic identity.[69] The idea that natural-textured hair was a political statement was apparent in the pages of *EJ*. During the 1970s natural-textured hair was associated with being young, with self-definition, and with political resistance.

Although natural-textured and straight hairstyles were almost equally represented in *EJ* illustrations, natural-textured hair was privileged in the narratives. As a marker of female attractiveness, natural-textured hair was depicted as more desirable by protagonists, and it received more accolades from members of the opposite sex, in the case of girls, and from one's peers, in the case of boys. But as the story of Rochelle Nichols noted, the desire for natural-textured hair was not without resistance from adults.

This point is made in the June/July 1973 article "Susa's Natural," by Norma Poinsett. The protagonist, Susa, asked her mother if she could cut her hair and wear a natural.

> Mama grabbed the back of a chair, unable to speak. She looked long and hard at Susa's head. It seemed that the voices on the radio suddenly hushed. The bubbling teakettle stopped singing, as Susa waited for an answer. Mama clenched her teeth and tried to unlock her mouth. "A natural!" she finally shouted. "Child, you took my breath." Mama sat down heavily in a kitchen chair. Suddenly she felt old and overweight though she was not. . . ."You don't need a natural," Mama said. "Look at your nice, long, black braids. They're awfully pretty to me."[70]

The extreme nature of the mother's response demonstrated the politicization of hair, the generational issues around hair, and the ways in which long, straight hair had historically been privileged as more beautiful. All of these issues became apparent in the mother's discussion about Susa's hair with her neighbor, Miss Adra:

> "That child nearly knocked me off my feet," Mama was near tears. "She wants to chop off all of her beautiful, long, black hair." . . . [M]other remembers pressing her own hair on the sly against her mother's wishes. Miss Adra said, "I wonder why hair has always been so important to Black folks?" "Maybe it's because it's so hard to keep it straight!" Mama answered. "That was true a while back," Miss Adra said. [Who then leaves. Alone to think, Mama says,] . . . "Aw, shoot! There's nothing wrong with naturals. That's our trouble. We've looked at too much television!"[71]

The importance of hair as it reflects beauty and politics was indicated in the mother's initial reaction to Susa's request by "being near tears." The mother's attachment to Susa's "beautiful, long, black hair" can be seen as her alignment with assimilation, in contrast to self-defining politics. Within this framework, there was clearly a distance between Susa (and her natural) and her mother (and her straight hair). But then Miss Adra helped Susa's mother recognize the politics behind hair: the issue of texture and the idea that straight hair is closer to White definitions of beauty and acceptability. Susa's mother realized the role of media in imposing arbitrary standards. Seeming to define Black beauty for herself, the mother allowed Susa to get a natural. But related to gender politics is the statement, "'Daddy and the boys have naturals,' Susa said. 'Why can't I have one too? Daddy would love for us both to wear a natural,' Susa added."[72]

In the 1970s, under Van Brunt Johnson's leadership, *EJ* valued self-definition and African American–centered hairstyles. Having, to some degree, relinquished her "assimilationist politics," and knowing that her husband would approve, the mother let Susa get a natural. The story ended with the mother stating, "Changing your hair doesn't change you. . . . You've got to be natural and kind inside if you want your natural to count."[73] *EJ*'s position on natural versus straightened hair was evident in the illustration at the end of the story: Susa had a natural and a halolike circle around her head.[74]

Finally, the boys of the 1970s *EJ* wore Afros of varying heights (e.g., "Sam Henry pulled his small brown body to the full height it had grown in 9 years. All 3 feet 10½ inches, although the extra 1½ inch was mostly his full, nicely shaped Afro."), but they did not wear the cornrows that I remember many young men of my 1970s community wearing.[75]

Although hair was not overtly problematized in articles after the first two issues, it was dealt with covertly through images. One example was the portrayal of Sunny and Honey and their doll. Beginning with the June/July 1973 issue, Sunny and Honey were both encoded as black. Honey's hair was in the highly popular, natural-textured Afro puffs, and Sunny's clothes were the latest style (an apple hat, plaid pants, and platform shoes). Even the doll wore an Afro. Earlier, in the May 1973 issue, Sunny and Honey were not encoded as Black; they were, for all intents and purposes, brown White children. Sunny had on a striped shirt, jeans, and nondescript shoes. Honey wore a nondescript top with a polka-dot skirt, and her straightened hair was in a ponytail with bangs. This small example illustrates how carefully the images were crafted to address and engage African American child readers who were constructed as being interested in their ethnic identity.

By the 1980s, for the most part, hair appeared to be a nonissue in the pages of *EJ*, as economics moved to the foreground. Again, I look to Sunny and Honey: In the 1980s Sunny, like other boys and men in *EJ*, continued to wear his hair in a mid-sized Afro, yet it was half its original size. Even though Honey and the doll's hair were still in what could be two Afro puffs, the puffs were very smooth and could be read as straightened hair styled into two buns.

Their transformation continued in the "*Ebony Jr! News*" column published in 1980. Honey's hair was relaxed and her Afro puffs were now clusters of curls. For the most part, both women and girls in other images tended to wear their hair straightened, although there were images of girls with natural-textured hair. In such cases, it was more related to the child's age than to a political statement.[76] Girls under eight years old typically wear their hair naturally; most cosmotologists suggest that parents wait until the child is nine or ten before they have their hair chemically straightened. Yet, even young girls will have their hair mechanically straightened, with a hot comb, for special occasions. Aligned with Racial Uplift, it is possible that since *EJ* was interested in the economic well-being of its readers, the hairstyles of the protagonists reflected that which would allow the readers to be viewed as acceptable and thus employable by White-dominated industry. Again, the African American community of the 1980s saw the backlash from the Civil Rights Movement along with urbanization and concentration of poverty: Loans were difficult for middle-class African Americans to acquire, there was still a disparity between the income of African Americans and Whites of equal similar backgrounds, and there was a concentration of the African American poor in underserved urban and rural centers. Hair, for *EJ*, had moved from a political statement about racial identity to an economic one.

But this does not explain why, in 2007, the online version of Honey wears her hair in a natural-textured hairstyle and Sunny wears cornrows. As shown in Afrocentric magazines such as *Essence* and *Ebony*, more African American women are wearing their hair in natural-textured hairstyles than in the 1980s. Currently it has less to do with politics and more to do with self-acceptance and a growing weariness of chemical processes. The proliferation of books encouraging women to stop relaxing their hair has exploded. In books such as *Good Hair*, by Lonnice Brittenum Bonner, authors begin with horror stories of getting their hair pressed, relaxed, chemically straightened, and curled using Jheri curl—think Michael Jackson in the 1980s. The saga continues with a discussion of the cost, daily maintenance, and resulting damaged hair from these processes. Eventually these women tired of trying to make their hair do something other than what is natural and then made the transition to natural-textured hair. Most of the books end with reminding Black women, many of whom have had their hair relaxed since at least high school, how to care for their hair in its original state. The underlying message is about self-acceptance—learning to love one's hair in its natural state. As such, Honey's hair is current, fashionable, and aligned with *EJ*'s mission to encourage self-esteem in its readers.

Similarly, Sunny's cornrows are representative of a fashion staple for males in 2007. Although many sources site Bo Derek wearing cornrows in the 1979 movie *10* as the moment when cornrows became popular, according to "Cornrows," a 1974 article in *EJ* by Janice Gray,

Cornrowing comes to us from Africa. There women cornrow their hair to make themselves look beautiful. Cornrowing has been done for many thousands of years. You may remember seeing actress Cicely Tyson or singer Roberta Flack with cornrows. Or maybe one of your friends wears them.[77]

While Gray tries to align child readers with their African heritage, African American women have always worn cornrows, even if they were under a scarf, wig, or weave (currently referred to as "hair extensions" by the mainstream).

Cornrows, whether worn by men or women, have long been a popular hairstyle in the African American community. Of course, as hairstyles do, they have fluctuated in popularity. Like Tyson, Flack, and innumerable African American men in the 1960s and 1970s, contemporary entertainers also wear cornrows. In the late 1990s the hairstyle resurged in popularity among African American males when NBA stars Latrell Sprewell and Allen Iverson began wearing them.[78] Both men were considered "bad boys" of the NBA. Cornrows became staples of mainstream popular culture when Justin Timberlake of *NSYNC wore them in 1998.[79] Black men report ease of styling, a desire to send a message that punctuates their ethnicity, being seen as rebellious, and making a fashion statement as reasons for wearing cornrows.[80] Sunny's cornrows define him as fashionable and place him firmly in 2007. While the political message is subtler than it was in the 1970s, Sunny's cornrows may also be a political statement affirming Blackness.

FOODWAYS AND AFRICAN AMERICAN IDENTITY

In addition to hair, food was racialized and posited to the child readers as part of their ethnic heritage and identity. During the post–World War II era, with the expansion of the Black middle class, came questions about what constituted "authentic" Blackness. Under attack as assimilationists by scholars such as E. Franklin Frazier, the Black middle class used multiple venues to create a strong sense of self-definition: art, politics, and, most relevant to this discussion, food.

Not only were systems such as art and politics evaluated and redefined, but also included in this self-defining discourse was the human body and everything associated with it, including food consumption.[81] Again, following Frazier's unflattering portrayal of the Black middle class, *Black Bourgeoisie*—which prompted questions about their racial authenticity—the Black middle class sought various venues through which to assert their racial identity.[82] According to William Van Deburg, the concept of "soul [that arose in the 1960s] was the folk equivalent of the Black Aesthetic. [As the essence of Black culture], soul was closely related to black America's need for individual and group definition."[83] In its culinary incarnation, "soul food" was associated with a shared history of oppression and inculcated by some with cultural pride. It was the food that bondsmen had eaten. It was also the food they incorporated into their diet after emancipation. Therefore, during the 1960s, middle-class Blacks used their reported consumption of soul food to distance them from the values of the White middle class, to define themselves ethnically, and to align themselves with lower-class Blacks. Irrespective of political affiliation or social class, the definition of "Blackness" or "soul," became part of the everyday discourse in the Black community.

Many factors contribute to the creation of a group-based identity: a common culture, history, and civic ideology, to name a few. According to Fischler, "Food is central to our sense of identity. The way any given human group eats helps to assert its diversity [and] hierarchy . . . and at the same time, both its oneness and the otherness of whoever eats differently."[84] And since meaning is attached to the separation of the culinary habits of various groups, food is also used to differentiate among groups. Foodways become "associated with nearly every dimension of human social and cultural life."[85] Specific foods become intertwined with holidays, group history, and the health of the community. According to cultural anthropologist Margaret Mead, the manner in which adults teach children to eat plays an important role in the production and reproduction of food moralities.[86] Foodways and identity intersect, as does the power relationship between adults and children. Adults, either explicitly and consciously, as in the case of the editor of *EJ*, or inexplicitly, as in the case of parents feeding their children, teach children foodways often associated with their ethnic identity.

A term coined in the North, *soul food*, was related to this overall self-defining discourse of the 1960s and 1970s. Some commentators, such as LeRoi Jones (now known as Amiri Baraka) "began valorizing it as an expression of pride in the cultural forms created from and articulated through a history of black oppression."[87] No matter who the scholar, soul food is said to be defined by three attributes: a connection to Africa and the diet of enslaved Blacks, something inherent in the Black body, and used as a tool to define a Black identity.[88] William Van Deburg stated that soul food originated in Western Africa and was transported to the American South with the slave trade.[89] Jones also used soul food to show connections within the African Diaspora, whether it was ingredients, such as black-eyed peas, collard greens, and okra, or cooking methods, such as deep-fat frying.[90] In *Black Hunger*, Doris Witt stated that "the emergence of soul food should be construed not just synchronically but also diachronically, as a part of an ongoing debate among African Americans over the appropriate food 'practices' of blackness."[91] Thus, soul food was encoded with Blackness.

Some scholars and culinary critics, such as Van Deburg and Craig Claiborne, differentiated between soul food and traditional southern foodways. For Van Deburg, ingredients such as "hog maws, neck bones, ham hocks, [and] chitterlings" were components of soul food, since "southern bondsmen" transformed them into "a gourmet's delight."[92] These ingredients—pieces of the pig that the White plantation owners did not want—along with cornmeal, were the core of the bondsmen's diet. As the diet of most Blacks' ancestors, these elements were considered the definitive ingredients of soul food. "Although collard greens, black-eyed peas, hush puppies, deep-fried chicken, and catfish may have appeared on both white and black tables in the antebellum South, it seemed to take a black hand in the kitchen before any recipe could be considered 'soulful.'"[93] Claiborne concurred, defining "typical Southern dishes as fried chicken, spareribs, candied yams and mustard or collard greens. . . . [And soul food as] trotters, neckbones, pigs' tails and chitterlings."[94]

While Van Deburg and Claiborne made such distinctions, most Blacks did not. For them, the difference between traditional Southern food and soul food was not contained in the ingredients but in the body of the cook. Only Blacks cooked soul food; Whites produced a "thin . . . parody."[95] Others, such as Elijah Muhammad, the leader of the Nation of Islam, and Dick Gregory, a Civil Rights activist and nutritional consultant, sought to distance the Black community from its slave past and diet by condemning it as an "unclean and/or unhealthful practice of racial genocide."[96] According to them, soul food was the "garbage" of White plantation owners, and Blacks deserved more than garbage.

FOODWAYS AND *EBONY JR!*: THE EARLY YEARS

As food was used to authenticate Black middle-class identity for adults, so, too, food in *EJ* was linked to ethnic identity and authenticity in the narratives, activity sheets, and cooking columns. Although there were various definitions of soul food among scholars and food critics, for the purposes of this article, I will use the common definition of soul food—traditional southern food cooked by Blacks—since it was the one used by the editors of *EJ*. While their definition incorporated intuition and cooking method, they did not differentiate among ingredients. For them, soul food was defined as traditional foods consumed by Blacks who had migrated from or still resided in the South. This idea was supported in a cartoon titled "Soul Cook-Out," in which three children were shown playing in the backyard of a home while a man stood over a barbecue grill with a spatula in his hand. This man wore a chef's hat and a white apron denoting him as the cook; there were hamburgers on the grill. The text read, "Even hamburgers have lots of soul when they're cooked with sauce over red hot coals."[97] This statement tells us that even something as mainstream as hamburgers can be transformed into soul food if they are cooked by a Black person. Furthering *EJ*'s definition of *soul food*, since Whites tended not to exist in *EJ*'s world, there was no need for the editors to differentiate between traditional southern Black food and that consumed by Southern whites. But they did differentiate between soul food as the core of the Black diet and everything else.

Yet the editors were cognizant of the portion of their audience who disavowed ingredients considered the garbage of White slave owners: hog maws, neckbones, pigs' tails and feet, along with chitterlings. Therefore, they tended not to mention these ingredients. Again, this may have been a marketing tool in an attempt not to alienate a portion of their Black audience.

At the beginning of her tenure, Van Brunt Johnson, the founding editor of *EJ*, took the opportunity to associate soul food with the reader's ethnic identity. In conceptualizing Blackness, *EJ* incorporated food as a way to immerse readers in their culture. Therefore, for the most part, only soul food and the foodways of the African Diaspora were used in *EJ*. This discourse was extended to the entire range of *EJ*'s audience (five- to eleven-year-olds), since the skill level of the recipes varied to include all elementary-school-aged children. Although they are not dishes associated with soul food, the recipes for "Icy Cold Treats" and "A Health Food Delight: Carrot Cookies" demonstrated that the food column included articles for all of *EJ*'s readers, regardless of their age.[98]

The "Icy Cold Treats" recipe for frozen treats made from Kool-Aid targeted the younger range of the intended audience, while "A Health Food Delight: Carrot Cookies" targeted older ones. Without posing harm, and only minimal mess, a child as young as five could easily make Icy Cold Treats. The recipe required the child to pour prepared Kool-Aid into an ice tray, cover the tray with plastic wrap, and insert toothpicks into the individual molds before putting the ice tray into the freezer. The child might spill Kool-Aid, but no sharp objects or the oven were required to make Icy Cold Treats, making it accessible to a five-year-old child. Since a knife, grater, and oven were required to make Searcy's Carrot Cookies, and adults were absent from the illustration and instructions, this recipe targeted older children.

Whatever the age of the target audience, for the most part, the Afrocentric orientation remained consistent. *EJ*'s first cooking column, "Baking Powder Biscuits," was accompanied by photographs of Teesha, a girl, and Thomas, a boy, who, according to the introduction, had written out the recipe. As in most of the child-centered recipes and food narratives, both genders were shown actively preparing the food. Aligned with the child-centered tenets of children's literature, even though the children were shown using an oven, there was no adult present. The biscuit recipe appeared to be handwritten by a child. Using a font that resembled the handwriting of an elementary school child, one who failed to write in a straight line, made it appear as if a child copied the recipe, thus facilitating the child readers in connecting with the text based on identifying with the text and possibly with *EJ* in general.

The introduction to the recipe for Baking Powder Biscuits continued: "The recipe comes from Johnson Publishing Company's, *The Soul of Good Cooking.*"[99] However, *The Soul of Good Cooking* is in fact only a portion of the title of the referenced cookbook: *The Integrated Cookbook: The Soul of Good Cooking*, which featured soul food and mainstream dishes. Even though Freda DeKnight published *The Ebony Cookbook: A Date with a Dish: A Cookbook of American Negro Recipes* with Johnson Publishing Company in 1948, 1962, and 1973, for some reason the editors chose the biscuit recipe from *The Integrated Cookbook: The Soul of Good Cooking*. The failure to reference the *Integrated Cookbook* portion of the title in the introduction might speak to the editors' desire to concentrate on formulating a Black identity through soul food.

Again, one of the primary goals of the magazine was to provide Black child readers with "a magazine which reflect[ed] the sounds and sights and colors of [their] community."[100] *EJ* served as a mirror for the Black child readers in which they could see their reflection by constructing an almost exclusively Black world—other races are rarely shown in *EJ*. The idea was to provide children with a foundation in Black history and culture to augment the Eurocentric education most Black children received in school. Therefore, grounding the reader in a Black identity was far more important than a discourse on integration. The editors might have deleted the portion of the cookbook that referenced integration, since it was not aligned with the primary intentions of the magazine. Surely it was not because of the complexity of the word *integrated*, since the editors regularly defined words for readers. Again, the editors may have been more concerned with defining Blackness through soul food and chose to delete the term *integration* to stay focused on their racialized agenda.

Let's return to the editors' decision to use biscuits as their first recipe. In her article "Soul, Black Women, and Food," Marvelene Hughes stated that homemade biscuits were a staple in breakfast of a "typical Black kitchen," a breakfast that, according to Hughes, "most often consists of grits, home-made biscuits, ham or bacon, molasses or canned preserves, fresh milk and fresh eggs."[101] She noted that "[t]here is supreme value, culturally, in the preparation of a 'hot meal' for breakfast. When the Black child goes to school, a caring other sees that she or he has had a 'hot meal.'"[102] Evidently the editors of *EJ* wanted children to know how to make a component of such a "hot meal" in accordance with the tenets of "a typical Black kitchen."

This thread continued in most of the narratives where food was mentioned, such as in the excerpt from Norma Poinsett's "Susa's Natural." Although it was a story about Susa's desire to wear an Afro—another marker of Blackness—food was nevertheless mentioned:

Mama finished washing the potatoes and emptied the peelings into the garbage can. She'd stew the potatoes and season them with butter, bacon bits and onions. She loved to season food just right. Then she'd add some grated cheese and just the right amount of salt and pepper. Food needed to have a bottom in it, soul, Mama thought. Then she cut up a chicken and seasoned it. She'd fry it for dinner. While at the refrigerator, she took out turnip and mustard greens. In no time she picked and washed the greens and stuffed them in a pot that was bubbling on the stove.[103]

Not only did the mother cook foods traditionally associated as soul food, she cooked according to some definitions of the soul food aesthetic, intuitively and with seasoning. Since the assumption in the Black community was—and might still be—that White foodways tended to adhere to standardized recipes and lacked improvisation, the reference to the intuition the mother used while cooking was aligned with those who defined "soul" as that which was located within the Black body and not within the ingredients of the dish. The mention of seasoning was necessary because White people's food was, and still is, considered bland by many Blacks. Again, White foodways inherently lacked "soul."

In addition to narratives, food was also the focus of some of the educational activity sheets. One example was "Picnic Lunch," where the reader was instructed to unscramble the words for the dishes in the picnic basket. The menu consisted of typical soul food fare: fried chicken, potato salad, baked beans, lemonade, watermelon, and, for some reason, hot dogs and celery, which were components neither of soul food nor of traditional southern food. The hot dogs may have been added to appeal to younger readers, while the addition of celery, a vegetable, would please nutrition-conscious adults. But the inclusion of non–soul food items was rare. Watermelon, long associated with Blacks, was the subject of the food segment in this same issue, with children making watermelon sherbet.

EBONY JR!'S RESPONSE TO DIFFERENCES WITHIN BLACK FOODWAYS

Alongside narratives and activity sheets, readers' responses were also constructed to support the soul food aesthetic. Darrick Wilson, winner of the October 1973 annual writing contest, included the following passage in his story "Mom's Sad and Happy Event": "Mom was in the kitchen cooking our favorite meal for dinner, which was red beans and rice, cornbread, baked neckbones and a peach cobbler."[104] Clearly the child reader was constructed as complicit in positing soul food as the culinary choice of *EJ*'s readers. But, interestingly enough, this was one of the rare occasions when a dish that might be controversial—a dish defined by scholars as soul food (neckbones)—is mentioned. Not only was pork problematized by Elijah Muhammad of the Nation of Islam as "unclean" and a type of "slave food," foods such as neckbones were particularly offensive.[105]

In essence, Muhammad instructed his community to reject soul food, by anyone's definition, because it was associated with slavery, was often the discarded foods of White slave owners, and was generally unhealthy—the incidence of diabetes, obesity, and heart disease in the Black community were evidence of such. He also wanted them to discard the slave-centered identity that was associated with these foods. Yet *EJ* reclaimed these foodways, disconnected them from slavery, and defined them as a commonality in the Black community. Thus, food was another tool used by Van Brunt Johnson to define and postulate a middle-class, Christian, and politically moderate (at least more so than the Nation of Islam) Black identity for child readers. Again, all of the foods Muhammad disallowed, except pigs' feet and tails and chitterlings, were regularly mentioned in *EJ* and almost none of the foods he suggested—"brussels sprouts, asparagus, eggplant, okra, squash and rhubarb"—were referenced. While one might say that not many of the latter foods were considered desirable by child readers, it should be noted that okra, squash, and mustard and turnip greens are components of the soul food diet and, with the exception of okra, are commonly consumed by some children.[106]

Let us not forget that *EJ* was published by Johnson Publishing Company, a family-owned corporation whose mission is to turn a profit. In evidence of this, John Johnson tended to avoid controversy that was not related to the Black Liberation Movement as much as possible. He also avoided any criticism of Blacks in his publications. As a publisher, he was always cognizant of sales. This position was evident in the foods included and avoided in *EJ*. First, the editors never faltered on the value of positing these foodways as relevant to the construction of a Black identity. But they tended to avoid mentioning foods that might be problematic for a significant portion of *EJ*'s audience: hog maws, neckbones, pigs' tails, and so on. While one might argue that it is these very ingredients that constitute soul food, the editors of *EJ* did not adhere to that definition. They considered soul food to be traditional southern food cooked by a Black person. Consequently, for the most part, the foods that are mentioned (e.g., fried chicken, watermelon, and beans) are more aligned with traditional southern foodways than with scholars' definitions of soul food.

In addition to class, politics, and possibly religion, gender issues intersected with food in *EJ*. Cognizant of gender politics and the Black Feminist Movement, *EJ*'s editors showed boys in the cooking segments almost in equal proportion to girls. But if a man was cooking, it was usually in a conventional male setting—outdoor barbecuing. For example, in Norma Poinsett's "The Main Dish," the protagonist, Victoria, was upset because she invited her teacher over for Thanksgiving dinner but forgot that the family's oven was broken and they could not afford to get it fixed.[107] Not wanting to embarrass Victoria, the family resolved to make dinner for the teacher. They all contributed to the meal: "Judson [her brother] and Lois [her sister] had washed and soaked fresh mustard and turnip greens from their garden and Mama picked them. Victoria washed the sweet potatoes and cut up the onions and peppers for the top-of-the-stove dressing."[108]

Of course, this was a soul food menu and adhered to the soul aesthetic. The greens were not only "fresh" but from the mother's garden, thus attaching more value to them. Notice that Poinsett used the southern term *dressing* as opposed to *stuffing*, a northern expression. Also noteworthy is the fact that Judson, Vicky's brother, helped cook inside the house. And the family could be forgiven for the top-of-the-stove dressing because the oven was broken. But "[e]verybody was busy except Daddy, who kept going out for walks in the back."[109] While she fretted over having gotten her family into such a predicament, Victoria sat on the front porch crying.

> She was still feeling bad [and] . . . wondering what her parents had done about the oven when the first spicy scent of barbecue passed her nose. It was coming from behind the house. "Barbecue!" Victoria shouted, sniffing the air again to make certain she was smelling right . . . . Victoria ran in the direction of the smell to see what was going on. Whoever heard of barbecue on Thanksgiving! She was out of breath when she finally ran into her father who was busy turning a spit with a beautiful golden reddish barbecued turkey on it. . . . He had dug a barbecue pit in the ground and filled it with hickory wood and was cooking up the best smelling turkey Victoria had ever sniffed![110]

While barbecuing a turkey is more aligned with traditional southern foodways, it is considered soul food by most Blacks when they do the cooking. Therefore, the barbecued turkey is a welcome component of a soul food meal. In relation to gender, barbecue has long been associated with males in the media, and *EJ* was no exception.

Even the stock cartoon characters Sunny and Honey were used to perpetuate this idea. In the November 1975 cartoon "Honey Baked a Turkey," Honey placed the cooked turkey on the table.[111] Sunny was seen in another room sitting in a chair, with his feet on an ottoman, reading a newspaper. In the next cell, Honey lit the candles in the candelabra and the text read, "I can tell that she baked plenty."[112] Then Honey looked around the corner as if calling Sunny to the table; all the while a doll was sitting at the table with her head turned to face the reader. One can assume that the doll was the speaker. As Honey called Sunny, the doll said, "But if Sunny gets his hands on it first, I'm sure we won't get any."[113] By this time Sunny was sitting at the table, holding the turkey and moving it toward his side of the table. Honey and the doll had gloomy expressions on their faces. The assumption was that Honey has baked the turkey but Sunny would eat the majority of it, leaving little for Honey and the doll. Because the column appeared in the November issue, Sunny and Honey were probably having their Thanksgiving dinner.

These traditional gender roles were also evident in the June/July 1975 issue, when Sunny, Honey, and the doll were again preparing to have dinner. Unlike the November issue, Honey and the doll were sitting at a picnic table while Sunny cooked. But he was not cooking inside the home: He was barbecuing spareribs—which he burned when Honey and the doll went inside to answer the phone.[114] Again, when men cooked in *EJ*, for the most part, they were barbecuing. While boys in cooking columns and articles often participated in cooking indoors, for the most part adult men, and occasionally boys, cooked outside exclusively.

As the foodways of *EJ* intersected with individual, familial, and gender identities, the magazine's approach was ultimately used to define and unite the Black community. The calendar's illustration of the 1975 Halloween issue was of two families and trick-or-treaters.[115] One couple was encoded as assimilationists, or at least as not being as racially conscious as the Black Nationalists. They had nondescript hairstyles and had a mainstream jack-o-lantern in their window. Their neighbors, on the other hand, were encoded as a Black Nationalist family: The man wore an Afro and had his fist in the air in the Black Power sign, and the woman had her hair in cornrows. In their window was half of a watermelon with a candle inside. Of course, the neighborhood children were going to the Black Nationalist couple's house, while the other couple looked on. It was the couple's nationalistic politics, as encoded in their fashion and food, that attracted the children. The message inherent in this illustration was that soul food, as represented by the watermelon, was linked to a Black identity—an ethnic identity the child readers shared with the characters in the illustration and one that the children could demonstrate and embody through their own foodways.

FOODWAYS AND *EBONY JR!*: THE LATER YEARS

From its inception, *EJ* connected Black readers to the African Diaspora. Although often precolonial, African history and culture was featured in most issues of *EJ*. Less common, but nevertheless consistent, were stories of the Caribbean and portions of South America that had a significant population of Blacks. For example, the Caribbean was one of the themes of the February 1982 issue. Stories included Karen Odom's "Freedom Fighters of the West Indies," activities such as a "West Indian Accents Crossword Puzzle," and a recipe column for "Jamaican Rub-Up Cake." Other issues featured lessons about and recipes for tropical fruits.

Unlike other recipe columns, the accompanying illustration for the Jamaican Rub-Up Cake was not a photograph of real children; instead, it was a drawing by Cliff Hayes. Consistent with *EJ*'s attempt to show gender equality in children, a girl and a boy were making the cake, but inconsistent with *EJ*'s history and children's literature in general—where the activity is child centered—the illustration also included an apron-clad woman standing in front of a rotisserie. The fact that the recipe called for the use of the oven did not account for the presence of an adult; as stated earlier, children were shown putting the biscuits in the oven without an adult present in the "Baking Powder Biscuit" recipe of May 1973. Children were losing their autonomy at this time in *EJ*'s tenure.

While the cake did connect an activity to the theme of the issue—one that attempted to associate the reader with the African Diaspora—it was not an appealing cake for most American children. While the child did get to "play" in the dough—step three stated, "[W]ith your fingertips, work the butter into the flour mixture and then add the sugar"—the cake did not have any frosting, typically children's favorite part.[116] The inclusion of adults in illustrations where they had never been—taking some agency from the child—and cakes with no frosting were indicative of the fact that the editors were losing touch with their audience.

Nevertheless, the editors continued to align the reader with the Diaspora. Another way of doing this was by featuring some of the tropical fruits grown in the Caribbean and South America in several issues. They were used as components of the science curriculum, as themes for food columns, and as a tool to make a connection to the Diaspora. Bananas, for example, were a theme in the June/July 1975 issue. The first activity sheet in this issue was a puzzle titled "Who Am I?" in which the reader answered a riddle for each letter of the puzzle. The reader was looking for the name of the "land of reggae, bananas and sun."[117] The clues did not give information about the island; instead they led the reader to the necessary letter to complete the puzzle. For example, "The first letter is in jar, jam and jive. The second letter is in apple, about and alive."[118] The answer, given on another page, was *Jamaica*. This activity sheet came right before an article, "A Bit about Bananas," that told how farmers in Jamaica, "one of our West Indian neighbors," grow, harvest, and package their bananas.[119]

The idea of the Diaspora was further perpetuated by the article's accompanying photographs showing Black Jamaicans: One showed women in a market and another showed two boys carrying hands of bananas on their heads. Having completed an activity and learned where and how bananas are grown and harvested, the reader was then offered a recipe featuring bananas: "Banana Icebox Pie."[120] Like "A Bit about Bananas," the recipe was accompanied by photographs of Black children preparing and eating the pie. Continuing the lesson on tropical fruit, "Oranges without Seeds for Christmas" appeared in the December 1975 issue. Unlike the straightforward nonfiction of "A Bit about Bananas," the article about oranges began with a folk tale about a "lonely little witch from the forest of Bahia, in Brazil," who wanted to give the people of the nearby village Christmas gifts.[121] She decided to give them the "biggest, sweetest, juiciest, oranges that they've ever seen"; her twist on these oranges was that they would be seedless.[122] After a brief discussion of how the witch used magic to produce the seedless oranges, the article continued with a nonfiction lesson on grafting orange trees and how these trees made their way to the United States.

Unlike the other articles, "Oranges without Seeds for Christmas" was accompanied by drawings of a Black woman in a peasant blouse and skirt. In the first image she carried oranges on her head in a hat and appeared to be walking past a grove of orange trees. In the second illustration, she pointed to a map of South America showing readers where Brazil is located.[123] Black women carrying baskets of fruit on their heads was also the illustration for the "Tasty Tropical Treats" food column in the December 1978 issue.[124] Readers were taught how to make pineapple sticks—basically, pineapple ice cubes that could be placed in punch. Apples and bananas were featured in the next recipe. What made them "tropical" was the illustration of a Black girl receiving a banana from a monkey hanging from a banana tree. The recipe connected to this illustration was similar to the pineapple sticks, calling instead for apples and bananas frozen in apple juice.

The lessons on where and how the fruit is grown also served as a component of *EJ*'s science curriculum. The fruits selected and the places featured supported the editor's efforts to make connections between the reader and the African Diaspora. Showing illustrations, particularly photographs, of Blacks across the Diaspora may have facilitated the connections. We know that non-Blacks live in all the places featured; therefore, the editors chose the images because the people featured in them were Black. This leads me to believe that the editors intentionally wanted to invite the reader into the Diaspora through these articles and images. Did it work? Were the middle-class readers of *EJ* eating soul food as a component of their diet? If not, could the children decode the connection between their Blackness and soul food?

SELF-DEFINITION OR STEREOTYPE: WHAT WERE MIDDLE-CLASS BLACKS REALLY EATING?

In positing a definition of Blackness, the editors of *EJ* choose universal symbols they believed children would recognize and associate with their own ethnicity. The texts were progressive in that they nationalized the issues of blackness for a people and posited self-definition and pride in an agreeable manner. Yet these symbols and the way they were encoded often essentialized Blackness. And depending upon the context in which the symbols would be read, they could be degrading. For an example, *EJ*'s first cover (May 1973) featured was a cartoon illustration of a jungle-like scene. In the foreground was a boy standing next to a seated lion; in the background a girl sat astride a giraffe, and "exotic" birds completed the scene. A self-defining, Afrocentric reading of this illustration would connect the African American children to their African ancestry. It would also associate the boy, more so than the girl, with the Ethiopian emperor Haile Selassie, who was featured in other JPC publications. As illustrated on the cover, the boy could be considered the rising young lion king.

But taken out of the context of the African American community, this same illustration could be considered stereotypical, and possibly White supremacist, in that it placed African American children in a jungle scene to symbolize their savageness and perennial closeness to nature.[125] Before the Civil Rights Movement, Black children were often depicted in racist advertisements as being in harm's way (e.g., a postcard with the image of a Black child on a beach about to be eaten by a crocodile with a caption that reads, "Wish you were here").[126] Of course, the children in the *EJ* illustration were not in danger, and the accompanying story was intended to be read within the context of the African American community.

The cover with the children in the jungle scene foreshadowed the story "Kwame and the Lion."[127] By naming the protagonist Kwame, the author made an indirect reference to Kwame Nkrumah, who served as president of Ghana from 1960 to 1966. When the protagonist Kwame visited the lion at the local zoo, instead of the "king of beasts . . . from the East," he found,

> The lion was lying on the ground, not making a sound.
> Kwame said, "This ain't hardly no king
> > He looks funny,
> > Like a old funny thing."
> The lion looked Kwame in the eyes and said with a surprise,
> "Son, I wants to tell ya something. . . .
> Long before you was born, I was in Africa nice and warm,
> I was king of beasts, the baddest dude in the East.
> Your ancestors and I were at home;
> > We were free,
> > Free to roam,
> > We were kings
> I was king of the jungle-nation
> And your ancestor was king of civilization."[128]

Clearly a connection was being made between the African lion and the African American protagonist, and, by extension, the child reader. Both found their ancestry in the continent of Africa, were descendants of royalty, used similar idioms, and shared a history of enslavement. The story continued with the lion telling Kwame about his being captured, caged, and brought to the zoo. The lion said, "They brought us here and rule us with fear,/They even took our roar."[129] Using the metaphor of losing his roar, the lion told of his oppression in the zoo. "Kwame wiped the tears from his eyes and the lion said,/'Son you are young and strong/and will live long. Don't weep for me/ because you can be free./Be FREEEEEEEE!'"[130]

Not only was Kwame connected to his African past, but the community's expectations for him as a child were outlined here, too. In the *Jet* article that celebrated *EJ*'s ten-year anniversary, Johnson reminded Black children that, as a generation, they benefited from the civil rights struggles of their ancestors, and that with these new opportunities "more will be required" of them.[131] This was a common ideology of the 1970s that I remember being instructed in through Black publications (e.g., *Essence* magazine), church, and from the older generation in general.

The *EJ* editors also used food to essentialize the African American identity by positing that most, if not all, Blacks were eating these foods as a regular part of their diet. But were they? What were middle-class Blacks really eating in the late 1970s? For an analysis of the eating habits of one middle-class Black community, I turn to Thomas Fitzgerald's 1979 study of the dietary habits of middle-class Blacks in a North Carolina community. Prior to Fitzgerald's study, "Norge Jerome, in her study on diet changes of Negroes migrating from the rural South . . . suggest[ed] that the basic core diet . . . [of traditional southern Black foods] undergoes little significant change. . . . It should be noted, [that this study] focused on low-income black households."[132]

Jerome's study supported the assumption by Jones and others who declared that the Black lower class primarily ate a soul food diet: that, in essence, their foodways were defined by and maintained their ethnic identity. In contrast to Jerome, Fitzgerald was interested in the diet of middle-class Blacks. He compared the foodways of a middle-class black community with their middle-class White neighbors:

> It is indeed rare to find studies in which subjects have been matched according to income level or comparable socio-economic status. The excuse often given is that there is too little variation in social class among blacks to permit any examination for the effects of social class in this group.[133]

Fitzgerald's work provides the research necessary to complicate the discourse that posited the Black middle class's supposed consumption of soul food to signify and reify their ethnic identity. One of the functions of the "soul food" discourse was to prove the retention of ethnic identity in middle-class Blacks as they ascended the socioeconomic ladder. Some suspected that as middle-class Blacks attained the advantages of class—college educations, professional employment, and desegregated housing and schools—they were discarding the vestiges of their ethnic heritage. In defending their Blackness, some middle-class Blacks pointed to their consumption of soul food as a marker of their allegiance to an Afrocentric identity. Again, I will use Fitzgerald's study to move past rhetoric to an empirical study of what middle-class Blacks in one community reported themselves as eating on a daily basis.

As discussed above, Marvelene Hughes stated that homemade biscuits were a staple in the breakfast of a "typical Black kitchen."[134] As such, breakfast food, specifically biscuits, were featured in *EJ*'s first cooking column. Since homemade biscuits were a staple of a "typical Black" breakfast, one can assume that the editors of *EJ* were trying to teach child readers how to make a soul food classic. Jerome's study stated that low-income Blacks who migrated to the North may have still been eating a core diet of soul food, which may have included homemade biscuits. As for the Black middle class,

> The notion that Southerners still eat a large breakfast of country ham, grits, eggs, fried sweet potatoes, and homemade biscuits is not borne out in this sample, among blacks or whites. In this suburban community, people tend to

eat very much like those in middle America—that is, cold cereal and milk, coffee, toast, and sometimes juice. Eggs and bacon or sausage are used only occasionally to break the monotony; there is no real difference here between blacks and whites. At least 30 per cent of those sampled claimed that they resort to the more traditional eggs/bacon/bread routine on weekends, if by weekend one means Saturday, Sunday for this church-going community is for Sunday school, hence early rising and lighter breakfasts . . . When biscuits were served, they had been purchased in a can or else prepared from biscuit mix. The traditional southern breakfast, then—for blacks and whites—is largely a thing of the past, perhaps still somewhat ceremonial (at times like Christmas) but fast in danger of extinction.[135]

Based on modernity, time constraints, and the availability of convenience foods, the middle-class Blacks of Fitzgerald's study were not eating a soul food breakfast—and, by extension, lunch or dinner—on a daily basis. As such, their eating habits had become a reflection of their work habits—of their social class. As accused, they were eating the same foods as their White neighbors. By extension, it can be assumed that some of the middle-class readers of *EJ* were not eating soul food as a component of their daily core diet. And I would suggest that because of the same factors—modernity, time constraints, and the availability of convenience foods—some lower-class Blacks had also moved away from the time-consuming dishes of a daily soul food diet.

Therefore, it is possible that many child readers, irrespective of their income, may not have been eating soul food as part of their core daily diet. But this does not mean that readers would not have known that the soul food of *EJ*'s cooking columns and narratives was encoded with Blackness. Readers would have made these connections based on consuming soul food on occasions that focused on family and community—Sunday and holidays; by having read other texts that made the connection between soul food and Blackness, which include oral stories told by their elders and the Black children's literature; and by being smart enough to decode the connection between food and ethnicity as it was presented in *EJ*.

Activists such as Jones had used the soul food discourse to align middle-class Blacks with their ethnic identity, so much so that the consumption of soul food transcended its class-based analysis.[136] In *EJ* the production and consumption of soul food as an ethnic identifier was used to inform Black children of all socioeconomic classes of their cultural identity. Although the food in *EJ* may not have reflected the food that some children ate on a daily basis, it was consistent with the traditional southern Black food served on Sundays, holidays, and special events that reified family, community, and ethnic identity. It was also consistent with the discourse on soul food and Black identity of the post–World War II era. *EJ* may have offered a Black identity through the use of food that may not have been a daily occurrence for many of its middle-class readers. Nevertheless, the child readers still would have understood the foodways to be traditional, valued, and linked to their ethnic identity.[137]

CONCLUSION

Although *EJ*'s racialized commentary became subtle over time, the images and symbols used to present Blackness as an ethnic identity remained and corresponded to the sociocultural and political moment. Black Nationalists were moving in the direction of increased self-definition, and children were included in the discussion through the arts and education. While *EJ* admirably attempted to ground itself in Black history and culture, thereby immersing the child in a racialized identity, it essentialized Blackness in ways that were understandable but nevertheless limiting. Within the Black community, these images represented racial pride, definition, and solidarity, but outside the community these same images could be constructed as racist and stereotypical (e.g., the continued references to fried chicken and watermelon). *EJ*, it should be noted, was not meant to be read and interpreted outside the context of the African American community. In addition to signifying "Blackness" as a component of the child reader's identity, *EJ*, like various factions of the African American community, constructed children. Yet their ideas differed based on factors such as class, religion, and political positions.

NOTES

1. Talmadge Anderson, *Black Studies: Theory, Method, and Cultural Perspectives* (Pullman: Washington State University Press, 1990), 128.
2. Norman R. Dixon, "Defining the Situation: Toward a Definition of Black Education," *Negro Educational Review* 14, no. 3 & 4 (1973); Akbar, as cited in Janice E. Hale-Benson, *Black Children: Their Roots, Culture, and Learning Styles* (Baltimore: Johns Hopkins University Press, 1982); Asa Hilliard, *Alternatives to IQ Testing: An Approach to the Identification of Gifted Minority Children* (Sacramento: California State Department of Education, 1976).
3. Dixon, "Defining the Situation," 114–15.
4. Ibid., 114.
5. Ibid.
6. Ibid., 115.
7. Akbar, as cited in Hale-Benson, *Black Children*.
8. Hilliard, *Alternatives to IQ Testing*, 42.

9. Hale-Benson's generalization about "distinct culture" does not imply an unawareness of the Black community's multifaceted makeup. Black culture has many versions but one primary historical root in chattel slavery.

10. Hale-Benson, *Black Children*, 4.

11. Dixon, "Defining the Situation," 115.

12. "A Page for You to Color," *Ebony Jr!*, May 1975, 11.

13. Frankie Cox, "That February," *Ebony Jr!*, February 1974, 49.

14. "School Is Hip," *Ebony Jr!*, June/July 1975, 36.

15. Sherry Ricchiardi, "At 23, She Lands Top Job on Magazine for Black Youths," *Des Moines Register*, May 2, 1973.

16. "Put It Together," *Ebony Jr!*, October 1973, 60.

17. "Can You Think Like Imhotep? A Story from the Nile," *Ebony Jr!*, May 1973, 21; Ricchiardi, "At 23, She Lands Top Job on Magazine for Black Youths."

18. "Can You Think Like Imhotep?" 21.

19. Ibid.

20. Julian Beckford, "The Mystery of Mobius Strip," *Ebony Jr!*, November 1973, 34–35.

21. Marlene Cummings, "Bobbie and Bubba Meet Mellow Mel," *Ebony Jr!*, November 1973, 58.

22. Ibid.

23. "There's a Job for Everyone," *Ebony Jr!*, March 1980, 7.

24. Mary C. Lewis, "'Mr. Black Labor' Himself, A. Philip Randolph," *Ebony Jr!*, March 1980.

25. Karen Odom, "The Good Buy Pig (The Three Little Pigs Retold)," *Ebony Jr!*, March 1980.

26. Ibid., 9.

27. William L. Van Deburg, *New Day in Babylon: The Black Power Movement and American Culture, 1965–1975* (Chicago: University of Chicago Press, 1992), 274.

28. William E. Cross, *Shades of Black: Diversity in African-American Identity* (Philadelphia: Temple University Press, 1991).

29. Ibid.

30. Ibid., 41.

31. Spencer J. Condie and James W. Christiansen, "An Indirect Technique for the Measurement of Changes in Black Identity," *Phylon* 38 (1977), 46–54.

32. F. James Davis, *Who Is Black? One Nation's Definition* (University Park: Pennsylvania State University Press, 1991).

33. James P. Comer and Alvin F. Poussaint, *Black Child Care: How to Bring up a Healthy Black Child in America: A Guide to Emotional and Psychological Development* (New York: Simon & Schuster, 1975), 20.

34. Eloise Greenfield, "Saturday," *Ebony Jr!*, May 1973.

35. Ibid., 46.

36. Ibid., 48.

37. Akbar, as cited in Hale-Benson, *Black Children*; Hilliard, *Alternatives to IQ Testing*.

38. Greenfield, "Saturday," 47–48.

39. Ibid., 48.

40. Ibid.

41. Ibid.

42. Frankie Cox, "The Big Day," *Ebony Jr!*, December 1973, 14.

43. Ibid.

44. Ibid.

45. Ibid., 14–15.

46. Ibid., 15–16

47. Ibid., 18.

48. Ibid.

49. Ibid.

50. Willie L. Morrow, *400 Years without a Comb* (San Diego: Black Publishers of San Diego, 1973); Esi Sagay, *African Hairstyles: Styles of Yesterday and Today* (Oxford: Heinemann International Literature and Textbooks, 1983).

51. Ayana D. Byrd and Lori L. Tharps, *Hair Story: Untangling the Roots of Black Hair in America* (New York: St. Martin's Press, 2001), 17.

52. Ibid., 19.

53. Ibid., 42.

54. Ibid.

55. Ibid., 37.

56. Ibid., 29–30.

57. Ibid., 37.

58. Ibid., 38.

59. Malcolm X, *The Autobiography of Malcolm X*, with the assistance of Alex Haley (1964; reprint, New York: Ballantine, 1992), 54.

60. Byrd and Tharps, *Hair Story*, 56.

61. Gloria J. Wade-Gayles, "The Making of a Permanent Afro," in *Pushed Back to Strength: A Black Woman's Journey Home*, ed. Gloria J. Wade-Gayles (Boston: Beacon Press, 1993).

62. Chemical relaxers—or perms, as they are commonly called—are a sodium hydroxide (lye) or calcium hydroxide (no lye) product applied to the hair to loosen the natural curl pattern, thereby straightening the hair.

63. William H. Grier and Price M. Cobbs, *Black Rage* (New York: Basic Books, 1968), 56.

64. Ibid., 42, 43.

65. Ibid., 44.

66. Ibid., 45.

67. Byrd and Tharps, *Hair Story*, 62.

68. Noliwe M. Rooks, *Hair Raising: Beauty, Culture, and African American Women* (New Brunswick, NJ: Rutgers University Press, 1996).

69. Wendy Cooper, *Hair: Sex, Society, Symbolism* (New York: Stein and Day, 1971).

70. Norma Poinsett, "Susa's Natural," *Ebony Jr!*, June/July 1973, 48.

71. Ibid., 49–50.

72. Ibid., 49.

73. Ibid.

74. Ibid., 50.

75. Frankie Cox, "Get It On!," *Ebony Jr!*, August/September 1973, 8.

76. From the late 1960s to the 1980s, for the most part, young African American girls' hair was not straightened until they reached adolescence. Now parents are straightening girls' hair at varying ages.

77. Janice Gray, "Cornrowing," *Ebony Jr!*, January 1974, 52.

78. Ray Smith, "Cornrows for Men Exploded This Year into the Mainstream," *Wall Street Journal*, July 31, 2000.

79. Stephen M. Silverman, "NSYNC: Head of the Class," *People* (1998), http://www.people.com/people/article/0,26334,617829,00.html.

80. Smith, "Cornrows for Men Exploded This Year into the Mainstream."

81. George De Vos, "Ethnic Pluralism: Conflict and Accommodation," in *Ethnic Identity: Cultural Continuities and Change*, ed. George De Vos (Palo Alto, CA: Mayfield, 1975).

82. E. Franklin Frazier, *Black Bourgeoisie* (Glencoe, IL: Free Press, 1957).

83. Van Deburg, *New Day in Babylon*, 195.

84. Claude Fischler, "Food, Self and Identity," *Social Science Information* 27, no. 2 (1988): 275.

85. Donna R. Gabaccia, *We Are What We Eat: Ethnic Food and the Making of Americans* (Cambridge, MA: Harvard University Press, 1998), 8.

86. Margaret Mead, "A Perspective on Food Patterns," in *Issues in Nutrition from the 1980s: An Ecological Perspective*, ed. Alice L. Tobias and Patricia J. Thompson (Monterey, CA: Wadsworth, 1980).

87. Doris Witt, *Black Hunger: Food and the Politics of U.S. Identity* (New York: Oxford University Press, 1999), 80.

88. LeRoi Jones, "Soul Food," in *Home: Social Essays*, ed. Amiri Baraka [LeRoi Jones] (New York: Morrow, 1966); Van Deburg, *New Day in Babylon*; Witt, *Black Hunger*.

89. Van Deburg, *New Day in Babylon*.

90. Jones, "Soul Food," 102.

91. Witt, *Black Hunger*, 80.

92. Van Deburg, *New Day in Babylon*, 203.

93. Ibid.

94. Craig Claiborne, "Cooking with Soul," *New York Times Magazine*, November 3, 1968, 109.

95. Van Deburg, *New Day in Babylon*, 203.

96. Witt, *Black Hunger*, 80.

97. "Soul Cook-Out," *Ebony Jr!*, June/July 1975.

98. Ike Sutton, "Icy Cold Treats," *Ebony Jr!*, February 1974; Shirley A. Searcy, "Banana Icebox Pie," *Ebony Jr!*, June/July 1975.

99. Norman L. Hunter (photographer), "Baking Powder Biscuits," *Ebony Jr!*, May 1973, 31.

100. John H. Johnson, "Why *Ebony Jr!*" *Ebony Jr!*, May 1973, 4.

101. Marvalene H. Hughes, "Soul, Black Women, and Food," in *Food and Culture: A Reader*, ed. Counihan Carole and Van Esterik Penny (New York: Routledge, 1997), 278.

102. Ibid.

103. Poinsett, "Susa's Natural," 50–51.

104. Darrick Wilson, "Mom's Sad and Happy Event," *Ebony Jr!*, October 1973, 25.

105. Witt, *Black Hunger*.

106. Elijah Muhammad and Fard Muhammad, *How to Eat to Live* (Chicago: Muhammad Mosque of Islam No. 2, 1967), 31.

107. Norma Poinsett, "The Main Dish," *Ebony Jr!*, November 1973.

108. Ibid., 8.

109. Ibid.

110. Ibid., 9–10.

111. Michael G. Davis, "Sunny and Honey," *Ebony Jr!*, November 1975, 22.

112. Ibid.

113. Ibid., 23.

114. Ibid.

115. "Calendar," *Ebony Jr!*, October 1975.

116. Marcia V. Roebuck, "Jamaican Rub-up Cake," *Ebony Jr!*, February 1982, 45.

117. "Who Am I?" *Ebony Jr!*, June/July 1975, 5.

118. Ibid.

119. Constance Lambie, "A Bit about Bananas," *Ebony Jr!*, June/July 1975.

120. Searcy, "Banana Icebox Pie."

121. Mary W. Wilson, "Oranges without Seeds for Christmas," *Ebony Jr!*, December 1975, 51.

122. Ibid.

123. Ibid.

124. Kanye K. Mugo, "Tasty Tropical Treats," *Ebony Jr!*, December 1978.

125. Poinsett, "The Main Dish," 8.

126. Riggs, *Ethnic Notions*.

127. "Calendar," *Ebony Jr!*, June/July 1975.

128. Marlon T. Riggs, *Ethnic Notions* (San Francisco: California Newsreel, 1987).

129. Ernest Gregg, "Kwame and the Lion," *Ebony Jr!*, May 1973, 27.

130. Ibid., 28.

131. Ibid.

132. Thomas K. Fitzgerald, "Southern Folks' Eating Habits Ain't What They Used to Be If They Ever Were," *Nutrition Today* 14 (1979): 16.

133. Ibid., 17.

134. Hughes, "Soul, Black Women, and Food," 278.

135. Fitzgerald, "Southern Folks' Eating Habits," 18.

136. Jones, "Soul Food."

137. Laretta Henderson, "*Ebony Jr!* and 'Soul Food': The Construction of Middle Class African American Identity through the Use of Traditional Southern Foodways," *Multiethnic Literature in the United States* 32, no. 4 (2007).

III

CONTEXTS AND ANALYSIS: CONSTRUCTING BLACK CHILDREN AND THEIR LITERATURE

6

Johnson Publishing Company's Construction of the Black Child

[An author creates] an image of himself and another image of his reader; he makes his reader, as he makes his second self.—Wayne Booth

To "make" or "construct" another human being is to attribute certain traits to that person—to contrive a persona that has meaning related to the "designer's" own standpoints. The language here is metaphoric, but as the following pages will illustrate, the "construction" business is very concrete. As we will see, the different sectors of African American society have "constructed" a Black child persona in different ways, in ways that generally harmonize with that sector's own worldviews, class interests, and philosophical orientations. Whether a corporation, an economic class, a political organization, or a religious group—all are building relationships with the young, and all have certain desired results in mind.

According to Aidan Chambers, a children's author and literary critic, child readers and children's creative authors implicitly "negotiate" the meaning of a story; a similar process can be identified in the wider arena of the child/author connections.[1] In short, adults "construct" the child and seek to build a relationship as they envision the unfolding shape of society and hope to influence that emerging shape.

The Brownies' Book, as *EJ*'s literary ancestor, illustrated the necessity of racializing childhood in direct response to the times. Johnson, like DuBois as editor of *The Crisis*, wrestled with what types of material to publish in relation to his child audience.[2] Fully conscious of the complexity of the issue, DuBois stated that *The Crisis* had a responsibility of publishing news about the oppression of the African American community even in the children's issues. The inclusion of this information, along with Black children's realities, evoked a letter from a child reader that called for more information on Black history and noted that even children hated white supremacists.[3] DuBois responded by describing his no-win dilemma: Education in hatred was a disaster, and ignorance of race-compelled hatred was equally disastrous.[4]

Encountering this same dilemma, how did Johnson, as publisher of *EJ*, perceive his responsibility to black child readers of the 1970s and 1980s?[5] How did he assess children's capacity to comprehend what was offered in *EJ*? According to Shirley Steinberg and Joe Kincheloe, "Childhood is a social and historical artifact, not simply a biological entity . . . that has been produced by social, cultural, political, and economic forces operating upon it."[6] Therefore, within the historical moment of *EJ*'s publication, how did the African American community conceptualize childhood? By way of background, I will consider how three different sectors of the African American community "constructed" the child during the time of *EJ*'s conception: the middle class, a Black Nationalist group (the Black Panthers), and the Black church.

THE MIDDLE-CLASS CONSTRUCTION OF THE CHILD

In this analysis of the African American child, I turn to Andrew Billingsley, a leading African American sociologist and author of *Black Families and the Struggle for Survival*, an analysis of and advice for the African American family.[7] I also look to James Comer and Alvin Poussaint's *Black Child Care: How to Bring up a Healthy Black Child in America: A Guide to Emotional and Psychological Development*.[8] As two physicians, Comer and Poussaint created an African American version of Dr. Benjamin Spock's *Baby & Child Care*.[9] Both the Billingsley and Comer/Poussaint texts offer a middle-class perspective and, like all the sources I consider in this analysis, operate under the assumption of African American children as oppressed beings but also as members of two cultures, White and Black. Then they address how to teach the child to deal with oppression and how both the family and the community have a role in relation to the child.

Childhood, and the ideology of innocence and protection associated with childhood in the modern era, does not protect the racialized child from suffering the injustices perpetrated by White supremacists. Both Billingsley and Comer/Poussaint commented on the double burden for African American children—the double consciousness stemming from life as an African American but still an American and part of the American system.[10] Or, as stated by DuBois: "One ever feels his two-ness,—an American, a Negro; two souls, two thoughts, two unreconciled strivings;

two warring ideals in one dark body, whose dogged strength alone keeps it from being torn asunder."[11] And both texts continued with ideas of how to teach children to cope. Comer and Poussaint stated:

> Today the black child is still made to feel inferior to whites. From his earliest days he senses that his life is viewed cheaply by white society and he enjoys little protection at its hand. For example, black youths are frequently the victims of racially motivated police abuse at an early age.[12]

They continued by stating that because of this oppression, the childhood experience has itself been thwarted. Children have had to learn to deal with "belligerent whites"; they have had to practice "cunning."[13]

To counteract this condition, both sources noted that children must be taught their human rights and have their self-esteem fostered and supported regularly. Billingsley told his reader, "It has been and continues to be an urgent and necessary prerequisite for the survival of our people that we teach our young ones to walk tall in a land which would deny the essence of their very being."[14] Comer and Poussaint agreed that self-esteem should be actively instilled in African American children to counteract White supremacy and children's feelings of degradation, but that adults should also politicize children somewhat: "We must help children become aware of their rights and opportunities. We must help them acquire the skills to take advantage of these rights and opportunities. We must help them learn to identify and fight racism."[15]

However, like DuBois and most other commentators, the authors of *Black Child Care* took a moderate position:

> [W]e don't have to help them become angry. Anger is a healthy human emotion. When youngsters are denied their rights and opportunities, anger will come naturally . . . unless they are crushed into line. This is not the case for most black children today.
> Making children supersensitive to all injustice in a world full of injustices will cause them to be indiscriminately reactive and angry . . . whether it will help or not. . . . [R]eactive and angry when, in fact, the offense was unintended or minor. . . . Hostility is not like healthy anger. . . . It does not help in the fight against racism.[16]

This political position, aligned with the nonviolent Civil Rights ideology, dissuades anger and, by extension, violence. Young adults had been very active in the Civil Rights Movement, and many portrayals of African American youth in the 1960s and 1970s implied that they were angry and violent. The middle-class segment of the African American community, armed with some entrée into the mainstream, was concerned about an anger that would prevent children from functioning in the mainstream.

They did not necessarily believe the anger was unwarranted—it was just counterproductive to integration. So children were seen as racially discriminated against, but they should be shielded from becoming too "reactive and angry" in responding to that oppression.

After discussing children as a part of the larger U.S. social system, these authors then located children within the family. The assumption was that the family into which a child is born determines the social conditions in which he or she will live. "A child's life chances are to an extent determined before his birth," wrote Comer and Poussaint.[17] This translated into a need to consider the health of the mother, prenatal care, any kind of economic and social "deprivation," and any lack of basic medical care. All these preconditions informed the child's life chances. Comer and Poussaint discussed how children who experience "good child-rearing practices . . . [in] an atmosphere of love and security, even in the poorest homes, will be prepared to face the challenges of tomorrow."[18] Commenting on the family structure, Billingsley showed how some basic Afrocentric activities supported children's social development as functional racialized beings. Families, Billingsley stated, should engage in activities such as singing, dancing, playing Afrocentric educational games, and reading books. He continued:

> Despite television, children still like to read and to be read to, especially in their early years. Our task is to capture their fascination for reading and help them develop a sustained interest in it, and to help expose them to reading material which depicts Black people in a positive light.[19]

He offered a list of books on Black history and culture, for example, Jean Carey Bond's *A Is for Africa* and John Shearer's *I Wish I Had an Afro*. Again, childhood does not protect African American children from oppression, but in the family, children can be taught how to cope. They can be supported in their efforts. As one traditional African American song states, "This is a mean world, to try to live in, to try to stay in . . . without a mother, without a father, without a sister, Lord, without a brother."[20]

And in the traditional African American sense, family is extended to the community. The community, according to all three of my sources, is also responsible for rearing the African American child in "this mean world." While Billingsley called upon authors and publishers to produce racially relevant reading materials, he also cited racialized community organizations such as the church and Operation PUSH, led by Jesse Jackson, whose organizational goal included teaching "the concept of somebodyness. 'I am somebody! . . . I may be poor, on welfare, in jail, persecuted, but I am somebody . . . I'm God's child!'"[21] The love that the child garnered from the family and the community, Billingsley stated, should transform into self-love, which was again the way that much of the African American middle class typically associated with Racial Uplift thought about combating the degradation of White supremacy.

According to Billingsley and Comer/Poussaint, even young children are aware of themselves as racialized beings.[22] Yet these children, as members of the African American and mainstream U.S. cultures, must learn to cope and be successful in both. To do so, the child's self-esteem should be fostered and supported by his/her family and community. Additionally, children should be minimally politicized, although they should be taught about their human and civil rights. "Excessive hostility," even in the face of oppression, is frowned upon as potentially counterproductive.

THE BLACK NATIONALIST CONSTRUCTION OF THE CHILD

In contrast, children were highly politicized by Malcolm X, the Black Panthers, and others in the Black Nationalist Movement of the 1960s and 1970s. Malcolm X, whom I have discussed previously, eventually parted with the Nation of Islam and began the Organization of Afro-American Unity (OAAU). Founded in 1965 and initially led by Malcolm X, the OAAU was a Black Nationalist organization that advocates unity and the self-determination of African peoples in the United States. In a speech to a "delegation of thirty-seven teenagers" from Mississippi, Malcolm X made his perceptions of the youth clear.[23] Primarily, he was adamant that children be made fully aware of themselves as racialized beings, which includes a thorough knowledge of their history and the tyranny of White supremacists. In addition to seeking knowledge, Malcolm X encouraged the young audience to be critical thinkers, which he defined as the ability to gather information from as many sources as possible and then to draw their own conclusions.

He stated, "The most important thing that we can learn to do today is think for ourselves."[24] Blind obedience to the system, and to some Black leaders (e.g., those who advocated Blacks serving in the military), was dangerous. Again, Malcolm X advocated independent and critical thought, because "[i]f you don't do it, you'll always be maneuvered into a situation where you are never fighting your actual enemies, where you will find yourself fighting your own self."[25] Armed with this critical approach, Malcolm X politicized children; he attempted to make them aware of themselves, as racialized beings, in relationship to the hypocrisies of the U.S. government, White supremacist discourse, and the ideas of Black leaders he thought were misguided. In addressing the youth directly and advocating critical thinking, self-defense and self-determinism, Malcolm X perceived the young as having agency, of being separate from adults and capable of acting on their own. But he knew they were young, and might not always be fully capable of discriminate and intelligent action on their own. In that case, he told his audience, "if you don't feel you're qualified to do it, we have some brothers who will skip in . . . and help train you and show you how to equip yourself and let you know how to deal with the man who deals with you."[26]

Another Black Nationalist/Self-Defining organization, the Black Panther Party, evolved from the Student Nonviolent Coordinating Committee and the Civil Rights Movement. As the members of the African American church have long referred to one another by using the titles "Brother" and "Sister," so too did the Black Nationalists. This sense of community as family extended to the construction of the child and child rearing. The Black Panther Party's newsletters are a useful resource for tracing the Panthers' perceptions of children.[27] From the newsletters, at the outset we see how they countered social scientists who blamed African Americans, particularly women, for many of society's social ills. The Black Panther Party applauded and encouraged parents. Unlike educators with a more middle-class perspective, the Black Panther Party politicized children before taking up their need for basic care and education. Additionally, the Black Panther Party disavowed materialism.

In the newsletter articles geared toward parenting and children, parents were supported and encouraged: "You have given much to your sons and daughters. You have overcome insurmountable forces of evil against you. You have paid the supreme price. You have given to the world your best. Stand behind it."[28] The writer continued by encouraging parents to allow children to be forthright in the struggle and to embrace the ideologies the Panthers thought would address White supremacy more effectively than the ideologies of the integrationists. "Don't let anybody tell you that you have failed. Don't sneak in corners and hide when your children cry 'All Power to the People.' . . . Support them in their struggle."[29]

Jewel Barker, on behalf of the Black Panthers, further politicized children. Barker wrote,

> I have but one child. I gave her to the cause. She works for you, because she knows where Vietnam really is. She said to me one day, she said "Mother, they are not oppressing us in Vietnam, they are not killing the soul brothers in Vietnam, they are not shooting through doors and killing Black women in Vietnam, they're doing it here!"[30]

Children, the Black Panthers asserted, should be knowledgeable about the political issues facing the African American community and the United States in general. Instead of being shielded, they should be encouraged to take a Black Nationalist stand, a position that affirms them as

African Americans, as in Shirley Williams's "Black Child Pledge." Here, children pledge allegiance to themselves and their community:

I pledge allegiance to my Black people.
I pledge to develop my mind and body to the greatest extent possible.
I will learn all that I can in order to give my best to my People in their struggle for liberation.
I will keep myself physically fit, building a strong body free from drugs and other substances which weaken me and make me less capable of protecting myself, my family and my Black brothers and sisters.
I will unselfishly share my knowledge and understanding with them in order to bring about change more quickly.
I will train myself never to hurt or allow others to harm my Black brothers and sisters for I recognize that we need every Black man, Woman, and child to be physically, mentally and psychologically strong. These principles I pledge to practice daily and to teach them to others in order to unite my People.[31]

Clearly, this oath encouraged the child to be grounded in and committed to the African American community. The sociopolitical duality of which the middle class spoke was absent from the Panthers' discourse. Further, the human body is seen as an instrument of the struggle, in contrast to the way Comer and Poussaint took a developmental approach to the child body.[32] And in its socialist ideology, the Black Panther Party put more emphasis on belonging to and bearing responsibility for the community. The relationship between child and community in the Panthers' discourse is more reciprocal than the relationship described in the middle-class discourse, which speaks solely of the responsibility of the community to the child.

In brief, the Black Panthers allowed children a greater sense of agency. But they also understood that children need to be cared for by adults and that adult intervention is even more critical in the lives of impoverished children. Therefore, the Black Panthers instituted the Free Breakfast for School Children Program "designed to serve the people."[33] According to Eldridge Cleaver, one of the party leaders, the

Breakfast for Children pulls people out of the system and organizes them into an alternative. Black children who go to school hungry each morning have been organized into their poverty, and the Panther program liberates them, frees them from that aspect of their poverty. This is liberation in practice.[34]

Clearly children were viewed by the Black Panther Party as being "programmed" into a "cycle of poverty," a cycle that could be counteracted by showing children that they could depend upon the African American community, as opposed to the White governmental structure, for their subsistence needs. But this program had a more immediate function as well:

> The Free Breakfast for School Children . . . was created because the Black Panther Party understands that our children need a nourishing breakfast every morning so that they can learn. . . . It is a beautiful sight to see our children eat in the morning after remembering the times when our stomachs were not full, and even the teachers in schools say that there is a great improvement in the academic skills of the children that do get the breakfast.[35]

In other words, in feeding the children breakfast, not only were their political minds fed, but their bodies were fed and they were better able to learn. The children the Black Panthers referenced, in contrast to those Billingsley and Comer/Poussaint address, were poor and in need of basic services.[36] But in addressing their basic needs, the Black Panthers encouraged the self-esteem the middle class discussed as being so important—but they did so in a more communal and socialistic way than the family-orientated approach of the middle class.

Finally, the Panthers rejected middle-class materialism. They suggested that adults

> make it real for our children. And this is the only way. The only way is through the struggle of our children and generations to come. Not through the birth control pill; no, not through hungry children, not through fine minks and big Cadillacs, and not through money.[37]

According to the Black Panthers, it was through self-definition, self-determination, political awareness, and community activism that African American children would become best prepared to cope with an oppressive society. This contrasted with the accommodationist position of the African American middle class, which tended to put a disproportionate burden on the children by telling them, in essence: "Be thick-skinned." "Bear up." "Learn to become stoical."

All the parties discussed here—Billingsley (a social scientist), Comer and Poussaint (two pediatric physicians), and members of the Black Panther Party—viewed the African American child as racialized and as subject to oppression. No one suggested that issues of race and oppression be kept entirely away from children because of their youth and their presumed innocence. In fact children, as such, were seen as more vulnerable to White supremacy than adults. Therefore, they believed adults should encourage a skill set that helped children cope and hopefully thrive in a discriminating environment. However, the manner by which this was to be accomplished in the middle class and in the Black Nationalist group contrasted noticeably. The middle class encouraged building children's self-esteem through family and community ties. The middle class would shield children from receiving too much knowledge, whereas the Black Panthers would have children become fully politicized and politically aware. Moreover, according to the Panthers, children were to be active members of the liberation struggle and encouraged in this role by the community. Self-esteem was important in the Black Panthers' construction of the child, but the Black Panther Party saw it as evolving in the struggle for human and civil rights. The unspoken question in this debate may well have been this: What are *we* (the adults) willing to do about it (the oppression of our children)?

THE BLACK CHRISTIAN CHURCH'S AND THE NATION OF ISLAM'S CONSTRUCTIONS OF THE CHILD

Everyone in the Black community of the late 1960s and early 1970s did not agree with the Black Nationalist agenda of groups like the Black Panthers. The National Baptist Convention, for example, rejected the Black Power ideology outright, as well as any church-affiliated organizations that sought to bridge the two (e.g., the National Conference of Black Christians).[38] This rejection of the Black Nationalist agenda by the church of the late 1960s was ironic "since at their inception, the black churches were highly nationalistic," if for no other reason than because they sought to have a culturally relevant theology and place to worship away from the prejudiced gaze of Whites.[39] According to Peter J. Paris, the church shunned the Black Power agenda because it "came from outside the established ecclesiastical framework" with "language and symbols . . . [that were] alien to the tradition of black churches" and, more importantly, because the church has historically refrained from engagement in controversial issues.[40] And like proponents of the Racial Uplift movement, the church leadership had always distanced itself from those who "implicitly or explicitly attacked the black churches and . . . [its] traditions."[41] The community, Paris stated, divided into basically two ideological camps: the Black Nationalist camp and the groups comprising the Black church. However, the National Conference of Black Christians did publish "A Statement by the National Committee of Negro Churchmen" (aka the National Conference of Black Christians) in the July 31, 1966, issue of the *New York Times*, concluding that Black Power was actually communal power.[42]

The Black church, then and now, meets a multitude of individual and community-based needs. In fact, it is the center of the Black community. It has a spiritual function, no doubt, but it also addresses academic and community-based education and provides economic, social, and political services and advocacy.[43] It is the largest Black organization in existence, and as such has a tremendous and often self-reflective influence on the entire community (of which children are a part). On the practical level, children are perceived by the Pentecostal church community as needing "training" for a future as committed Black Christians. While academic education is important, as seen in the annual graduation and commencement awards and ceremonies that highlight school-based success, religious education is also important and twofold—scriptural education as well as church etiquette are offered. Sunday school and morning worship services are both places where religious "training" is conducted. The construction of the child through the structure of services reflects the church's curriculum and pedagogical ideologies as well as economic influences.

Prior to the 1960s, "old churches" were usually one- or two-room buildings. In the late 1960s and early 1970s, as congregations became more financially able, they purchased larger buildings with a sanctuary, pastor's office, and small basement with cooking and dining facilities.[44] Here, Sunday school classes would be divided throughout the sanctuary and the basement. The class divisions were, and still are: Cradle (0–3 years old), Sunshine Band (4–7 or 8 years old), Youth Group (8–10 or 12 years old), Teens (13–18 years old), Young Adults (18 to approximately 26, but always single with no children), Adult (over 26, married or a parent).[45] Each class would have an age-appropriate version of the Sunday school text. The teachers for the Cradle through to the Teen classes were usually women, and literacy was expected of the students. The teachers for the Young Adult and Adult classes were usually men, or a woman and a man working together, and the participants, as products of migration and Jim Crow school systems, were not necessarily expected to be fully literate.

Children in the church of the late 1960s and 1970s were discussed by the leadership as the "Church of Tomorrow" and as such were trained to take leadership roles through such events as Youth Day, often a designated Sunday (e.g., the third Sunday of the month), where the Sunshine Band sang and the youth filled the roles usually held by adults, from usher to the speaker for the day.[46] Another training opportunity existed in the Sunday school. Derral Anderson, pastor of Assembly of Love Full Gospel Center in Markham, Illinois, stated that this system was called "triple training" among the pastors of the local community.[47] The program allowed for at least three generations of women to be ministered to on any given Sunday. Since the Sunday school held age-based classes, mothers had an opportunity to fully engage in worship services or classes unencumbered with child care, and the young children received age-based care or spiritual education.

The training did not end there. The Sunday school teachers who taught the children were established members of the church community and were often schoolteachers. Most of these teachers had a girl or young woman (10–19 years old) assigned to them who acted as a teacher's aide.[48] In her role as teacher's aide, the young woman taught—and learned—the biblical curriculum, church etiquette, and child care skills, all of which she was expected to use in the family as an assistant to her mother and in her life as a Christian. The young woman's training completed the third portion of the triple training program in which three members of the family—the mother, the young child, and the adolescent girl—were all ministered to and groomed for a Christian life of leadership. Women were knowingly targeted for this training program because they constituted the majority of the church's membership, and because "the scope and breath of the church was such that its teachings encompassed the whole of life within the Black community."[49] By contrast, boys were often groomed to be deacons, ministers, and pastors.

Also wanting a religious-based education for their children, the Nation of Islam (NOI) maintained schools, the University of Islam (K–8) in Detroit and Chicago for its children. A Muslim sect, the Nation of Islam was founded in 1931 by Fard Muhammad. It was based on a syncretic version of Islam that enmeshed biblical scriptures and Qur'anic verses.[50] Elijah Poole (aka Elijah Muhammad) was the second leader of the NOI. Under his leadership, the NOI remained relatively unknown by the majority of Blacks. It was not until Malcolm X became a minister of the NOI that its membership and notoriety escalated.

As the most well-known minister of and spokesman for the Nation of Islam during the 1960s, Malcolm X offers a glimpse of how the Nation constructed the child. Malcolm X's mission was to teach the truth, a truth that would free Blacks from oppressive Christian ideologies. His goal was to instill spiritual and ethnic pride.[51] The first step toward this goal was education, and for Malcolm X that meant knowledge of Black history and White tyranny. According to Hank Flick, he

> used the concept of Blackness to foster pride and to change the self-concepts of Blacks. Not only did he wish to have his auditors accept their Blackness, but to wear it with pride. Blackness was seen as an asset and not as a badge of personal inferiority.[52]

By focusing on Blackness, Malcolm X was able to connect African Americans to their African past and present. The foundation of the Nation's message, as explained by Malcolm X, was that (1) Allah (God) is Black, (2) "Blacks were descendants of the original man, and (3) Blacks were the Bible's lost sheep and were destined to be separated from white America."[53] Resisting the well-known images of a European (White) Christ and the accompanying belief that God is White, Elijah Muhammad portrayed Allah as Black. He stated, "We were black in the very beginning of the creation of the father who was black."[54]

Not only is Allah Black, but all humans evolved from Black people:

> Original Man was Black, in the continent called Africa where the human race had emerged on the planet Earth. The Black man, the original man, built great empires and civilizations and cultures while the white man was still on all fours in caves.[55]

With this foundation, the Nation asserted that Blackness, although associated with a painful history in the United States, was a source of pride.

With self-esteem restored, the next step in Malcolm X's agenda was racial segregation based on the idea that Blacks are the biblical lost sheep:[56]

> [T]he so-called Negroes, are the people who are the lost sheep, who are returned to their own in the last days. He [Elijah Muhammad] says that we are also referred to in the Bible, symbolically, as the lost tribe. . . . lost until the end of time. Lost in a house that is not theirs, lost in a land that is not theirs, lost in a country that is not theirs, and who will be found in the last days by the Messiah who will awaken them and enlighten them, and teach them the desire to come together among their own kind and go back among their own kind.[57]

The teachings of the Nation of Islam and Black history were the venues through which the "lost sheep" would find a "new land and a new identity."[58] According to Malcolm X, this "new land" was exclusively Black, since "White America is doomed. Death and devastating destruction hang at this very moment in the skies of America."[59] Further, separation from Whites was necessary, since, as Malcolm X stated, "[n]owhere in the scriptures did God ever integrate his enslaved people with their slave masters. God always separates his oppressed people from their oppressor and then destroys the oppressor."[60]

Malcolm X's message to the Black community sought to increase Black self-esteem through a discourse that reversed the ideology of White supremacy with Allah and the original man being Black (not White) and that—for cultural, religious, and economic health—encouraged racial segregation. For children, this message encouraged racial and religious segregation. Children were constructed as benefiting from a critical education of their history as racialized beings and were taught to be proud of their ethnic heritage.

Overall, the Black religious organizations, the traditional Christian churches, and the Nation of Islam all sought to educate their children spiritually and practically. In the churches of my community, this educational agenda was rhetorical and logical, and evolved through the 1960s and 1980s in relation to children as "tomorrow's church" and children as "today's church." Children moved from being marginal members of the larger congregation to members with services geared toward them. The Nation's emphasis sought to educate its children through a discourse that emphasized their history as African Americans and as the children of a Black God. With religious education as their mainstays, in a political atmosphere that sought racially relevant education, both the Nation and the Christian church instituted schools of their own. Beyond their theological and political positions, both the Nation of Islam and the Christian church valued education and ethnic pride and tried through training and rhetoric to instill the same in their children.

The community agreed that Black children, like their White counterparts, needed to be prepared for their economic futures. But unlike White children, Black children were perceived as needing to be prepared to live their lives as racialized beings. Every aspect of their lives—cultural, political, and economic—would be informed by race.

JOHNSON PUBLISHING COMPANY AND THE CHILD

Johnson Publishing Company did not begin its "construction" of the child with the publication of *Ebony Jr!* The child and related parenting issues were a part of JPC publications from the very beginning. As mentioned in previous chapters, there was something related to children in each JPC magazine. Beginning with *Negro Digest*'s "Color in Social Work," children were described as racialized beings, and the color of an adopted child, as well as the adopting parents, was deemed important. In conformity with its overarching Racial Uplift ideology, JPC saw children as in need of self-esteem. But unlike the approach of Black Nationalists, JPC's approach did not construct children as needing to be too aware of their political position as African Americans.

For example, the cover story for the inaugural issue of *Ebony Magazine* was "Children's Crusade," an article written by "Reverend A. Ritchie Low, a White pastor who was trying to eliminate [racial] bias by taking Harlem Blacks to Vermont farms for their annual vacation."[61] Noteworthy is the integrationist and middle-class position of this article. Children were constructed as racialized, and integration and interracial understanding were encouraged. Children were considered so integral to the community that they were included in the romance magazines such as

Tan (in a child care column and in "Teen Talk"). One of the most important moments in JPC's history covering the child was the report of the
lynching of fourteen-year-old Emmett Till. This incident and its published
description, more than any other, demonstrated the palpable reality of the
child as a racialized entity in the United States.

JPC also took an active role in speaking to racialized children, not
only in its magazines but in its hardcover books as well. All the titles
published by JPC Hardcover Division were written for and about
Blacks, and a significant number of them targeted children. All told,
children have always had a place in JPC's publications and have been
seen as needing a racialized education. The intended result was an increase in their self-esteem and preparation for a literate future as middle-class citizens.

THE CONSTRUCTION OF THE CHILD READER OF *EBONY JR!*

Some of these same assumptions were carried about the politicization
of children from various factions of the African American community
into the pages of *EJ*. The child was treated as someone with an imposed
race-defined identity. That is, the Black child would be judged in the
dominant society only in terms of White-constructed mythologies
about race and about Africans in particular. Consequently, children
needed lessons on their racial and ethnic history and culture, an education that would probably (if presented in the school system) be inac-
curate and incomplete. Further, children were thought to bring an interest in their African and African American history and culture with
them to their reading of *EJ*. Children were not explicitly told how important learning history would be to them; their interest was assumed.
Moreover, African American mores and values were presented in *EJ* in
an unquestioned manner, since children were perceived as having ac-
cepted these values or being in need of indoctrination. But children
were not politicized in the manner of the Black Panther Party or other
Black Nationalist groups. Articles dealing with politics and current affairs were noticeably absent. Child readers were positioned in relation
to other children who looked like themselves, presumably with the assumption that seeing a Black child in a text was rare and that it would
increase the readers' self-esteem.

Two constructions of the child appear at the outset. It is assumed that
the child readers of *EJ* were interested in literacy-building materials, as
were the parents. The first construction was that children were interested in their African and African American historical and cultural connections. Second, children were racialized beings, and knew it. One has

only to look at the format of *EJ* and note the centrality of narratives, theme, activity sheets (under Van Brunt Johnson's tenure), reader responses, and academic exercises. The perception of the child as interested in literacy events was actually the foundation of *EJ*, as seen in the way John H. Johnson highlighted "reading mastery" and the child's "highly literate future."[62]

Additionally, *EJ* assumed an interest in literary materials, as in Phyllis Johnson's "Langston Who? The Langston Hughes I Knew." The author stated, "Would you like to hear more about this man, Mr. Langston Hughes? You can find out about him in the library. If you can't get to the library by yourself, do as Mr. Hughes suggested in one of his books entitled 'Ask Your Mama!'"[63] In addition to presupposing that the child was interested in literacy, literature, and a famous poet, *EJ* assumed that the family and community were interested as well. This assumed that readers had access to a library in either the school or the community that had racialized children's literature.

From the first issue of *EJ*, African and African American history and culture were at center stage. Many groups within the African American community were discussing and defining *Blackness* and the need for a racially relevant education, but irrespective of the adult conversations, the child readers were perceived as a good audience for African and African American subject matter. In the inaugural issue, Africa was brought to the foreground as the ancestral home of African Americans. And, as per the *EJ* formula, the craft project coincided with the theme of the issue, with a column about how to make "An African Mask Is in Your Kitchen." The text of the column stated,

> You can make an African mask at home with some of the things you have in your kitchen. Before you begin, there are a few things you should know about African masks. The African artist never made a mask to look just like a person. The artist used his imagination when he made a mask. . . . Sometimes the artist made masks of animal spirits with horns or long teeth.[64]

As discussed earlier, college students of the 1960s had been calling for a racially relevant education and had been largely supported by the Black leadership. The underlying assumption of *EJ* was that the child readers were also interested in an ethnic-specific curriculum and specifically in the recapturing of ancient history and art forms.

In relation to self-awareness as well as self-esteem, it was assumed that children needed instruction in defining themselves as African American or that they needed a channel through which to negotiate these issues.

Reader responses illustrated this point further. In the October 1976 issue, the second-prize winner of the writing contest for ten- to twelve-year-olds, Jossie Dunham, wrote a story about a Blackfoot Indian chief who wanted to beautify his land. Jossie stated that Chief Chaka "called everybody and said, 'Our home looks like a slum, it's so dumb looking. Other tribes will think we're bums. I want you all to paint our home. Let's put a little soul in it!'"[65] Historical and cultural inaccuracies aside, this text reinforced the idea that the African American child was comfortable with language that connected with a Black lexicon and speech pattern.

But the Black child was constructed holistically. Like mainstream children, the *EJ* child readers were assumed to like adventure; to want to be independent of adults; to have a life outside of school that was equally as important as school, if not more so; and to be socially oriented. Therefore, children were seldom shown as receiving adult assistance. They were primarily depicted in community settings with other children, as opposed to school settings and in the company of adults.

READERS' RESPONSES AS JPC CONSTRUCTED THE CHILD

Johnson Publishing Company constructed the child reader in part through the readers' responses. Not only was *EJ* overflowing with children's original stories, poems, letters to the editor, and artwork, these items were probably "discussed" (screened) by the editors. According to Johnson, letters to the editor for *Ebony Magazine* were "discussed"—that is, excised if too critical and/or not aligned with his goals for JPC. Johnson's micromanagement style may have extended to the close supervision of readers' responses for other columns in *EJ* as well.[66] Such a practice—whatever the intention—along with the magazine's layout, articles, tone, and graphics, "constructed" the child reader in accordance with JPC's ideologies of childhood and its desire to sell the magazine through adult buyers.

With this in mind, I will use Wolfgang Iser's interpretation of Kurt Wolff's idea of the "intended reader" to discuss how JPC "constructed" the Black child reader. "Wolff—with his intended reader," Iser stated, "sets out to reconstruct the idea of the reader which the author had in mind."[67] In order to "reconstruct" this child, one must, according to Wolff, offer

> relatively detailed knowledge of the contemporary reader and of the social history of the time, if the importance and function of this intended reader are to be properly evaluated. But in any case, by characterizing this fictitious reader it is possible to reconstruct the public which the author wished to address.[68]

The reader envisioned by the text, or in this case by JPC, within the historical moment of the text, came to the surface in the magazine's well-calculated reader response sections.

Columns that featured the readers included *"Ebony Jr!* News," "Writing Readers," "From Our Readers," *"Ebony Jr!* Art Gallery," and the annual writing contest. These columns, and the printed responses, supported *EJ*'s mission and also produced a profile of its intended reader. It was rare to see a reader's response that disagreed with an issue or in any way disapproved of *EJ*. Almost all the responses followed a formula that I discuss below. Again, in the Racial Uplift tradition of JPC, no negative criticism was allowed. Such a policy is still in effect with *Ebony*.

Children's responses corresponded to the following pattern. The child identified him- or herself: "My name is Craig Stephen Powell. I'm eleven years old and I'm in the fifth grade."[69] Then the appreciative reader praised *EJ* and talked about the many things he or she enjoyed in the magazine, or rather the "book." (For some reason the children, irrespective of age, usually referred to *EJ* as a book, not a magazine.) Dewayne Thomas wrote, "I enjoy reading your books. I think *Ebony Jr!* is a great book because it helps young people. I like the play called 'The Other Side of the Mirror: A Look at Black History," in the February 1981 issue."[70] This writer took the trouble to provide the date of the issue, whereas most of the children just listed some articles or characters they enjoyed.

The formula continued with the child either stating how important reading was to him or her or continuing the praise of *EJ* by encouraging the publisher to "keep up the good work." Dewayne Thomas continued, "I hope that you keep on making more and more plays like this one. I just hope and pray that you keep publishing these books because I wouldn't be able to do without them. I enjoy reading Sunny and Honey."[71] Sometimes the reader created the notion of a community of readers, of *EJ* being popular, as when Ryan Johnson stated, "I saw one of the issues that my friend let me hold and I went out for my own."[72]

Under Van Brunt Johnson's leadership, more so than the other editors, photos accompanied the readers' responses and the children listed their schools. Since the photos were handled in such a uniform manner, I am led to believe that *EJ* staff members took the photos at school while on a sales call or classroom visit. In addition, in many, the telltale cinderblocks of many schools' interior construction are evident in the background of the photo. In the 1980s the photos continued but were less frequent and less uniform, suggesting that some were sent in with the letters or gathered with the letters from whatever source. The photos functioned as a mirror for the child readers. Especially in the early 1970s, when there were not many images of African American children in mainstream print, the photos were a way to suggest to the readers that they were part of a community of racialized readers who all read *EJ*.

In conjunction with the use of photos as images of the readers, the editor also contrived the *"Ebony Jr!* Art Gallery." In the May 1973 issue, there was a call for drawings:

> Black people have beautiful and exciting faces. We come in many different colors and have a wide variety of features. If you follow the steps on this page you will be able to draw a picture of your own face. When you have finished your drawing, send it to me so that I can see how beautiful you are![73]

Again, *EJ* provided one of the few opportunities for the African American children to see themselves reflected in print, and this opportunity would be used to reflect images of them that were defined as beautiful.

BUILDING A WORLDWIDE COMMUNITY

More than any other editor, Constance Van Brunt Johnson attempted to make connections between the African American child reader and the Diaspora.[74] Van Brunt Johnson, whose vision structured *EJ*, included numerous stories, features, and "games and things to do" about Africa and, to a lesser degree, other parts of the Diaspora. She aligned the messages of *EJ*'s narrative with the definition of Diaspora as that which

> embodies the following: the voluntary and forced dispersion of Africans at different periods in history and in several different directions; the emergence of a cultural identity abroad without losing the African base, either spiritually or physically; the psychological or physical return to the homeland, Africa. Thus viewed, the African diaspora [sic] assumes the character of a dynamic, ongoing and complex phenomenon stretching across time and geography.[75]

When Karen Odom became editor, stories about the Diaspora decreased greatly although there were the occasional "games and things to do" that featured the Diaspora. While Africa loomed largest in the overall discourse, the Caribbean was included to a lesser degree, with South America rarely mentioned.

As discussed previously, the inaugural issue of *EJ* was specific in that it represented Van Brunt Johnson's view of *EJ* without reader response. As such, this issue contained three stories that had Africa as their theme: "A Story from the Nile," about Egyptian architects; "Kwame and the Lion," the story of the connection between an African American boy and a caged lion; and "Over the Ocean, Over the Sea," which told of the pride a female protagonist felt when an important visitor from Africa commented on how her beautiful, natural-textured hairstyle reminded him of home. There was also an activity sheet, "Lost with the Maroons," that discussed how Africans enslaved on an island ran away and hid in the mountains.

In the mountains, "legend says that every Black man who got away or escaped slavery was sure to find a pot of gold at the end of the rainbow."[76] In an activity sheet readers were instructed to find the letters in the illustration to spell the name of the island: Bermuda.

All of these features were an attempt to construct the child readers' identity as it connected readers with their African ancestry and to those of African ancestry around the world. This precedent continued. Throughout Van Brunt Johnson's tenure as editor, Africa, and sometimes the Caribbean, was presented in each issue of *EJ* via history, folklore or contemporary fiction and nonfiction, and activity sheets. Johnson's work focused on the migration from Africa to North America: connecting the African American child readers to Africa as their ancestral home or to the Caribbean as a place with others from the same ancestral home; defining Africa, and by extension the African American child, as beautiful; and, aligned with *EJ* tradition, representing the Diaspora primarily free of Whites.

As mentioned before, the editors of *EJ* assumed that the child readers had some basic information about slavery, including that Africans were captured, enslaved, and transported to North America and the Caribbean (South America was rarely featured) and that these Africans were the child readers' ancestors. The migration of Africans to North America was discussed primarily through metaphor, as in Robert Green's "The Ebony Tree and the Spirit of Christmas." After being told how beautiful, strong, and resilient he was by his mother, the mother told the little ebony seed that "[i]n due time . . . a wind will come and blow you away. You will land someplace in the forest's soil and become a great ebony tree yourself!"[77] The wind did come and carry the seed away; eventually the "wind became stronger and stronger. Soon a terrible wind storm swept through the forest!"[78] Eventually he landed on the deck of a ship and was placed in the pocket of a little boy who was "very sad about being taken away" from his homeland in Africa.[79]

After retrieving the seed from a rat whose strong jaws could not break the seed's shell, the boy picked up the shell, put it in his pocket, and was pleased to have a remnant from his homeland to comfort him on his journey. Through the journey and landing in North America, the seed and the boy had the same emotional and physical experience: "When the little boy was frightened, his heart pounded and pounded. The little seed was frightened whenever he heard the pounding of the little boy's heart because their journey was very fearful."[80] Once he arrived on a plantation, an old woman who spoke the little boy's language told him that he had arrived during "a time called 'Christmas' which was much like the first harvest season at home."[81] After reminiscing about the harvest season, the little boy realized that "if the seed were going to live to be a greet tree, like its ancestors in the forests at home, it would have to be planted soon."[82]

After planting the tree the boy recited

> words that his own father had spoken to him. . . . "Little seed, grow into a tree
> so tall and strong that you will lift your branches toward the heavens, for there
> is the source of strength. Sink your roots deep into the soil for there is the
> source of life. Stand firm in rain and wind, for there is the source of endurance.
> Drink deep from the waters of life, for there is the source of love and beauty."[83]

Eventually, the boy became a man and the seed became "the greatest tree in the forest."[84]

Although ebony trees are indigenous to West Africa, one cannot fail to make the connection between *EJ* as the seed and *Ebony* magazine as the adult tree and between the seed and the child reader. The story clearly was a message to the child readers that, as did their ancestors in the guise of the little ebony seed and/or the little boy, they came from beautiful, strong people who had endured the middle passage, slavery, and a racist society, and that if they were connected to spirit, were grounded in community, and loved life, they would, like the seed and the boy, grow into remarkable adults. But before this occurred, they would have to endure "a wind [that] will come and blow you away"—a wind that may become a storm.[85] Clearly, the wind and storm are life's challenges. Within the context of the story, these challenges may be race related. Again, race related or not, obstacles can be overcome.

The mentioning of the rat also spoke to the living conditions aboard ship. Could the rat also be a metaphor for White oppression and the hard shell being that which was necessary for the Africans' physical and psychic survival? And as they usually did in stories about Africa, in an attempt to connect the United States and Africa—and, by extension, the child readers and their African heritage—a correlation is made here between Christmas in the United States and the harvest season in Africa. The prayer the little boy spoke over the seed was for himself, the tree, and, by extension, the reader. The seed and the little boy used spirit, community, stamina, and love of life to endure life's challenges and White supremacy. These sources of personal strength were ones that adhered to all the political agendas prevalent in the African American community of the 1970s. They are also ones that child readers could incorporate to endure a racist society.

The use of the storm to represent life's challenges is a common theme in *EJ*'s stories appearing in other narratives, such as Jean Brannon's "Phillis Wheatley" in January 1976. Of Wheatley's journey, Brannon wrote,

> The trip across the ocean was long, frightening and terrible for the small African. She was chained and crowded among hundreds of other slaves who had been kidnapped. She had to endure hunger, thirst and all types of extreme weather conditions while sailing the rough waters.[86]

Clearly, for those knowledgeable about African American history, this referenced the weather and traveling conditions of the Middle Passage.

But not all the lessons on how African Americans arrived in North America were through metaphor. While the capture, enslavement, and transportation of Africans was *rarely* discussed in *EJ*, the story "Phillis Wheatley" told of how, as a young girl of seven or eight, Phillis was "taken from her mother and placed aboard a slave ship bound for the continent of North America."[87] Once she made it to North America, she was sold to Mr. Wheatley, who took her home to his wife who "welcomed the child, bathed her, dressed and fed her hot porridge."[88] Phillis, "happy in her strange, new surroundings" learned English, how to read and write, and eventually wrote poetry and a letter to George Washington.[89]

The absent White presence that "takes Phillis and places her aboard a slave ship" and the benevolence of her master, as discussed earlier, avoided insulting White advertisers. It also avoided the quandary DuBois faced with *The Brownies' Book*—teaching African American children about their history and the backlash of anger that was destined to arise in them. Most relevant to this discussion, this story was one of the few that told the reader that Africans were kidnapped and brought to North America, as, for the most part, basic knowledge about slavery was assumed. Also noteworthy about this piece was its adherence to the self-help agenda of *EJ*—that even though she was a slave, Phillis worked hard academically and was a success, based on the limitations of her sociopolitical position. This message, through *EJ*, was clearly one the editors wanted the child readers to get.

Although they were among the few times when African migration to North America was discussed, these two stories represented the nature of the image of Africa Van Brunt Johnson posited in *EJ*. Africa was presented as the homeland of all Blacks, but specifically African Americans. Other narratives postulated and affirmed an Afrocentric cultural identity and gave credence to the necessity of a psychological return to Africa for the child readers' emotional and cultural well-being.

In addition to providing information about the Diaspora, *EJ* offered a counternarrative of Africa and her people as beautiful with a rich and varied history, compared to the demeaning one children may have garnered from the mainstream press or school.

For example, although it was produced in 1949 and eventually censored, I remember seeing "Which Is Witch" as a child in the 1970s. In this Bugs Bunny cartoon, Dr. I. C. Spots, an African "witch doctor," prepared a concoction for which he needed a rabbit as an ingredient.[90] Dr. I. C. Spots was portrayed in the minstrel style as a short, jet-black man with white lips and a big red nose. He lived in "Kuka Munga," a small village

of huts surrounded by a jungle that included palm trees. His home had
African masks on the walls and a big cauldron in the center of the room
where he made his potion. After the addition of each ingredient, he
danced around the pot with a spear and shield. His language was a
stereotypical minstrel-like representation of African speech patterns. The
women, who walked through a number of frames, were silhouettes—
faceless black figures with large, protruding lips; they walked in the lazy,
slow-witted style of Stepin Fetchit.[91] Because Dr. I. C. Spots needed a rabbit for his potion, he tried to capture Bugs Bunny. But as we all know,
Bugs is a trickster and eventually evaded Dr. I. C. Spots.

The physical and linguistic representation of Dr. I. C. Spots and the
women of his community were derogatory and aligned with White
stereotypes of Africa, and of African Americans as uncivilized, uneduca-
ble White mimics. These are the images *EJ* fought to resist through its historical, current, and folkloric representation of Africa.

In "Treetop Terri," Teresa Ann (aka Terri), who at eleven years old was
five feet, seven inches tall, was ridiculed by her classmates because of her
height. For her, "[b]eing a tall girl just wasn't fun."[92] One day Terri grew
tired of the teasing and bolted from the classroom. Having run for quite a
distance, Terri found herself outside the Garvey Theater.

> Soon she had slipped through the heavy theater door and stood swaying
> with the drumbeat and staring at the graceful dancers on the stage. Terri
> forgot all about being too tall and drifted with the proud sway of the
> dancers. "Hello there." The soft voice startled Terri and she whirled around
> to find herself looking up into the dark face of one of the tallest girls she'd
> ever seen![93]

The girl, whose name was Lisette, was a member of the National Dance
Troupe of Burundi. She explained to Terri, who again lamented her
height, that "in our homeland, many of us grow to be near 7 feet or more.
We are the Watusi and we are famous the world over for our tall beauty
and graceful dancing."[94] Terri continued to complain about her height,
saying that as an eleven-year-old she was still growing, to which Lisette
responded, "Oh, how lucky you are. . . . Already, I'm 14 and not yet 6 feet
in height! I wish I grew as you do. Then I could join the dance troupe instead of only minding the costumes. I want to grow tall enough to be one
of the dancers so badly!"[95]

Hearing her new friend's emotional response, seeing how she "stood
tall and proud, like a queen," Terri, who slumped to appear shorter,
"straightened herself up and held her chin high just as Lisette did. Terri
wanted to be as tall and graceful and beautiful as Lisette and the
dancers."[96] After saying goodbye to her new friend, Terri returned to

school a changed girl. She decided that "being Treetop Terri isn't bad at all."[97] When the teacher asked her where she had been, "Terri smiled and stood gracefully, even beautifully, 'I went to learn about the Watusi dancers. I may grow tall enough to be one someday you know. . . . And even if I don't grow tall enough to be a Watusi dancer, I'm going to be the tallest, most beautiful treetop you've ever seen!'"[98]

Clearly Terri's introduction to the Watusi and an Afrocentric orientation gave her another framework by which to evaluate herself, one that was more aligned with her physicality and one that affirmed her. This paradigm also defined Terri as beautiful and facilitated her construction of herself as graceful and thus proud of her body. Further, it was no coincidence that the theatre is named after Marcus Garvey. This created a clear correlation, to the informed reader, between Garvey's Black Nationalist politics and activism, the nature of the dancers' performance, and the theme of the story. References to Garvey were slight, for example, the theater or a street named after him, but they were, under Van Brunt Johnson's editorship, present.

As soon as Van Brunt Johnson's editorship ended, Africa was featured much less frequently. Articles still appeared, but they did not emphasize the Diaspora and the child's place within this worldview. Instead, they featured articles such as Independence Day celebrations of various countries; other stories featured the natural resources of various nations within the Diaspora.

Even though *EJ* constructed the child as a racialized being (although not always an oppressed one), *EJ* itself was constructed as solely an educational magazine, without advertisements for material goods other than JPC products related to *EJ* and articles highlighting books to buy. In December 1973 JPC started to advertise *Ebony Jr!* Books. The ad read, "This Christmas Give *Ebony Jr!* Books for the younger reader." The ad then listed five books for readers of various ages, from *Li'l Tuffy and His ABCs*, by Jean Pajot Smith, to *The Ebony Book of Black Achievement*, by Margaret Peters and illustrated by Cecil L. Ferguson, for older readers. The only other regular advertisement was for Sunny and Honey dolls that were sold beginning in the December 1973 issue:

> In time for Christmas! Just what you've been waiting for your own Sunny and Honey. They follow you from the pages of *Ebony Jr!* right into your home. Sunny and Honey will be with you in person as you read their humorous antics in *Ebony Jr!* A unique and inspirational toy for young readers.[99]

Social awareness was an aspect of African American life that reached new heights in the late 1960s and 1970s.[100] It was a cornerstone of the Black Nationalist discourse and of works by African American educators such as Na'im Akbar and Asa Hilliard.[101] These scholars joined the discussion as they encouraged pedagogical methods focused on "sociocentric" methods.[102] The child reader of *EJ*, prior to the 1980s and continuing afterward, although to a lesser degree, was constructed as being socially oriented but also as someone to be shielded much more than either Hilliard's or DuBois's pedagogical philosophy would suggest.[103] DuBois noted in *Black Reconstruction*:

> One is astonished in the study of history at the recurrence of the idea that evil must be forgotten, distorted, skimmed over. . . . We must forget that George Washington was a slave owner . . . and simply remember the things we regard as creditable and inspiring. The difficulty, of course, with this philosophy is that history loses its value as an incentive and example; it paints perfect men and noble nations, but it does not tell the truth.[104]

In a similar vein, Hilliard advised against any suppression of the historical record—the scholar's best chance in the quest for truth. He wrote in "Why We May Pluralize the Curriculum":

> Under the old white supremacy system, the white European culture was considered both "universal" and "superior" . . . [Curriculum must] proceed . . . from the assumption that there is truth in the whole of human experience. Valid scholarship must be the source of curriculum content. Children can handle the truth, warts and all.[105]

The stress on individualism in the 1980s was, arguably, more compatible with JPC's endeavors than the collective solidarity and candor that were imperative in the civil rights struggle. Including children in that solidarity and candor may have constituted, ultimately, the best shield.

CONCLUSION

Like any other publication targeting children, *EJ* constructed the child according to the political position of its publisher. The staff of *EJ*

> intended to motivate reading mastery and strengthen the preparedness of Black children for a highly literate future. . . . [This would be done through] biographies of famous people, stories, games, science stories and child-centered Black history.[106]

With this precise agenda, *EJ* constructed the child as racialized culturally and linguistically and as liking to learn. But the child readers of *EJ* were not viewed as needing an awareness of political or current events, although they were exposed to African American history and culture, which was arguably a political act itself. Through the reader response columns, we saw that children enjoyed *EJ*, specifically an article or two, reading *EJ* with family or friends, and encouraging *EJ* to continue to be published. Children often discussed how important the information about Africa and African American history and cultures was to them. In addition, readers had an opportunity to see images of children who looked like them racially. Because *EJ* incorporated children throughout the Diaspora, it attempted to create a sense of community throughout the world. This attempt to construct the child was one that reinforced *EJ*'s mission, and one, I assume, the editors believed would sustain sales.

NOTES

1. Aidan Chambers, "The Reader in the Book," in *The Signal Approach to Children's Books: A Collection*, ed. Nancy Chambers (Metuchen, NJ: Scarecrow Press, 1980), 253.

2. An arm of the NAACP, *The Crisis* was begun in 1910 by W. E. B. DuBois as a tool to combat the oppression of Blacks. It is still being published.

3. W. E. B. DuBois, "The True Brownies," *Crisis*, October 1919.

4. Ibid.

5. In my construction of the child reader of *EJ*, I am considering the mainstream African American child. I do not consider "deviants" or children being serviced by the social welfare system.

6. Shirley R. Steinberg and Joe L. Kincheloe, "Introduction: No More Secrets— Kinderculture, Information Saturation, and the Postmodern Childhood," in *Kinderculture: The Corporate Construction of Childhood*, ed. Shirley R. Steinberg and Joe L. Kincheloe (Boulder, CO: Westview Press, 1997), 1.

7. Andrew Billingsley, *Black Families and the Struggle for Survival* (New York: Friendship Press, 1974).

8. James P. Comer and Alvin F. Poussaint, *Black Child Care: How to Bring up a Healthy Black Child in America: A Guide to Emotional and Psychological Development* (New York: Simon & Schuster, 1975).

9. Benjamin Spock, *Baby & Child Care* (London: Bodley Head, 1969).

10. Billingsley, *Black Families and the Struggle for Survival*; Comer and Poussaint, *Black Child Care*.

11. W. E. B. DuBois, *The Souls of Black Folk* (1903; reprint, New York: Dover, 1994), 2.

12. Comer and Poussaint, *Black Child Care*, 11.

13. Ibid., 12.

14. Billingsley, *Black Families and the Struggle for Survival*, 58.

15. Comer and Poussaint, *Black Child Care*, 64.

16. Ibid., 64–65.

17. Ibid., 9.

18. Ibid., 13.

19. Billingsley, *Black Families and the Struggle for Survival*, 62.

20. Bernice Johnson Reagon, "This Is a Mean World," in *Sweet Honey in the Rock: In this Land* (New York: Warner Bros. Records, 1985).

21. Jackson, cited in Billingsley, *Black Families and the Struggle for Survival*, 57.

22. Ibid.; Comer and Poussaint, *Black Child Care*.

23. Malcolm X, "To Mississippi Youth," in *Malcolm X Speaks: Selected Speeches and Statements*, ed. George Breitman (New York: Grove Press, 1965), 137.

24. X, "To Mississippi Youth,"137.

25. Ibid., 138.

26. Ibid., 146.

27. Philip S. Foner, ed., *The Black Panthers Speak* (New York: Lippincott, 1970).

28. Jewel Barker, "A Word for Panther Parents," in *The Black Panthers Speak*, ed. Philip S. Foner (New York: Lippincott, 1970), 164.

29. Ibid., 165.

30. Ibid., 164–65.

31. Shirley Williams, "A Black Child Pledge," in *The Black Panthers Speak*, ed. Philip S. Foner (New York: Lippincott, 1970), 24.

32. Comer and Poussaint, *Black Child Care*.

33. Eldridge Cleaver, "Community Activities," in *The Black Panthers Speak*, ed. Philip Sheldon Foner (New York: Lippincott, 1970), 167.

34. Ibid.

35. "Free Breakfast for School Children," in *The Black Panthers Speak*, ed. Philip S. Foner (New York: Lippincott, 1970).

36. Billingsley, *Black Families and the Struggle for Survival*; Comer and Poussaint, *Black Child Care*.

37. Foner, *The Black Panthers Speak*, 165.

38. Wilmore, as cited in Peter J. Paris, *The Social Teaching of the Black Churches* (Philadelphia: Fortress Press, 1985).

39. Errol Henderson, "War, Political Cycles, and the Pendulum Thesis: Explaining the Rise of Black Nationalism, 1840–1996," in *Black and Multiracial Politics in America*, ed. Yvette M. Alex-Assensoh and Lawrence J. Hanks (New York: New York University Press, 2000).

40. Although the SNCC, the organization from which the modern black nationalist movement arose, had its beginnings in the church it nevertheless distanced itself through its attack of traditional black leaders, as stated in Paris, *The Social Teaching of the Black Churches*.

41. Paris, *The Social Teaching of the Black Churches*, 120.

42. Ibid.

43. Hank Flick, "A Question of Identity: Malcolm X's Use of Religious Themes as a Means for Developing a Black Identity," *Negro Educational Review* 31, no. 3–4 (1980).

44. Derral J. Anderson, personal interview, 2003.

45. Ibid.

46. Ibid.

47. Ibid.

48. Girls are also groomed for positions such as missionary, members of the Hospitality Committee, choir director and/or member, and church secretary.

49. Flick, "A Question of Identity: Malcolm X's Use of Religious Themes as a Means for Developing a Black Identity."

50. Randall O. Ali, "The Foundation: Women in the Nation of Islam" (unpublished thesis, University of Iowa, 1998).

51. Flick, "A Question of Identity."

52. Ibid., 147.

53. Ibid.

54. Ibid.

55. Elijah Muhammad, "Are We the Black Muslims?" in *The Rhetoric of Black Americans*, ed. James L. Golden and Richard D. Rieke (Columbus, OH: Merrill, 1971), 407.

56. The parable of the lost sheep is located in two places in the Bible: Matt. 18:12–14, which I cite here, and Luke 15:3–7. In the book of Matthew, Jesus is recorded as stating,

> If a man have an hundred sheep, and one of them be gone astray, doth he not leave the ninety and nine, and goeth into the mountain, and seeketh that which is gone astray? And if so be that he find it, verily I say unto you, he rejoiceth more over that sheep than over the ninety and nine which went not astray. . . . [I]t is not the will of your Father, who is in heaven, that one of these little ones should perish.

C. I. Scofield, Arthur L. Farstad, and Thomas Nelson Publishers, eds., *The New Scofield Study Bible: King James Version* (1909; reprint, Nashville: T. Nelson, 1967).

57. James Farmer and Malcolm X, "Separation or Integration," in *The Rhetoric of Black Americans*, ed. James L. Golden and Richard D. Rieke (Columbus, OH: Merrill, 1971), 433.

58. Ibid.

59. Malcolm X, "God's Judgement of White America (The Chickens Come Home to Roost)," http://www.malcolm-x.org/speeches/spc_120463.htm.

60. Benjamin Goodman, ed., *The End of White Supremacy: Four Speeches by Malcolm X* (New York: Merlin House, 1971), 72.

61. John H. Johnson and Lerone Bennett, *Succeeding against the Odds* (Chicago: Johnson Publishing, 1989), 160.

62. Flick, "A Question of Identity," 151.

63. "Johnson Introduces Magazine Designed for Black Children," *Jet*, May 10, 1973, 52.

64. "An African Mask Is in Your Kitchen," *Ebony Jr!*, May 1973, 32.

65. Josie Dunham, "The Painted Desert," *Ebony Jr!*, October 1976, 11.

66. Johnson and Bennett, *Succeeding against the Odds*, 9.

67. Ibid.

68. Wolfgang Iser, *The Art of Reading: A Theory of Aesthetic Response* (Baltimore: Johns Hopkins University Press, 1978), 32–33.

69. Ibid., 33.

70. "From Our Readers," *Ebony Jr!*, February 1981, 40.

71. Ibid.

72. Ibid.

73. Ibid.

74. First used to describe a session, "The African Abroad or the African Diaspora," of the 1965 International Congress of African Historians held in Tanzania (Ranger, cited in Joseph E. Harris, "Introduction," in *Global Dimensions of the African Diaspora*, ed. Joseph E. Harris [Washington, DC: Howard University Press, 1982], 3), the term Diaspora gained notoriety when it was used in the title of a 1979 conference at Howard University—the First African Diaspora Studies Institute. This conference was "aimed to assess African diaspora (sic) studies and to explore new ways of strengthening links between African and African American scholars" (p. 4).

75. Ibid.

76. Ibid., 5.

77. Robert Green, "The Ebony Tree and the Spirit of Christmas," *Ebony Jr!*, December 1973, 56.

78. Ibid., 57

79. Ibid.

80. Ibid.

81. Ibid.

82. Ibid., 61.

83. Ibid.

84. Ibid.

85. Ibid., 56

86. Jean Brannon, "Phillis Wheatley," *Ebony Jr!*, January 1976, 12.

87. Ibid.

88. Ibid.

89. Ibid.

90. Fritz Freleng, "Which Is Witch" (Warner Bros., 1949).

91. Stepin Fetchit was the stage name of Lincoln Theodore Monroe Andrew Perry, a controversial African American character actor whose performances as lazy and slow witted insulted many African Americans.

92. "Treetop Terri," *Ebony Jr!*, November 1974, 7.

93. Ibid., 8.

94. Ibid.

95. Ibid., 9.

96. Ibid.

97. Ibid., 10.

98. Ibid.

99. "In Time for Christmas!" *Ebony Jr!*, December 1973, 45.

100. Billingsley, *Black Families and the Struggle for Survival*; Comer and Poussaint, *Black Child Care*.

101. Akbar, as cited in Janice E. Hale-Benson, *Black Children: Their Roots, Culture, and Learning Styles* (Baltimore: Johns Hopkins University Press, 1982); Asa Hilliard, *Alternatives to IQ Testing: An Approach to the Identification of Gifted Minority Children* (Sacramento: California State Department of Education, 1976).

102. Hale-Benson, *Black Children*.

103. Hilliard, *Alternatives to IQ Testing*.

104. W. E. B. DuBois, *Black Reconstruction* (1935; reprint, Cleveland, OH: World Meridian, 1964), 722.

105. Asa Hilliard, "Why We Must Pluralize the Curriculum," *Educational Leadership* 49, no. 4 (1992): 13–14.

106. "Johnson Introduces Magazine Designed for Black Children," 52.

Conclusion

The Ebony Tree and the Spirit of Christmas

The little ebony seed lived in the forest with his father, mother and hundreds of aunts and uncles, who were the great ebony tees. As was the tradition, his mother told him the story of the great ebony trees and how they were the strongest and toughest trees in the forest. She told him that the ebony trees were prized for their beautiful, hard, black wood. [The seed was blown onto a ship and taken from] his homeland in Africa and was very sad about being taken away. . . . [E]ven the strong jaws of the rat could not break the hard shell of the little ebony seed. The rat tried and tried, but could not open the little seed's hard shell! [On board the ship the seed meets a little boy who keeps him warm and takes him with him.] Soon the little boy was rushed off the ship and over the land to a huge plantation. He was taken to a tiny cabin where other men, women and children from his homeland were living. . . . One old woman, who spoke the boy's language, told him that he was lucky to come at such a cold time of the year [since it was Christmas]. [Eventually, the little boy planted the tree and said a prayer over it.] [T]ime passed and the little boy grew and returned many times to the place where he planted the ebony tree. And as he did he saw that the tree grew taller and stronger. . . . The little ebony seed, after traveling so long and hard a journey, had begun its new life as the greatest tree in the forest of the new land.—*Ebony Jr!* author Robert Green

During the late 1960s and early 1970s, there were multiple calls for racially relevant and culturally accurate literature for Black children. Black and White educators, as well as the Black community in general, knew of the dearth of literature for Black children and supported literary achievements in the 1970s and 1980s through such sources as the Coretta Scott King Book Award, the Council for Interracial Books for Children, and Title VI monies. Children were also the focus of some Civil Rights activism, as in their participation in school desegregation. And in its efforts to garner adequate educational opportunities for children, the NAACP developed its anti–Jim Crow struggle by reforming nationwide educational programs that were allegedly "separate but unequal."

Winning the *Brown v. Board of Education* case was only a small step toward desegregating public facilities and obtaining an adequate education for Black children. The legal battles of the NAACP were complemented by the initiatives of Civil Rights activists, who boycotted, marched, and braved White-induced violence to desegregate southern schools. In the North, busing was the primary tool used to desegregate schools. White-led violence accompanied these efforts as well. While a case can be made that desegregation eliminated one form of "tracking," it actually meant that many Black children who were transferred to White schools with better facilities were placed in slow and remedial courses, which effectively segregated the classroom, if not the school.

However, desegregated schools were not the only way to access better education for Black children. Black Nationalists such as those in the Nation of Islam chose segregated Black-run schools with racially relevant curriculums. Other Black Nationalists called for racially relevant curricula at all levels of public education. As this work demonstrates, a sociopolitical analysis of *EJ* clarifies the manner in which the leading political ideologies of Racial Uplift, Civil Rights activism, Black Nationalism, and, possibly, the Black church informed the "construction" of children in the community and in the pages of *EJ*.

Responding to the call for a magazine for Black children, John H. Johnson looked to the precedent available in White children's magazines. Since there was nothing similar for Black children, he made the decision to call for a racially relevant education and set about publishing *EJ* from 1973 until 1985. *EJ*, as alluded to in the story "The Ebony Tree," sought to increase Black children's self-esteem through an educational magazine. It posited the importance of basic literacy skills (e.g., reading, math, and science skills) along with a Black history curriculum that connected African American children to a racialized history in the United States and the Diaspora. As such, it was rare and accompanied by only a few other magazines throughout history that attempted to do the same. Although children's periodicals experts applauded *EJ*, and sales sustained it for twelve years, *EJ* was not without it critics.

POLITICAL CONSCIOUSNESS AND *EBONY JR!*

While Black Nationalist politics surely informed *EJ*, it was predominantly aligned with the Racial Uplift agenda. Consequently, one can look to Black Nationalism for a severely critical (if indirect) treatment of *EJ*. Although much of the criticism is of *Ebony* and other JPC publications, Black Nationalists have provided insights that may well have pertained to *EJ*. Larry Neal "insisted [that African American] journals be black at all levels of involvement, from owner to reader" and *EJ* as a JPC magazine fit that bill.[1] But that was not enough. According to Eddie Ellis, *Ebony* "was headed distinctly in the wrong direction, straight into the pockets of white businessmen profiting off the delusions of many Afro-Americans."[2] In Ellis's two-part article "Is *Ebony* a Negro Magazine?" he stated, "*Ebony* has no loyalties to the Negro people. . . . *Ebony* has NO identification with, or loyalties to, the other 30 million BLACK captives in America."[3] The assumption here is that these "30 million Black" people adhered more to a Black Nationalist agenda than to one connected with Racial Uplift. In support of his position, Ellis (and later Jerry Watts) noted the advertisements in JPC publications for items that were racially problematic. Ellis referred to products

> for lightening the skin and straightening the hair—and the models looking like Anglo-Saxons [which] encouraged readers to "de-identify" with blackness. The advertisers of Dr. Fred Palmer's Skin Whitener, among other items, were profiting off *Ebony*, and they were almost exclusively white.[4]

While Ellis's criticism of Johnson's business tactics is understandable from a political perspective, it did not take account of the day-to-day realities of running a business in a racist society. Nor did it consider that Johnson, in essence, was a businessman—not a politician, scholar, or political activist. But in an effort to assist Johnson in redirecting his publications along Black Nationalist lines, Neal stated, "We [Black Nationalist writers] must support existing firms like Johnson publications, force them to publish meaningful work by deluging them with the best that we have."[5]

Later criticisms of *Ebony* were also enlightening. For example:

> Every month since 1945, the slick pages and photo-heavy profiles of *Ebony* magazine have chronicled its readers' upwardly mobile obsessions. Singers' homes are saluted (the June cover story is "Luther Vandross's $8.5 Million Hide-away"); athletes' salaries celebrated; mayors, judges, and congresspeople coddled. . . . Overall *Ebony*, the flagship of the black-owned Johnson Publishing empire, provides regular indoctrination in the Positive Image Mentality that dominates the public utterances of black leaders.[6]

What Nelson George called "Positive Image Mentality" (PIM) was actually the Racial Uplift ideology that has dominated JPC publications from the beginning. It was, according to George,

> tunnel vision that sees all success stories as benefiting the race-role models for the young, proof we can compete on white terms. It is an elitist worldview that serves establishment blacks—the middle-class Dr. King's efforts helped expand—but doesn't help the black masses. PIM loves achievement and ignores accountability. PIM creates a conspiracy of silence that muffles self-criticism.[7]

Not only did the continuation of a Racial Uplift agenda "silence [healthy] self-criticism," it also, as an outdated ideological position, alienated many younger readers from JPC publications.

Jerry Watts also criticized *Ebony*, calling it and *Jet* "frivolous," with "obscene displays of black conspicuous consumption."[8] "Historically," Watts stated, "*Ebony* has aggressively celebrated the anti-intellectual core of black bourgeois ostentatiousness."[9] While Watts degraded *Jet* as a "modern-day ethnic gossip column," he also noted that it "carries ethnic news that cannot be found in other magazines."[10] Like George, Watts criticized the regular inclusion of athletes' and entertainers' "de facto press releases."[11] In short, he took issue with the bourgeois leaning of JPC and its Racial Uplift agenda.

I suspect that Watts, George, and Neal would all applaud *EJ* for its African American–centered orientation and educational curriculum. But I think they would also have strong reservations about its conservative representation of Black history, its exclusion of a White subject (culprit) in the Black history narratives, its consumerist and classist tone in the 1980s, and its failure to overtly prepare children for a political future.

In essence, because JPC has been the most stable African American magazine publisher and the only publisher of Black magazines in many categories over a number of years, JPC magazines have often been the only thing the African American community has had. Like it or not, *Ebony*, as a Black picture magazine, has no contemporary. Similarly, *EJ* had no contemporaries that combined academic and racialized curricula. In its beginning, it was "cool" and "hip" and politically relevant as it presented an appropriate, racially sensitive curriculum encased in historically accurate narratives and activities.

However, as the political climate for Blacks changed, *EJ* did not change sufficiently. Many of the popular culture references were removed in the late 1970s. And while the editors began to offer career education in response to the tightening economic climate in the Black community, they did so (I would argue) in a manner that child readers would probably find uninteresting. In addition, the layout changed, with the print appearing smaller and the number of words increasing per page—all things that I find unattractive. In essence, the times changed and *EJ* did not change significantly enough to stay active. Therefore, what began as an educational tool ended as a relatively irrelevant and bland magazine. And "[b]y virtue of its allegiance to PIM, [one of] the most famous black [children's] publication in the world . . . [became] anachronistic and maybe even obsolete."[12]

For the purpose of this study, the more important question is: What was JPC trying to teach African American children? Certainly its intentions were admirable:

> *Ebony Jr!* seeks to reflect the happiness, spontaneity and tremendous creativity which are a part of black childhood, and to provide opportunities for the development of the skills and self-confidence which are so essential to the transformation from childhood to productive and successful adult life.[13]

EJ's educational curriculum was in accordance with this transformative goal. The curriculum was well rounded in that it offered reading, math, science, social science, and arts and crafts activities. The activity sheets allowed the reader to interact with *EJ* as well as to practice some of the skills that the children should have been learning in school. And in the beginning *EJ* was marketed as a supplement to the standard White-dominated educational curriculum. Aligned with various segments of the Black community (e.g., the church), *EJ* attempted to increase children's self-esteem and racial pride by offering an African American–centered magazine that taught Black history and culture and excluded whites (thereby skirting the problem of "teaching hatred" to children). *EJ* also avoided politicizing the child, although readers were encouraged to embrace community-centered values. Missing were any references to political positions, in contrast to the Black Panthers' child-centered programs. In short, happiness and racial pride were fostered; creativity was encouraged through writing contests and arts-and-crafts columns; and an educational tone was sustained that made *EJ* marketable to its buyers: adults.

Hans Robert Jauss argued that "we ought to study the way a contemporary audience receives a literary work and to pay attention to the way the attitude toward a work alters over time."[14] Jauss suggested that one interesting project might be to take a nineteenth-century text and present it to a modern audience. Questions to consider would include "[w]hat made the books popular, the reasons for their disappearance, and their current revival (at least in the academy)."[15] This would allow access to how "readers are formed and how trends change."[16] This study has investigated the way the Black child reader of *EJ* was constructed as a racialized being in the 1970s and 1980s. The next section considers *EJ* as a component of African American literature.

EBONY JR! AS PART OF THE
AFRICAN AMERICAN LITERARY TRADITION

Literature and politics have always been linked for the African American community; to be sure, the literature had its very origins in slave narratives and, canonically, has maintained the struggle for human rights as its focus. In this section, I will briefly discuss the history of African American adult and children's literature and theory, locating *EJ* within each genre. Since JPC publications were aligned with Racial Uplift, they present African Americans in the best light for themselves and for Whites. In addition, JPC provided a venue for the Black Arts Movement through *Black World*. But it would be erroneous to say that *EJ* was specifically aligned with the Black Arts Movement, since Johnson held many of the tenets of the Black Arts Movement prior to its articulation in the late 1960s.

For example, from its inception JPC's goal was to address a Black audience with news about and images of itself. That said, *EJ*'s publication coincided with the Black Arts Movement, and its editorial staff was surely informed by it. *EJ* presented its materials from an Afrocentric perspective; its narrative subjects and form (as well as illustrations) were grounded in the African American experience; it offered a collective history; and it reflected the cultural, social, and political concerns of the community and its children. It did not offer "melting pot" texts in which the child protagonist could be any child.[17] It was not produced for the enlightenment of Whites. *EJ* was written for and about African American children, so that no other groups, save Africans, were included on a regular basis. *EJ* was also grounded in teaching an Afrocentric education. The educational component of this orientation aligned *EJ* with other children's periodicals of its time. The racialized component of the instruction addressed the call for culturally relevant education, and served as a marketing ploy for parents.

The illustrations in *EJ* during Constance Van Brunt Johnson's tenure as managing editor emphasized the African American community and popular culture. Although Sunny and Honey appeared to be darkened White children in the May 1973 issue, their appearance was changed in the June/July 1973 issue and clearly encoded as African American children. Honey had her hair in Afro puffs, a popular Afrocentric hairstyle of the day, and Sunny was stylishly dressed in platform shoes and plaid pants.[18] Noteworthy was the fact that it was the illustrations that changed, not the narrative content. Sunny and Honey remained dressed and groomed in accordance with the current African American fashion of the day until, as mentioned in chapter 1, Mary Lewis became editor. During this time, the illustrator for Sunny and Honey changed from Michael Davis to Buck Brown, and the illustrations changed accordingly.

Ebony Jr! always privileged the African American perspective, and Africans and African Americans were always the topics. Even though the discourse on multicultural education and desegregation loomed large at the time, throughout *EJ*'s entire run, the editors made no attempt to present a multicultural view that included those outside the Diaspora. In short, there were very few non-Black people existing in the world *EJ* constructed. As for a multiethnic cast of characters, one of the few examples I found (other than popular culture celebrities) was in the February 1974 issue. "Nandi's Surprise" was about the first day of school for a child from Africa and the many questions the children had about the continent. Because of the students' interest in "other cultures," the teacher decided to sponsor an international festival. In response, one student said, "I'll bring some Chinese food. . . . [While another said,] I can bring a dancer's costume from Mexico."[19] The girl who offered to "bring the dancer's costume from Mexico" was identified as a Latina, presumably from Mexico, in that her name was Esperonza. The illustrations for this piece included children who were coded as ethnically diverse: two Asian boys and one Asian girl, one Latino boy and one Latina girl, several Black children, four White children, and a Black teacher. Other than this, and a few other instances, the world of *EJ* was Black, with people from other cultures rarely appearing. In every issue, there was at least one article that focused on Africa, one about African American history, and something about culture or prominent members of the community in an effort to educate and instill ethnic pride.

For example, in the August/September 1976 issue, an article appeared about the Harlem Globetrotters, titled "Magical Scenes from the Harlem Globetrotter's [*sic*] Popcorn Machine"; an article about Yvonne Burke, "A Congresswoman's Scrapbook"; and a craft project about making East African dolls. In a political climate where African American students were fighting for a relevant curriculum in high schools and colleges, *EJ* offered such curricula to young readers. It offered a version of our "collective memories or consciousness" in that stories of mostly precolonial Africa, slavery, the South, Emancipation, and northern migration were commonly highlighted. Further, the editors assumed that readers had some knowledge of these topics prior to their reading. It must be said, however, as noted above, that the version of history told by *EJ* was firmly middle-of-the-road.

Although the purist may say that *EJ* was not literature proper, it did adhere to the tradition of African American literature in the way it acknowledged the struggle for civil and human rights. And while I believe that *EJ*'s politics (as well as the politics in most JPC publications) were grounded in the Racial Uplift ideology, it did adhere to many of the tenets of the Black Aesthetic. But knowing where *EJ* was located in African American literature still leaves us with the question: Where was *EJ* located in the history and tradition of African American children's literature?

As discussed before, various issues sparked an increase in the publication of African American children's literature from the late 1960s to the 1980s. These factors included the call for racially relevant education, Nancy Larrick's article that highlighted the omission of Black children from text and trade books of the 1960s, the rise of the Civil Rights Movement and a corresponding call for racially relevant education, the $1.4 billion available to schools under the Elementary and Secondary Education Act of 1965, and the Coretta Scott King Book Award.

All of these motivated publishers to produce more materials about African Americans.[20] "Liberal consciences had been deeply pricked by the events of the previous decade, and federal money made it possible for school districts and libraries to spend large sums on books. Thus, a market was created for books about Black children."[21] I turn to Rudine Sims's *Shadow & Substance* for an overview of the status of the image of African Americans in this literature.[22] Using her work will help situate *EJ* within the field of children's literature and discuss how it offered counternarratives to stereotypical representation of African Americans.

Sims conducted a review of children's books written between 1965 and 1979 that included Black children and adults.[23] In so doing, she identified and labeled three basic categories: melting pot books, culturally conscious books, and social conscience books. Sims defined a melting pot book as one totally devoid of Black culture other than including a dark-colored (Black) child in the illustration; the same kind of child existed in social conscience books to "help whites know the condition of their fellow humans."[24] On the other hand, the culturally conscious texts "were written primarily, though not exclusively, for Afro-American readers. These books attempted to reflect and illuminate both the uniqueness and the universal humanness of the Afro-American experience from the perspective of an Afro-American child or family."[25]

Here I will discuss melting pot and social conscience texts and how they intersected with *EJ*. I do not discuss culturally conscious texts, since they did not contain material that *EJ* would have to resist. By so doing, I suggest that while *EJ* was popular ("low") culture, it was nevertheless in a dialogue with the so-called high culture literature and is worthy of analysis in relation to the trends of literature for Black children of the 1970s and 1980s. Although Sims did not say so, she seemed in sync with the Black Aesthetic, as when she wrote that "consideration of the audience to whom books about Afro-Americans are primarily addressed cannot be dissociated from other factors that influence the quality of such books."[26] If a Black child was the target audience, it should be considered in the construction of the text. In addition, Sims noted that although some White authors, such as Ezra Jack Keats, may have produced acceptable African American children's literature, it was the lived experience that offered a greater insight and often a more authentic narrative.

As stated earlier, *EJ*'s form was aligned more with magazines than literature. But neither exists in a vacuum, and *EJ* did resist some of the clichés that Sims noted as recurring in socially conscious and melting pot books. Moreover, *EJ* resisted common stereotypes of African Americans in popular culture and the media. Some of these stereotypes had been gaining support from social scientists. One such social theory was the infamous Moynihan Report: *The Negro Family: The Case for National Action*, published in 1965 by Daniel Patrick Moynihan.[27] It stated that the "deviant Negro family was the 'fundamental weakness of the Negro community.'"[28] Moynihan cited the large number of single female–headed households as the cause of many of the social ills that plagued the African American community. His report perpetuated the misconception that the prominence of Black women in the family structure, not racism, was responsible for "the problems" of the Black family.[29]

Noted Moynihan, "Unless the damage [from this 'abnormal prominence of women'] is repaired, all the effort to end discrimination, poverty and injustice will come to little."[30] Because of the African American's "cultural depravity," Moynihan suggested that the government enter a period of "benign neglect." For the next decade, sociologists, anthropologists, and educators responded to Moynihan by demonstrating that "blame" was being placed on African American institutions, not on the oppressive mainstream culture, organizations, and individuals. "[T]he logical outcome of analyzing social problems in terms of the deficiencies of the victim is the development of programs aimed at correcting deficiencies" as opposed to addressing structural inequalities in institutions.[31] The editors of *EJ* were fully aware of the White supremacist social theories about African Americans and constructed *EJ* in response to such.

In her review of children's literature that included African American characters, Sims found that the images of the African American family changed from melting pot books to social conscience books and in conjunction with prevailing social theories (as, for example, Moynihan's theories about a dysfunctional Black family).[32] Unlike Sims, I will begin with an analysis of the issues in social conscience books and how *EJ* responded to them, since they are similar to many of the political battles the community faced in general. Sims noted that in social conscience books, the authors "had been reading 1960s descriptions of the so-called disadvantaged. The single most frequently occurring phenomenon in the social conscience books is the absent Black father."[33] Sims may have had Moynihan in mind, since he stated that the "deviant Negro family was the 'fundamental weakness of the Negro community'" and the principle culprit was the single Black woman.[34] Since Moynihan was a Harvard-trained academic as well as a U.S. Senator, his report was extremely influential.

But as scholars disputed Moynihan's research, so too did some children's literature. In the melting pot books, says Sims,

> The fatherless families of the social conscience books have been replaced, where families are included, by nuclear families. . . . [F]or the most part, the Black children in the melting pot books have responsible fathers present in the home.[35]

Sims continued,

> Some families are less well off financially, but not because of absent fathers. . . . The nuclear family is the model middle-class American family, although the rising divorce rate suggests that fewer and fewer such families exist.[36]

The family, as constructed by scholars, was reflected in children's literature. One of the ways this evolving family was defined in Black children's literature was by the family members present in the story, with the father often being the interchangeable pawn. Most often, social class was associated with his presence or absence. *EJ* responded to the discourse about the dysfunctional African American family by encouraging solidarity and extolling the family. And the African American community as a whole countered the aspersion on the family by solidarity against White supremacy in academic and popular forms.[37]

In the pages of *EJ*, where there was a family, there was a father. Even if he was not an active character in the story, he was, nevertheless, mentioned and his absence explained (e.g., he was described as being at work). Through the entire tenure of *EJ*, images of the family included a father. For example, Van Brunt Johnson instituted the Phonics Loonicans, a cartoon family that exposed child readers to phonics lessons. As stock characters, the Phonics Loonicans family was complete with a father. Not only did the cartoon families have fathers, so did families in the fiction and nonfiction narratives. For instance, in November 1973, the Goins family was highlighted in an article titled, "Goins and Goins: Family Racers." The Goins family was described as being rare because "[t]here are not very many other Black drag racers in the whole country"—not because it was a nuclear family with the father in the home.[38]

In the 1980s, Karen Taha's short story, titled "Tina's Present," was about a girl who talked incessantly and who (because she had not planned appropriately) gave her father the gift of her silence for his birthday.[39] In text and in illustration, the father was present. In the same issue, "Brother Obie's Saturday" depicted the way Obie walked around the neighborhood doing errands for his mother. Although the father was not present in the story, he was nevertheless mentioned as being present in the home.[40] The editors of *EJ* consciously resisted the image of the Black family as fatherless by including a father in the story even when he wasn't necessary for the plot. As such, it sought to "talk back" to the stereotype Moynihan perpetuated.

Another issue *EJ* addressed was making the language familiar and engaging to children without using idioms and grammatical structure that parents and teachers would find problematic. Aligned with the academic and popular culture discourses about identity, language, and education, *EJ* incorporated idioms and the rhyme and rhythm of Black speech while it steered clear of Black English Vernacular grammar and terms that adults resist as being, if not undesirable, then unnecessary in an educationally oriented publication. And although it did use slang expressions such as "cool," it did not use idioms such as "ain't "or "fixin' to." Although many adults would agree that Blacks need to be competent in Standard English (for economic success) and Black English Vernacular (for community-based social interactions), they do not think that Black English Vernacular should be used with children in a teaching forum such as *EJ*. As an educational tool, *EJ* was sensitive to the issues of the African American community and the pedagogical methods that would accommodate the language the children used on a daily basis in school and in the community.

Sims noted, "For the most part, the Afro-American in the social conscience books speak Standard English, or at least the same variety as that spoken by the non-Afro-American characters."[41] This made the text less than realistic, since for many African Americans in a Black context, Standard English was either not used or, at least, was peppered with words from the Black English Vernacular. In addition, even if Standard English was used, the rhythm of the language usually adhered to the patterns of Black speech.

Ebony Jr!'s editors were very conscious of the rhythm of Black speech and some of its idioms. While the magazine did not incorporate Black English Vernacular, it maximized wordplay through rhyme and rhythm and by incorporating popular terminology. The first issue of *EJ* was full of rhyming, even in texts that were not in poetic form. For example, in "Over the Ocean: A Story from the Nile" from the May 1973 issue, the text rhymes: "Imhotep built a suntower known as 'The Pyramid of Steps,' the first building of its kind and Zozser's final place of rest. Yet even though the Pyramid of Steps was a stairway to the sun, the Egyptian builders at Ghizeh said, 'Our work is not yet done!'"[42]

Another example is "Bobbie and Bubba and The B-A-A-D Babble Apple Mystery." This was a skit about the mystery of a walking, talking apple.[43] Telling Bobbie about the apple, Bubba stated,

> It said, "My name is Fred," and jumped right over my head!
> Bobbie: What said its name is Fred and jumped over your head?
> Bubba: I don't know just what to say! Did you see an apple come this way?[44]

Notice the use of the term "B-A-A-D" as a popular term for that which is really hip. Also notice the verbal quality of the two "A's," as well as the way the text, although not a poem, still rhymes. Even as an adult, I find the rhythm of the language appealing and playful, and I would suspect that I might have felt the same as a child. Another illustration of language usage that might have been appealing to the child reader was "Get It On!" a story by Frankie Cox. "Get it on" is a common expression used to begin a fight, as in "let's get it on"; it was also the title of a very popular Marvin Gaye (1971) song, where it meant to have sex. It is the fighting, not the sexual, connotation that was used in *EJ*. The story, like the title, led the reader to believe that two boys would have a fight, and a battle did occur (a battle with marbles, not with fists). As Sims noted, the use of Black English Vernacular, popular vocabulary, and the rhythms of Black speech go a long way in making a text authentic—and, I would add, appealing to the reader.[45] Since the Black community was the target audience, *EJ* reflected the African American culture in terms of language.

Another issue of interest in the community, one that *EJ* covertly addressed, was colorism. As discussed earlier, JPC had a history of including African Americans of varying hues in their publications. It privileged brown-skinned models, excluding dark brown or ebony-colored models.[46] The color of the models was noteworthy in that during the mid-1900s and beyond, when Johnson was publishing, lighter-skinned African Americans were considered, even in the African American community, to be more attractive. In much of the literature that Black children of the mid-to-late-twentieth century were exposed to, lighter-skinned Blacks were noticeably privileged. Sims noted,

> *It you're white, all right; if you're brown, stick around; if you're black, stay back.*
> This attitude is expressed in several of the social conscience books, often by a Black character. It suggests that beauty, and perhaps goodness, are determined by how closely one's physical characteristics resemble those of Euro-Americans.[47]

The editors of *EJ* were cognizant of this issue and addressed it in various places. Readers were told that African Americans come in varying shades and that all the shades are beautiful, as in "Draw Yourself," by Maya Sharpe in the May 1973 issue. The instructions stated that Black people have "beautiful and exciting faces."[48] Of the culturally conscious texts, like *EJ*, that showed varying hues, Sims stated,

> The culturally conscious books provide an interesting contrast to the social conscience books in terms of the image used to describe the various skin coloring of Afro-Americans. While Huck suggests that such descriptions are unusual in children's fiction, they abound in the culturally conscious books.[49]

More importantly, the coloring mirrored for children the communities in which they probably lived, and hopefully showed them their own beauty. The (White) mainstream and even their own community may have been saying otherwise. The popular singer/composer James Brown sang, "Say it Loud, I'm Black and I'm Proud" in 1969, but Toni Morrison's first novel, *The Bluest Eye*, discussed what could happen to the African American who is not considered beautiful and who is not proud. In showing multiple skin colors (except for the darkest brown), the editors of *EJ* tried to increase the African American child readers' self-esteem. By incorporating issues such as colorism, *EJ* made itself relevant to the racialized reader.

It also made it culturally authentic, another issue Sims examined. In her survey, she found that

> the recurring phenomenon that most readily distinguishes the melting pot books from the social conscience books and the culturally conscious books [was that] without the illustrations one would have no way of knowing that the story was about an Afro-American child. . . . Nor do they project any distinctly Afro-American experiences or traditions.[50]

The underlying reason for this silence was that many of the books were not written for or about African American children, but instead were most likely written for White children, who represented a normalized reader, or what Sims referred to as "Any Child."[51] Many of the melting pot books, like social conscience books, "though listed in bibliographies of books about Blacks, actually have non-Afro-Americans as main characters."[52] Actually, most vestiges of African American culture were deleted from melting pot books as they "deliberately ignore racial and subcultural differences in their texts."[53] Since, by definition, melting pot books

> assume a kind of cultural homogeneity for their subjects, it is likely that the same assumption applies to their presumed primary audience; melting pot books are not only about Any Child, they are written for Any Reader. It has already been pointed out that they are not intended to reflect any distinct Afro-American cultural experiences.[54]

Ebony Jr! was a virtual "balm in Gilead" for African American child readers in that they, as racialized and cultured beings, were reflected in the pages of the magazine. Although not describing *EJ*, Sims's definition of a culturally conscious text is applicable. *EJ* fits Sims's description of books whose "primary intent is to speak to Afro-American children about themselves and their lives," although, as has been pointed out, they were by no means closed to other children.[55] And as Sims required, the elements of *EJ* (the text, structure, and illustrations) were all clearly and firmly grounded in the African American community.

Like African American adult literature, *EJ* was based in the African American community as it struggled for its civil and human rights. The topics addressed in *EJ* were, for the most part, reflections of the concerns of at least a fraction of the community. Therefore, *EJ*, as a popular culture magazine, should be considered in the trajectory of African American children's literature. It coordinated with the Black Aesthetic and with Sims's definition of culturally conscious texts in that it spoke to the racialized child in form and content. It used some of the idioms of the community and addressed relevant issues of the day such as colorism, Black English, and functional family life.

Sims belongs to a group of African American literary scholars and artists dating from the 1970s and beyond. Other distinguished contributors to African American children's literature and criticism—for example, Eloise Greenfield, Walter Dean Myers, and Sharon Bell Mathis—had their works occasionally included in the pages of *EJ*. But they were also part of the continuous debates about cultural authenticity in children's literature and about the effectiveness of school policies and practices vis-à-vis African American children. As commentators on such matters, they manifested a more radical mindset than the one shaping *EJ*.

For example, poet/storyteller Eloise Greenfield warned of "a gross and arrogant misuse of talent" if writers for children failed to "encourage human development."[56] She emphasized social responsibility in the arts, since

[i]t is true that politics is not art, but art is political. Whether in its interpretation of the political realities, or in its attempts to ignore these realities, or in its distortions, or in its advocacy of a different reality, or in its support of the status quo, all art is political and every book carries its author's message.[57]

People who are writers use word-weapons, noted Greenfield, in these varied political strategies, yet they often "disclaim all responsibility for what they say."[58] They insist upon being "merely objective observers . . . or secretaries transcribing the dialogue of characters over whom they have no control. Is it the writer's fault that the characters just happen to be racists?"[59] Accountability, in other words, cannot be dispensed with in the name of "artistic license" or "entertainment." Greenfield continually reminded the literary world what is owed to children and what is owed to posterity.

From this perspective, *EJ* can be perceived as contributing to the "human development" of readers by attempting to increase their racialized self-esteem. *EJ*'s Afrocentric orientation was consciously constructed by its publisher and editors to boost children's self-image. Moreover, every facet of the black community, from the scholars to the churches, agreed that education was high on the agenda, and John H. Johnson marketed *EJ* on this platform. This education was political in that JPC was owned and operated by African Americans and was competing with the top White-owned corporations. But *EJ* was also political in that the editors chose to delete the White presence from Black history. Greenfield would surely have disagreed with this decision in that it denied the truth of racism and committed omissions similar to the ones committed by White historians. But this position would discount the business necessities of publishing and Johnson's need to maintain White advertisers for his other publications.

Novelist Walter Dean Myers showed the relationship between that powerful authority figure, the school, and the development of self-esteem. He noted the difficulty of helping Black children

> deal with the concept of being less worthy because they are Black, especially when that concept is being reinforced in the school. If you choose to deal with my children then you must deal with them as whole people, and that means dealing with their blackness as well as their intellect.[60]

Ebony Jr! went to great lengths to supply the appreciation of Blackness that Myers deemed basic to children's well-being, while at the same time embracing Racial Uplift conservatism.

Beryle Banfield, a scholar and educator who was also the president of the Council on Interracial Books for Children, was an indefatigable worker on behalf of children's civil rights.[61] In her essay "Racism in Children's Books: An Afro-American Perspective," she outlined the premises on which racism and literature can be effectively studied. For example, she noted that literature reflects "the values of society" and helps reinforce them; that intellectual disciplines provide theoretical "support for these values"; and that communication media broadly disseminate those values.[62] Given such features in education and the media, children's books have a much greater role than simply producing entertainment. If a society is racist, children's books may be a means of perpetuating that negative social reality.[63] Such commentaries from Black professionals suggest the reasons why *EJ* needed to come into being and enter the educational scene as well as the recreational lives of Black children. *EJ* can rightly be seen as working in tandem with other strands in the fabric of Black children's literature. Its demise weakened the whole cloth.

THE DEMISE OF *EBONY JR!*

In his autobiography, John H. Johnson explained why he decided to terminate the production of *EJ*:

> [There was a] declining circulation of a new magazine *Ebony Jr!* . . . [It] hit a peak circulation of 100,000 before dropping to 40,000. The major problems—identification of parents with children in the target age groups and city-by-city sales campaigns focused on boards of education—were solvable, but required more time and more than I was willing to give at the time. After investing more than $2 million, I decided to cut my losses and concentrate on the profitable divisions.[64]

But, as Jerry Watts said of Johnson's response to the end of *Black World*, "This explanation [of the ruin of *EJ*] seems disingenuous."[65] Circulation was only the symptom of a larger problem in *EJ*'s downfall. For one thing, the economic and political conditions in the African American community changed significantly from 1973, when *EJ* began, and 1985, when it folded. The call for self-definition gave way to a call for economic stability. The African American middle class was growing, but at a price: that is, it was often isolated from the community as a whole. Further, the poor were getting poorer and more isolated in urban and rural areas. The clash between them was apparent in *EJ*. Also, Lewis removed the educational activity sheets that, I contend, made it so appealing to teachers and parents concerned with basic literacy, and through which children could have a much higher level of interaction with each issue. Although reading, in and of itself, is a powerful educational tool, many parents may have believed that the worksheets, like the ones they had as children, were an invaluable teaching tool. Without the worksheets, *EJ* was just a literary magazine, and during the 1980s the African American children's and young adult publishing field was supplied with better literature, specifically those highlighted by the Coretta Scott King Book Award.

EBONY JR! RETURNS

After the death of her father in 2005, Linda Rice Johnson assumed the position of CEO of JPC. Like her father, one of her goals for the company is to discover new markets and products. JPC has a history of developing new products to support the corporate structure and the mainstay of the company, *Ebony*. When these products are no longer profitable and cannot be revised, they succumb to the next venture. After the demise of *EJ* in 1985, there was—and still is—no literary periodical targeting African American children. But times and technology have changed in the twenty-two-year gap.

Foreshadowing *EJ*'s online future, a 1982 article, "Classy Computers," summarized the history of computers, their use in schools, and their growing prevalence. The article's focus was allied with *EJ*'s intention to provide entertaining education. According to the article, the appeal of computers for children was that they had become "the most popular form of playtime; a variety of games—from hand-held sports toys to big machines at arcades—are high on any child's list of favorites."[66] The sales pitch for parents was, as always for *EJ*, rooted in education: "Computers have entered the classroom as the latest tool to make learning more fun. . . . [Computer use is becoming more prevalent] as more teachers discover the best ways to include a computer in their lesson plan."[67] Like *EJ*, this article put computers forward as a form of edutainment. It also alluded to the importance of computer access and literacy for children.

In 2002, 83 percent of all U.S. family households with at least one child reported computer ownership, whereas only 71 percent of African American families owned computers.[68] This was a substantial increase over the 39 percent of African American families that owned computers in 2000.[69] Children may also have access to the Internet at school or in the library. This translated into children ages nine to twelve spending an average of 4.4 hours per week online, and those between ages six and eight spending 2.7 hours per week online.[70] Whatever one's position on the intersection of Internet usage and reading, many children are reading less print material and more online texts. These online texts are far less expensive to produce than written texts. Within this environment, JPC has launched an online version of *EJ*. Because there is a lack of literary magazines targeting African American children and use of the Internet has become so widespread, an online version of *EJ* might prove successful for JPC. One can only stay tuned to the site to see how it develops. I suspect that it will not stray far from Johnson and Van Brunt Johnson's original vision.

At the time of this writing, the *EJ* Web site was sparse, but I anticipate that it will be expanded. So far, the Afrocentric focus, stock characters, and urban (Chicago) setting are the same as the print version of *EJ*. The inclusion of a school named JPC Academy may indicate that an educational component will be added. For now, Sunny and Honey continue to use popular vernacular and wear fashionable clothes. In an effort to appeal to contemporary African American children, instead of a doll as their companion, Sunny and Honey have a dog, a cell phone, and video games.

What came to light in my research was the way *EJ* constructed the reader within the context of the Black community. Clearly, *EJ* worked to create a sense of the Black community by defining Blackness and by focusing on Black achievements that were ignored by schools and the White press. Although it admittedly offered a conservative version of Black history, it was fairly consistent in presenting an Afrocentric worldview and in encouraging racial pride and self-esteem in its readers.[71] Black children are currently without an educational and/or cultural magazine targeted toward their growth and their joy. The question remains as to whether the *EJ* online version will have the depth, breath, and readership of the print version.

NOTES

1. Neal, as cited in Abby Arthur Johnson and Ronald Maberry Johnson, "Scholarly Journals and Literary Magazines," in *The Oxford Companion to African American Literature*, ed. William L. Andrews, Frances Smith Foster, and Trudier Harris (New York: Oxford University Press, 1997), 165.

2. Ellis, as cited in Ibid., 5.

3. Eddie Ellis, "Is *Ebony* a Negro Magazine? [Part One]," *Liberator* 5 (1965): 5.

4. Ellis, as cited in Johnson and Johnson, "Scholarly Journals and Literary Magazines," 167.

5. Ibid.

6. Larry Neal, "Some Reflections on the Black Aesthetic," in *The Black Aesthetic*, ed. Addison Gayle (New York: Anchor Books, 1971), 8.

7. Nelson George, "The Ebony Agenda," in *Buppies, B-Boys, Baps & Bohos: Notes on Post-Soul Black Culture*, ed. Nelson George (1989; reprint, New York: HarperCollins, 1989/1992), 115.

8. Ibid., 116.

9. Jerry G. Watts, *Amiri Baraka: The Politics and Art of a Black Intellectual* (New York: New York University Press, 2001), 214.

10. Ibid.

11. Ibid.

12. Ibid.

13. "*Ebony Jr!* Seeks to Reflect the Happiness," *Ebony Jr!*, May 1975, 45.

14. Jauss, as cited in George, "The Ebony Agenda," 116.

15. Jauss, as cited in Roderick McGillis, *The Nimble Reader: Literary Theory and Children's Literature* (New York: Twayne Publishers, 1996), 179.

16. Ibid.

17. Rudine Sims, *Shadow & Substance: Afro-American Experience in Contemporary Children's Fiction* (Urbana, IL: NCTE, 1982).

18. "Sunny and Honey," *Ebony Jr!*, June/July 1973, 22–23.

19. Beverly Mae Brown, "Nandi's Surprise," *Ebony Jr!*, February 1974, 8.

20. Nancy Larrick, "The All-White World of Children's Books," in *The New Press Guide to Multicultural Resources for Young Readers*, ed. Daphne Muse (1965; reprint, New York: New Press, 1997).

21. Sims, *Shadow & Substance*, 3.

22. Ibid.

23. Ibid.

24. Ibid., 14.

25. Ibid., 18.

26. Ibid., 8.

27. For the complete text of the Moynihan report see L. Rainwater, *The Moynihan Report and the Politics of Controversy: A Trans-action Social Science and Public Policy* (Cambridge, MA: MIT Press, 1967).

28. Moynihan, cited in William Ryan, "Blaming the Victim," in *Race, Class and Gender in the United States: An Integrated Study*, ed. Paula S. Rothenberg (1971; reprint, New York: St. Martin's Press, 1998), 520.

29. Paula Giddings, *When and Where I Enter: The Impact of Black Women on Race and Sex in America* (New York: Morrow, 1984), 325.

30. Ibid.

31. Ryan, "Blaming the Victim," 521.

32. Sims, *Shadow & Substance*.

33. Ibid., 25.

34. Moynihan, cited in Ryan, "Blaming the Victim," 520.

35. Sims, *Shadow & Substance*, 42.

36. Ibid.

37. This praise of the family is evident in Sly and the Family Stone's 1972 song, "It's a Family Affair":

It's a family affair, it's a family affair
One child grows up to be
Somebody that just loves to learn . . .
Blood's thicker than mud
It's a family affair, it's a family affair.

38. "Goins and Goins: Family Racers," *Ebony Jr!*, November 1973, 29.

39. Karen T. Taha, "Tina's Present," *Ebony Jr!*, June/July 1981.

40. Cris Parker, "Brother Obie's Saturday," *Ebony Jr!*, June/July 1981.

41. Sims, *Shadow & Substance*, 25.

42. "A Story from the Nile," *Ebony Jr!*, May 1973, 19.

43. Marlene Cummings, "Bobbie and Bubba Meet Mellow Mel," *Ebony Jr!*, November 1973, 10–13.

44. Ibid., 11.

45. Sims, *Shadow & Substance*.

46. It should be noted that my research is being done from microfilm, therefore the shade of the hardcopy may be different than what I can discern from the film.

47. Sims, *Shadow & Substance*, 26.

48. Maya Sharpe, "Draw Yourself," *Ebony Jr!*, May 1973, 40.

49. Sims, *Shadow & Substance*, 70.

50. Ibid., 33–34.

51. Ibid.

52. Ibid., 34.

53. Ibid., 43–44.

54. Ibid., 41.

55. Ibid., 49.

56. Eloise Greenfield, "Writing for Children: A Joy and a Responsibility," in *The Black American in Books for Children: Readings in Racism*, ed. Donnarae MacCann and Gloria Woodard (Metuchen, NJ: Scarecrow Press, 1985), 19.

57. Ibid., 20.

58. Ibid.

59. Ibid.

60. Walter D. Myers, "The Black Experience in Children's Books: One Step Forward, Two Steps Back," in *The Black American in Books for Children: Readings in Racism*, ed. Donnarae MacCann and Gloria Woodard (Metuchen, NJ: Scarecrow Press, 1985), 222.

61. Beryle Banfield, "Racism in Children's Books: An Afro-American Perspective," in *The Black American in Books for Children: Readings in Racism*, ed. Donnarae MacCann and Gloria Woodard (Metuchen, NJ: Scarecrow Press, 1985).

62. Ibid., 23.

63. In a race-centered society, race is continually reintroduced as a political tool. John H. Stanfield noted that "in race-centered societies, races are created as social and cultural constructions and used as political weapons." This means that people are socialized into "the belief that it is 'natural' to assume that . . . phenotypic features predict values, personality, intellectual attitudes, behavior, moral fiber, and leadership abilities." This turns race into an "organizing principle of everyday life, because it facilitates decision making in such matters as self-concept, concept of others, residential choice, hiring and firing in labor markets, and selection of mates and friends." John H. Stanfield and Rutledge M. Dennis, *Race and Ethnicity in Research Methods* (Newbury Park, CA: Sage, 1993), 15.

64. John H. Johnson and Lerone Bennett, *Succeeding against the Odds* (Chicago: Johnson Publishing, 1989).

65. Watts, *Amiri Baraka*.

66. Mary C. Lewis, "Classy Computers," *Ebony Jr!*, January 1982, 10.

67. Ibid.

68. Grunwald Associates, "Connected to the Future: A Report on Children's Internet Use from the Corporation for Public Broadcasting" (2003), http://cpb.org/ed/resources/connected.

69. Ibid.

70. Ibid.

71. McGillis, *The Nimble Reader*, 179.

Bibliography

CRITICAL REFERENCES

Ali, Randall O. 1998. "The Foundation: Women in the Nation of Islam." Unpublished thesis, University of Iowa.

American Library Association. *The Coretta Scott King Book Awards for Authors and Illustrators.* Vol. 2007. Chicago: American Library Association, 2006.

Anderson, Derral J. 2003. Personal interview.

Anderson, Talmadge. *Black Studies: Theory, Method, and Cultural Perspectives.* Pullman: Washington State University Press, 1990.

Andrews, William L., Frances Smith Foster, and Trudier Harris, eds. *The Concise Oxford Companion to African American Literature.* New York: Oxford University Press, 2001.

Asante, Molefi K. "Afrocentricity." In *Dictionary of Race and Ethnic Relations,* edited by Ernest Cashmore, 24–25. London: Routledge & Kegan Paul, 1984.

Bahr, Howard M., Bruce A. Chadwick, and Joseph H. Stauss. *American Ethnicity.* Lexington, MA: Heath, 1979.

Bailey, Ronald W. "Black Studies." In *The Concise Oxford Companion to African American Literature,* edited by William L. Andrews, Frances Smith Foster, and Trudier Harris, 80–82. New York: Oxford University Press, 1997.

Baker, Houston A. *Blues, Ideology, and Afro-American Literature: A Vernacular Theory.* Chicago: University of Chicago Press, 1984.

Banfield, Beryle. "Racism in Children's Books: An Afro-American Perspective." In *The Black American in Books for Children: Readings in Racism,* edited by Donnarae MacCann and Gloria Woodard, 23–38. Metuchen, NJ: Scarecrow Press, 1985.

Baraka, Imamu A., and Larry Neal. *Black Fire: An Anthology of Afro-American Writing.* New York: Morrow, 1968.

Barker, Jewel. "A Word for Panther Parents." In *The Black Panthers Speak*, edited by Philip S. Foner, 164–66. New York: Lippincott, 1970.

Beasley, Edward W. "Father Is Also a Parent." *Tan*, November 1950, 45, 52.

Billingsley, Andrew. *Black Families and the Struggle for Survival*. New York: Friendship Press, 1974.

Byrd, Ayana D., and Lori L. Tharps. *Hair Story: Untangling the Roots of Black Hair in America*. New York: St. Martin's Press, 2001.

Carmichael, Stokely, and Charles V. Hamilton. *Black Power: The Politics of Black Liberation*. New York: Random House, 1967.

Chambers, Aidan. "The Reader in the Book." In *The Signal Approach to Children's Books: A Collection*, edited by Nancy Chambers, 250–75. Metuchen, NJ: Scarecrow Press, 1980.

Claiborne, Craig. "Cooking with Soul." *New York Times Magazine*, November 3, 1968, 102–9.

Clark, Kenneth B. *Prejudice and Your Child*. Boston: Beacon Press, 1955.

Clarke, Caroline V. "A New Johnson Is CEO." *Black Enterprise*, June 2002, 136–37.

Cleaver, Eldridge. "Community Activities." In *The Black Panthers Speak*, edited by Philip S. Foner, 167. New York: Lippincott, 1970.

Coles, Robert. *The Political Life of Children*. Boston: Houghton Mifflin, 1986.

Collins, Patricia Hill. "When Fighting Words Are Not Enough: The Gendered Content of Afrocentrism." In *Fighting Words: Black Women and the Search for Justice*, edited by Patricia Hill Collins, 155–83. Minneapolis: University of Minnesota Press, 1998.

Combahee River Collective. "A Black Feminist Statement." In *All the Women Are White, All the Men Are Black: But Some of Us Are Brave*, edited by Gloria T. Hull, Patricia Bell Scott, and Barbara Smith, 13–33. New York: Feminist Press, 1982.

Comer, James P., and Alvin F. Poussaint. *Black Child Care: How to Bring up a Healthy Black Child in America: A Guide to Emotional and Psychological Development*. New York: Simon & Schuster, 1975.

Condie, Spencer J., and James W. Christiansen. "An Indirect Technique for the Measurement of Changes in Black Identity." *Phylon* 38, no. 1 (1977): 46–54.

Cooper, Wendy. *Hair: Sex, Society, Symbolism*. New York: Stein and Day, 1971.

Cooperative Children's Book Center. *Children's Books by and about People of Color Published in the United States*. http://www.education.wisc.edu/ccbc/books/pcstats.htm.

Cross, William E. *Shades of Black: Diversity in African-American Identity*. Philadelphia: Temple University Press, 1991.

Cruse, Harold. *The Crisis of the Negro Intellectual*. New York: Morrow, 1967.

Dalton, Edwin. "Color in Social Work." *Negro Digest*, December 1942, 62–64.

Daniel, Walter C. *Black Journals in the United States: Historical Guides to the World's Periodicals and Newspapers*. Westport, CT: Greenwood Press, 1982.

Davis, F. James. *Who Is Black? One Nation's Definition*. University Park: Pennsylvania State University Press, 1991.

Dawson, Richard E., and Kenneth Prewitt. *Political Socialization: An Analytic Study*. Boston: Little, Brown, 1968.

De Vos, George. "Ethnic Pluralism: Conflict and Accommodation." In *Ethnic Identity: Cultural Continuities and Change*, edited by George De Vos and Lola Romanucci-Ross. Pal Alto, CA: Mayfield, 1975.

Dixon, Norman R. "Defining the Situation: Toward a Definition of Black Education." *Negro Educational Review* 14, no. 3 & 4 (1973): 114–15.

Dodge, Mary Mapes, ed. *St. Nicholas: Scribner's Illustrated Magazine for Girls and Boys.* New York: Scribner's Sons, 1873.

DuBois, W. E. B. *Black Reconstruction.* 1935. Reprint, Cleveland: World Meridian, 1964.

———. *The Souls of Black Folk.* 1903. Reprint, New York: Dover, 1994.

———. "The True Brownies." *Crisis,* October 1919, 285–86.

"The Ebony Bookshop." *Ebony,* December 1963, 36.

"*Ebony Jr!* Celebrates Its Tenth Anniversary with Special May Issue." *Jet,* May 9, 1983, 14–16.

"*Ebony Jr!* Seeks to Reflect the Happiness," *Ebony Jr!,* May 1975, 45.

Ellis, Eddie. "Is *Ebony* a Negro Magazine? [Part One]," *Liberator* 5 (1965): 5.

Farmer, James, and Malcolm X. "Separation or Integration." In *The Rhetoric of Black Americans,* edited by James L. Golden and Richard D. Rieke, 422–38. Columbus, OH: Merrill, 1971.

Farrison, W. Edward. "Looking Back at Booker T." *Negro Digest,* May 1942, 55–57.

Fischler, Claude. "Food, Self and Identity." *Social Science Information* 27, no. 2 (1988): 275–92.

Fitzgerald, Thomas K. "Southern Folks' Eating Habits Ain't What They Used to Be If They Ever Were." *Nutrition Today* 14 (1979): 16–21.

Flick, Hank. "A Question of Identity: Malcolm X's Use of Religious Themes as a Means for Developing a Black Identity." *Negro Educational Review* 31, no. 3–4 (1980): 140–55.

Foner, Philip S., ed. *The Black Panthers Speak.* New York: Lippincott, 1970.

Frazier, Edward Franklin. *Black Bourgeoisie.* Glencoe, IL: Free Press, 1957.

"Free Breakfast for School Children." In *The Black Panthers Speak,* edited by Philip Sheldon Foner, 168. New York: Lippincott, 1970.

Fry, Edward. "Fry's Readability Graph: Clarifications, Validity, and Extension to Level." *Journal of Reading* 21, no. 3 (1977): 242–52.

Fuller, Hoyt. "Towards a Black Aesthetic." In *The Black Aesthetic,* edited by Addison Gayle, 3–11. Garden City, NY: Doubleday, 1971.

Gabaccia, Donna R. *We Are What We Eat: Ethnic Food and the Making of Americans.* Cambridge, MA: Harvard University Press, 1998.

Gaines, Kevin K. *Uplifting the Race: Black Leadership, Politics, and Culture in the Twentieth Century.* Chapel Hill: University of North Carolina Press, 1996.

Gayle, Addison, Jr. "Cultural Strangulation: Black Literature and the White Aesthetic." In *Within the Circle: An Anthology of African American Literary Criticism from the Harlem Renaissance to the Present,* edited by Angelyn Mitchell, 207–12. Durham, NC: Duke University Press, 1994.

George, Nelson. "The Ebony Agenda." In *Buppies, B-Boys, Baps & Bohos: Notes on Post-Soul Black Culture,* edited by Nelson George, 115–18. New York: Harper-Collins, 1992.

Giddings, Paula. *When and Where I Enter: The Impact of Black Women on Race and Sex in America.* New York: Morrow, 1984.

Goodman, Benjamin, ed. *The End of White Supremacy: Four Speeches by Malcolm X.* New York: Merlin House, 1971.

"Great Achievements of a Great Man." *Jet,* August 29, 2005, 39.

Greenfield, Eloise. "Writing for Children: A Joy and a Responsibility." In *The Black American in Books for Children: Readings in Racism*, edited by Donnarae MacCann and Gloria Woodard, 19–22. Metuchen, NJ: Scarecrow Press, 1985.

Greenstein, Fred I. *Children and Politics*. New Haven, CT: Yale University Press, 1965.

Gregory, Dick. *Dick Gregory's Natural Diet for Folks Who Eat: Cookin' with Mother Nature!* New York: Harper & Row, 1973.

Grier, William H., and Price M. Cobbs. *Black Rage*. New York: Basic Books, 1968.

Grover, Stephen. "Children's Magazines Thrive on Devotion, and Get Oodles of It." *Wall Street Journal*, April 21, 1975, 1, 7.

Grunwald Associates. "Connected to the Future: A Report on Children's Internet Use from the Corporation for Public Broadcasting." (2003). http://cpb.org/ed/resources/connected.

Hale-Benson, Janice E. *Black Children: Their Roots, Culture, and Learning Styles*. Baltimore: Johns Hopkins University Press, 1982.

Harley, Sharon. *The Timetables of African-American History: A Chronology of the Most Important People and Events in African-American History*. New York: Simon & Schuster, 1995.

Harris, Joseph E. "Introduction." In *Global Dimensions of the African Diaspora*, edited by Joseph E. Harris, 3–14. Washington, DC: Howard University Press, 1982.

Harris, Violet J. "African American Children's Literature: The First One Hundred Years." *Journal of Negro Education* 59, no. 4 (1990): 540–55.

Henderson, Errol. "War, Political Cycles, and the Pendulum Thesis: Explaining the Rise of Black Nationalism, 1840–1996." In *Black and Multiracial Politics in America*, edited by Yvette M. Alex-Assensoh and Lawrence J. Hanks, 337–74. New York: New York University Press, 2000.

Henderson, Laretta. "*Ebony Jr!*: The Rise—and Demise—of an African American Children's Magazine." *Journal of Negro Education* 75, no. 4 (2006): 649–60.

Hilliard, Asa. *Alternatives to IQ Testing: An Approach to the Identification of Gifted Minority Children*. Sacramento: California State Department of Education, 1976.

———. "Why We Must Pluralize the Curriculum." *Educational Leadership* 49, no. 4 (1992): 12–15.

Hoover Report. "Minding Black Business of America: Johnson Publishing Company, Inc." (2002). http://www.blackstocks.com/Features/Bizlegends/jj/jj2.html.

Houston, Helen R. "Amelia E. Johnson." In *Notable Black Women*, edited by Jessie C. Smith. New York: Gale Research, 1996.

Hughes, Marvalene H. "Soul, Black Women, and Food." In *Food and Culture: A Reader*, edited by Carole Counihan and Penny Van Esterik, 272–280. New York: Routledge, 1997.

"Ike's New Black Cabinet." *Hue*, May 1953, 4–5.

Iser, Wolfgang. *The Art of Reading: A Theory of Aesthetic Response*. Baltimore: Johns Hopkins University Press, 1978.

Jackson, Mary, and Lelia Wishart. *The Integrated Cookbook: Or, the Soul of Good Cooking*. Chicago: Johnson Publishing, 1971.

Johnson, Abby Arthur, and Ronald Maberry Johnson. *Propaganda and Aesthetics: The Literary Politics of Afro-American Magazines in the Twentieth Century*. Amherst: University of Massachusetts Press, 1979.

———. "Scholarly Journals and Literary Magazines." In *The Oxford Companion to African American Literature*, edited by William L. Andrews, Frances Smith Foster, and Trudier Harris, 567–69. New York: Oxford University Press, 1997.

"Johnson Introduces Magazine Designed for Black Children." *Jet*, May 10, 1973, 52–54.

Johnson, John H. "Editorial." *Tan Confessions*, November 1942.

———. "Why *Ebony Jr!*" *Ebony Jr!*, May 1973, 3.

———. "Why *Hue?*" *Hue*, November 1953, 66.

Johnson, John H., and Lerone Bennett. *Succeeding against the Odds*. Chicago: Johnson Publishing, 1989.

———. "The Pedagogy and the Promise of Du Bois' *The Brownies' Book* Magazine." In *Telling Tales: The Pedagogy and Promise of African American Literature for Youth*, edited by Dianne Johnson-Feelings, 15–37. New York: Greenwood Press, 1990.

Jones, LeRoi. "Soul Food." In *Home: Social Essays*, edited by Imamu Amiri Baraka, 101–4. New York: Morrow, 1966.

Katz, William A. *Magazines for Libraries: For the General Reader, and School, Junior College, and Public Libraries*. 2nd ed. New York: Bowker, 1972.

———. *Magazines for Libraries: For the General Reader, and School, Junior College, and Public Libraries*. 2nd supp. ed. New York: Bowker, 1974.

"Kid Speed Boat Racer." *Hue*, May 1953, 10–11.

Knowles, Francine. "Twenty-Eight Black-Owned Illinois Firms on Magazine's Lists of Biggest." http://www.findarticles.com/p/articles/mi_qn4155/is_20020530/ai_n12466027.

Koste, Margaret I. "An Evaluation of Magazines Published for Children in America." Unpublished Ph.D. diss., The Ohio State University, 1962.

Kryder, Daniel. "War and the Politics of Black Militancy in the Twentieth Century U.S." Paper presented at the Annual Conference of the American Political Science Association, Washington, DC, 1997.

Larrick, Nancy. "The All-White World of Children's Books." In *The New Press Guide to Multicultural Resources for Young Readers*, edited by Daphne Muse, 19–25. New York: New Press, 1997.

Lee, Robert A. "Periodicals: Black Periodicals." In *The Concise Oxford Companion to African American Literature*, edited by William L. Andrews, Frances Smith Foster, and Trudier Harris, 565–67. New York: Oxford University Press, 1997.

Lorde, Audre. "The Uses of Anger: Women Responding to Racism." In *Sister Outsider: Essays and Speeches*, edited by Audre Lorde, 124–33. Trumansburg, NY: Crossing Press, 1984.

MacCann, Donnarae. "Effie Lee Newsome: African American Poet of the 1920s." *Children's Literature Association Quarterly* 13, no. 1 (1988): 60–65.

———. *White Supremacy in Children's Literature: Characterizations of African Americans, 1830–1900*. New York: Garland, 1998.

Madhubuti, Haki. *Blacks, Jews, and Henry Louis Gates, Jr. Claiming Earth: Race, Rage, Rape, Redemption*. Chicago: Third World Press, 1994.

Malcolm X. *The Autobiography of Malcolm X*, with the assistance of Alex Haley. 1964. Reprint, New York: Ballantine, 1992.

——. "God's Judgement of White America (The Chickens Come Home to Roost)." http://www.malcolm-x.org/speeches/spc_120463.htm.

——. "To Mississippi Youth." In *Malcolm X Speaks: Selected Speeches and Statements*, edited by George Breitman, 137–46. New York: Grove Press, 1965.

Marable, Manning. *Race, Reform, and Rebellion: The Second Reconstruction in Black America, 1945–1990*. 2nd ed. Jackson: University Press of Mississippi, 1991.

Maryland State Archives. "Rev. Dr. Harvey Johnson: Last of the Old Guard." http://archive1.mdarchives.state.md.us/msa/stagser/s1259/121/6050/html/12414101.html.

McDougald, Elise J. "The Task of Negro Womanhood." In *The New Negro*, edited by Allen Locke, 369–82. 1919. Reprint, New York: Simon & Schuster, 1997.

McGillis, Roderick. *The Nimble Reader: Literary Theory and Children's Literature*. New York: Twayne, 1996.

Mead, Margaret. "A Perspective on Food Patterns." In *Issues in Nutrition from the 1980s: An Ecological Perspective*, edited by Alice L. Tobias and Patricia J. Thompson, 225–29. Monterey: Wadsworth, 1980.

Morrow, Willie L. *400 Years without a Comb*. San Diego: Black Publishers of San Diego, 1973.

Moynihan, Daniel P. *The Negro Family: The Case for National Action*. Washington, DC: Office of Policy Planning and Research United States Department of Labor, 1965.

Muhammad, Elijah. "Are We the Black Muslims?" In *The Rhetoric of Black Americans*, edited by James L. Golden and Richard D. Rieke, 408–11. Columbus, OH: Merrill, 1971.

Muhammad, Elijah, and Fard Muhammad. *How to Eat to Live*. Chicago: Muhammad Mosque of Islam No. 2, 1967.

Myers, Walter D. "The Black Experience in Children's Books: One Step Forward, Two Steps Back." In *The Black American in Books for Children: Readings in Racism*, edited by Donnarae MacCann and Gloria Woodard, 222–26. Metuchen, NJ: Scarecrow Press, 1985.

Neal, Larry. "Some Reflections on the Black Aesthetic." In *The Black Aesthetic*, edited by Addison Gayle, 12–15. Garden City, NY: Doubleday, 1971.

"Negro Who's Who." *Negro Digest*, January 1943, 17.

Nodelman, Perry. *The Pleasures of Children's Literature*. New York: Longman, 1992.

Paris, Peter J. *The Social Teaching of the Black Churches*. Philadelphia: Fortress Press, 1985.

Patterson, Philana. (2005.) "*Ebony's* License to Grow." *Black Enterprise*. http://www.blackenterprise.com/exclusivesekopen.asp?id=1203&p=0.

Perkus, Cathy, and Nelson Blackstock, eds. *COINTELPRO: The FBI's Secret War on Political Freedom*. New York: Monad Press, 1975.

Peters, Pearlie-Mae. "*Ebony Jr!*" In *The Oxford Companion to African American Literature*, edited by William L. Andrews, Frances Smith Foster, and Trudier Harris, 246. New York: Oxford University Press, 1997.

Ranlet, Louis F. "Magazines for Tens and 'Teens.'" *Horn Book* 20 (1944): 271–77.

Reagon, Bernice Johnson. "This Is a Mean World." In *Sweet Honey in the Rock: In this Land*. New York: Warner Bros. Records, 1985.

"Remembering John H. Johnson, 1918–2005." *Jet*, August 29, 2005, 12–43.

Ricchiardi, Sherry. "At 23, She Lands Top Job on Magazine for Black Youths." *Des Moines Register*, May 2, 1973, 13.

Riggs, Marlon T. *Ethnic Notions*. San Francisco: California Newsreel, 1987.

Rooks, Noliwe M. *Hair Raising: Beauty, Culture, and African American Women*. New Brunswick, NJ: Rutgers University Press, 1996.

Rose, Ada Campbell. "Are Children's Magazines Dying on the Vine?" *Catholic Library World* 47, no. 4 (1976): 370–73.

Sagay, Esi. *African Hairstyles: Styles of Yesterday and Today*. Oxford: Heinemann International Literature and Textbooks, 1983.

Saunders, Doris E., ed. *The Ebony Handbook*. Chicago: Johnson Publishing, 1974.

Schein, Amy. "Johnson Publishing Company, Inc." Hoover's. (2007). http://www.hoovers.com/johnson-publishing/—ID__40251—/free-co-factsheet.xhtml.

Scofield, C. I., Arthur L. Farstad, and Thomas Nelson Publishers, eds. *The New Scofield Study Bible: New King James Version*. 1909. Reprint, Nashville: T. Nelson, 1967.

Silverman, Stephen M. "NSYNC: Head of the Class," *People*. (1998). http://www.people.com/people/article/0,26334,617829,00.html.

Sims, Rudine. *Shadow & Substance: Afro-American Experience in Contemporary Children's Fiction*. Urbana, IL: NCTE, 1982.

Sinnette, Elinor Desverney. "*The Brownies' Book*: A Pioneer Publication for Children." *Freedomways* 5, no. 1 (1965): 133–42.

Small, Stephen. *Racialised Barriers: The Black Experience in the United States and England in the 1980s*. Critical Studies in Racism and Migration. London: Routledge, 1994.

Smith, Ray. "Cornrows for Men Exploded This Year into the Mainstream." *Wall Street Journal*, July 31, 2000.

Spock, Benjamin. *Baby & Child Care*. London: Bodley Head, 1969.

Stanfield, John H., and Rutledge M. Dennis. *Race and Ethnicity in Research Methods*. Newbury Park, CA: Sage, 1993.

Stead, Deborah. "A Look at Children's Magazines: Not All Fun and Games." *Interracial Books for Children Bulletin* 6, no. 2 (1975): 1, 6–7.

Steinberg, Shirley R., and Joe L. Kincheloe. "Introduction: No More Secrets—Kinderculture, Information Saturation, and the Postmodern Childhood." In *Kinderculture: The Corporate Construction of Childhood*, edited by Shirley R. Steinberg and Joe L. Kincheloe, 1–30. Boulder, CA: Westview Press, 1997.

Stewart, Jeffrey C. *1001 Things Everyone Should Know about African-American History*. New York: Doubleday, 1996.

"'Talented Tenth' Builds on Family Prestige." *Hue*, May 1953, 20–21.

"Thousands Join in Historic Farewell Celebration for Publisher John H. Johnson in Chicago." *Jet*, August 29, 2005, 4–10, 59–61.

Ulrich's Periodical Directory. "Black Stars." ProQuest-CSA LLC. http://www.ulrichsweb.com/ulrichsweb/Search/fullCitation.asp?navPage=1&tab=1&serial_uid=326471&issn=10252665.

Van Deburg, William L. *New Day in Babylon: The Black Power Movement and American Culture, 1965–1975*. Chicago: University of Chicago Press, 1992.

Vaughn-Roberson, Courtney, and Brenda Hill. "*The Brownies' Book* and *Ebony Jr!*: Literature as a Mirror of the Afro-American Experience." *Journal of Negro Education* 8, no. 4 (1989): 494–510.

Vecchione, Judith. *Eyes on the Prize: American Civil Rights Years, 1954–1965.* Alexandria, Virginia: PBS Video, 1990.

Wade-Gayles, Gloria, J. "The Making of a Permanent Afro." In *Pushed Back to Strength: A Black Woman's Journey Home,* edited by Gloria J. Wade-Gayles, 133–58. Boston: Beacon Press, 1993.

Walker, David. *David Walker's Appeal: In Four Articles, Together with a Preamble, to the Coloured Citizens of the World, but in Particular, and Very Expressly, to Those of the United States of America.* 1829. Reprint, New York: Hill and Wang, 1995.

Walker, Jan. "High School Is Dangerous." *Tan,* November 1950, 26, 66.

Walker, Juliet E. K. *The History of Black Business in America: Capitalism, Race, Entrepreneurship.* Twayne's Evolution of Modern Business Series. New York: MacMillan Library Reference USA, 1998.

Washington, Booker T. *Up from Slavery: An Autobiography.* 1901. Reprint, Garden City, NY: Doubleday, 1963.

Watts, Jerry G. *Amiri Baraka: The Politics and Art of a Black Intellectual.* New York: New York University Press, 2001.

Whitehead, Tony, and Psyche A. Williams-Forson. "African American Foodways." In *Encyclopedia of Food and Culture,* edited by Solomon H. Katz and William Woys Weaver, 425–37. New York: Thompson-Gale, 2002.

Williams, Juan. *Eyes on the Prize: America's Civil Rights Years, 1954–1965.* New York: Viking, 1987.

Williams, Shirley. "A Black Child Pledge." In *The Black Panthers Speak,* edited by Philip S. Foner. New York: Lippincott, 1970.

Witt, Doris. *Black Hunger: Food and the Politics of U.S. Identity.* New York: Oxford University Press, 1999.

"World's Richest Negro Woman." *Hue,* May 1953, 12–13.

Wright, Richard. "Blueprint for Negro Writing." In *Within the Circle: An Anthology of African American Literary Criticism from the Harlem Renaissance to the Present,* edited by Angelyn Mitchell, 97–106. Durham: Duke University Press, 1937; reprint, 1994.

CHILDREN'S LITERATURE

Alger, H., Jr. *Ragged Dick.* 1865. Reprint, New York: Penguin Books, 1985.

"An African Mask Is in Your Kitchen." *Ebony Jr!,* May 1973, 32–33.

Aspinall, Josephine. "The Secret." *Ebony Jr!,* August/September 1973, 47–49.

Beckford, Julian. "The Mystery of Mobius Strip." *Ebony Jr!,* November 1973, 34–35.

Brown, Beverly Mae. "Nandi's Surprise." *Ebony Jr!,* February 1974, 7–11.

Brown, Buck. "Sunny and Honey." *Ebony Jr!,* November 1981, 22–23.

Burnett, Frances Hodgson. *Little Lord Fauntleroy.* New York: Scribner's Sons, 1887.

"Calendar." *Ebony Jr!,* June/July 1975, 2.

"Calendar." *Ebony Jr!,* October 1975, 2.

"Can You Think Like Imhotep? A Story from the Nile." *Ebony Jr!,* May 1973, 21.

"A Cookie Painted Picture." *Ebony Jr!,* December 1973, 28–30.

Cox, Frankie. "The Big Day." *Ebony Jr!,* December 1973, 14–18.

———. "Get It On!" *Ebony Jr!,* August/September 1973, 7–9.

———. "Tough Enough." *Ebony Jr!*, June/July 1973, 7–9.

Cox, Frankie. "That February." *Ebony Jr!*, February 1974, 49.

Cummings, Marlene. "Bobbie and Bubba Meet Mellow Mel." *Ebony Jr!*, November 1973, 58.

Davis, Eloise Greenfield. "Nothing to Do." *Ebony Jr!*, January 1974, 37–41.

Davis, Michael G. "Sunny and Honey." *Ebony Jr!*, November 1975, 22–23.

"Ebony Jr!: Sunny & Honey." http://ebonyjr.com/.

"From Our Readers." *Ebony Jr!*, January 1974, 39.

"From Our Readers." *Ebony Jr!*, December 1974, 60.

"From Our Readers." *Ebony Jr!*, February 1981, 40.

"Goins and Goins: Family Racers." *Ebony Jr!*, November 1973, 28–30.

Gray, Janice. "Cornrowing." *Ebony Jr!*, January 1974, 52–53.

Greenfield, Eloise. "Saturday." *Ebony Jr!*, May 1973, 45–48.

Gregg, Ernest. "Kwame and the Lion." *Ebony Jr!*, May 1973, 26–28.

"Help Robert Smalls Escape." *Ebony Jr!* , November 1973, 12.

Hunter, Norman L. (Photographer). "Baking Powder Biscuits." *Ebony Jr!*, May 1973, 31–32.

"If You Miss Me from the Back of the Bus." *Ebony Jr!*, January 1974, 61.

"In Time for Christmas!" *Ebony Jr!*, December 1973, 45.

Jones, Anne Rowry. "Phonics with the Loonicans." *Ebony Jr!*, August/September 1981, 12.

King, Renee. "Great Galaxies, What a Mess!" *Ebony Jr!*, January 1980, 20–21.

Lambie, Constance. "A Bit about Bananas." *Ebony Jr!*, June/July 1975, 7–9.

Lawrence, Jacob. "Harriet and the Promised Land." *Ebony Jr!*, June/July 1973, 16–20.

"A Letter from Sunny and Honey." *Ebony Jr!*, May 1978, 3.

Lewis, Mary C. "Classy Computers." *Ebony Jr!*, January 1982, 10–11.

———. "James Van Der Zee." *Ebony Jr!*, May 1978, 28–30.

———. "'Mr. Black Labor' Himself, A. Philip Randolph." *Ebony Jr!*, March 1980, 20–22.

———. "Super Shutterbug." *Ebony Jr!*, May 1978, 31–33.

Lowery, Jan. "How to Be a Sharpshooter." *Ebony Jr!*, May 1978, 7–10.

"Mama Write-On's Scribblin' Scope." *Ebony Jr!*, October 1973, 24.

Mathis, Sharon Bell. *"Ebony Jr!* News." *Ebony Jr!*, February 1974, 38–39.

Mugo, Kanye K. "Tasty Tropical Treats." *Ebony Jr!*, December 1978, 26–27.

Normet, Lynn. "Welcome to Success." *Ebony Jr!*, August/September 1981, 6–7.

Odom, Karen. "The Good Buy Pig (The Three Little Pigs Retold)." *Ebony Jr!*, March 1980, 8–11.

"Our Ninth Annual Writing Contest." *Ebony Jr!*, May 1981, 14.

"A Page for You to Color." *Ebony Jr!*, May 1975, 11.

Parker, Cris. "Brother Obie's Saturday." *Ebony Jr!*, June/July 1981, 34–36.

Poinsett, Norma. "The Haunted Ship in Charleston Harbor." *Ebony Jr!*, May 1973, 7–11.

———. "The Main Dish." *Ebony Jr!*, November 1973, 7–10.

———. "Susa's Natural." *Ebony Jr!*, June/July 1973, 47–51.

"Put It Together." *Ebony Jr!*, October 1973, 60.

Roebuck, Marcia V. "Jamaican Rub-up Cake." *Ebony Jr!*, February 1982, 45.

"School Is Hip." *Ebony Jr!*, June/July 1975, 36.

Searcy, Carol. "Peter's Tenth Christmas." *Ebony Jr!*, December 1973, 37–41.

———. "Sneezing Powder." *Ebony Jr!*, January 1974, 7–10.

Searcy, Shirley A. "Banana Icebox Pie." *Ebony Jr!*, June/July 1975, 54–55.

"Selma to Montgomery." *Ebony Jr!*, January 1974, 44.

Sharpe, Maya. "Draw Yourself." *Ebony Jr!*, May 1973, 40.

"Soul Cook-Out." *Ebony Jr!*, June/July 1975, 56.

Stevenson, Robert L., and Rosalind E. Woodruff. "The Fox Who Came Out of the Hole." *Ebony Jr!*, June/July 1976, 19–21.

"A Story from the Nile." *Ebony Jr!*, May 1973, 16–20.

"Sunny and Honey." *Ebony Jr!*, June/July 1973, 22–23.

Sutton, Ike (Illustrator). "Icy Cold Treats." *Ebony Jr!*, February 1974, 50.

Taha, Karen T. "Tina's Present." *Ebony Jr!*, June/July 1981, 14–16.

Taylor, Janice. "Dr. Martin Luther King Jr.—Leader." *Ebony Jr!*, January 1982, 42.

"There's a Job for Everyone." *Ebony Jr!*, March 1980, 7.

"Treetop Terri." *Ebony Jr!*, November 1974, 7–10.

"Who Am I?" *Ebony Jr!*, June/July 1975, 5.

Wilson, Darrick. "Mom's Sad and Happy Event." *Ebony Jr!*, October 1973, 25–27.

Wilson, Mary E. "Oranges without Seeds." *Ebony Jr!*, December 1975, 50–53.

Index

About the Author

Laretta Henderson is an assistant professor in the School of Information Studies at the University of Wisconsin–Milwaukee, where she teaches courses in children's and young adult literature. She has published articles in *MELUS*, the *Journal of Negro Education*, and *Children's Literature in Education: An International Quarterly*.